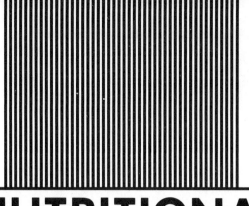

NUTRITIONAL
CARE OF THE
TERMINALLY ILL

Charlette R. Gallagher-Allred, Ph.D., R.D.
Volunteer Consulting Nutritionist
Hospice at Riverside
Columbus, Ohio

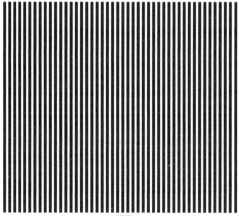

AN ASPEN PUBLICATION®
Aspen Publishers, Inc.
Rockville, Maryland
1989

Library of Congress Cataloging-in-Publication Data

Gallagher-Allred, Charlette R.
Nutritional care of the terminally ill/ Charlette R. Gallagher-Allred.
p. cm.
"An Aspen publication."
Includes bibliographies and index.
ISBN: 0-8342-0060-0
1. Diet therapy. 2. Terminally ill-Nutrition. I. Title.
[DNLM: 1. Critical Care. 2. Diet Therapy. 3. Palliative Treatment. WB 400 G 162n]
RM217.G35 1989 615.8'54--dc19 DNLM/DLC
for Library of Congress
89-381
CIP

The authors have made every effort to ensure the accuracy of the information herein, particularly with regard to drug selection and dose. However, appropriate information sources should be consulted, especially for new or unfamiliar procedures. It is the responsibility of every practitioner to evaluate the appropriateness of a particular opinion in the context of actual clinical situations and with due consideration to new developments. Authors, editors, and the publisher cannot be held responsible for any typographical or other errors found in this book.

Editorial Services: Marsha Davies

Library of Congress Catalog Card Number: 89-381
ISBN: 0-8342-0060-0

Printed in the United States of America

1 2 3 4 5

This book is dedicated to my
husband
and my family,
co-authors of all that is
best in my life

Table of Contents

Foreword

Finally, an authoritative and complete text on the nutritional needs of dying persons in palliative care settings—a first and only one of its kind!

Dr. Gallagher-Allred is uniquely qualified to write this book with her ten years of experience as a volunteer consulting nutritionist to Hospice at Riverside—the first hospice in the United States to combine all three components of home care, inpatient care, and day care in a single free-standing facility.

Most of us now accept the conviction of Dame Cicely Saunders that care of the person with terminal illness is as important as treatment of the underlying disease. To care means that we accept the patient and family and deal with the issues and concerns that are important to them. Nutrition is often one of their major concerns.

This book should be prerequisite for every dietitian working with terminally ill patients. It sets the stage for full-fledged entry of dietitians into palliative care teams by instructing the practitioner on specific and appropriate nutritional techniques, effective counseling skills, and how to participate in interdisciplinary team meetings.

This book is also a must on the shelf of every hospice library because it provides information that is important to physicians, nurses, and administrators. Here, health care professionals will find answers to many of the questions and concerns of dying patients, their families, and team members, such as:

"Would vitamins and laetrile help me?"
"But doctor, if my wife doesn't eat, she will starve to death!"
"He used to love my beef stew; why won't he eat it now?"
"Is dehydration painful; would tube feeding lessen his suffering?"

While living, some people live to eat—who could ever forget those scenes of ripened fruit and raw oysters in *Tom Jones* or vintage wines in *Babette's Feast*? But, while dying we all eat to live.

The author is vitally aware that meeting the nutritional needs of the dying patient and his or her family must be with the knowledge that we are caring for the living. Our degree of caring is measured by the spirit of love we express as we accept and affirm our patients. That spirit of love is evident throughout this book, which as American poet Robert Frost penned, ". . . and that has made all the difference."

Warren L. Wheeler, M.D.
Medical Director
Hospice at Riverside
Columbus, Ohio

Preface

In 1978 when I began volunteer work with terminally ill patients in a local hospice program, I found meager literature to guide me in my professional role. After 10 years of experience with dying patients, their families, and diverse inpatient and home care team members, the time has come to share those insights that I wish I had found in my early quest.

Dietitians working part time or full time with terminally ill patients, whether in an inpatient, home care, long-term care, or day care facility, will find this book helpful in defining their roles and responsibilities, in providing nutritional care to terminally ill patients and their families, and in interacting with health care professionals.

The tables, exhibits, figures, and appendixes provide practical, readily usable information and will guide the dietitian in making decisions that are clinically appropriate and ethical. Many of the suggestions contained in this book have come from patients. It would be their hope, as well as mine, that these pages will challenge the reader to seek ways in which the sufferings of the dying can be made easier, and that food and nutrition issues would be considered equally important to other palliative care therapies.

Part I

Palliative Care and the Professional Dietitian

It is an exciting time to be a dietitian. Changes in the health care system are allowing dietitians to show how the services we provide are cost beneficial and cost effective. New avenues for practice are opening, and dietitians are showing that we are prepared for the challenge of facing a new era in health care.

Amidst change, some things remain unchanged. People are or will become terminally ill, and death from chronic degenerative disease is an ever-present threat to us all. Over the past century, hospital care has become cure oriented and highly technological, often seeming to lose the caring component. The palliative care movement in the 1960s and 1970s has reawakened the challenge of putting humanity back into medicine.[1]

The provision of palliative nutritional care to terminally ill patients and their families represents an entrepreneurial opportunity for dietitians and a benefit to health care institutions. The territorial domain of the dietitian in terminal care is uncharted. Few paths cross its realm. Opportunities for dietitians in palliative care are explored in Chapter 1.

The dietitian can help the patient and family achieve a comfortable and dignified death. In order to do so, it is essential to understand the process of dying, including the physiological and psychological changes that occur during the dying process. These changes are explored in Chapter 2.

The purpose of Chapter 3 is to create a picture of palliative care today by presenting its definition, history, philosophy, objectives, standards of care, types of programs, and financial and reimbursement characteristics. With this knowledge, the dietitian's role can be more fully understood and appreciated. The dietitian's contributions in developing a palliative care program are also discussed in this chapter.

Patients and families are the center of palliative care programs. In order to help patients live to the fullest, even while dying, many more aspects of living and dying need to be addressed than can be done by one person. Therefore, palliative care programs are frequently composed of many and varied team members, the combined efforts of whom can help dying patients and their families live as fully as possible until the patient dies. Chapter 4 includes a discussion of palliative care team members and the patient and family around which the team revolves.

Dying patients who place their lives in our care ask two things—that we understand and that we respond. In order to understand, we need an opportunity to explore our personal feelings regarding death and dying as well as a lifetime of experiences. Chapter 5 will help us to explore our own mortality and to recognize symptoms of burnout that may occur from caring for terminally ill patients and their families.

NOTE

1. Sir George Young, "The Hospice Concept," in *Hospice: The Living Idea*, ed. Dame Cicely Saunders, Dorothy H. Summers, and Neville Teller (London: Edward Arnold Publishers, Ltd., 1981), 3.

Chapter 1

Terminal Illness: Opportunities for Dietitians

Every moment of every day we are living and we are dying. The focus of this book is on those patients who are alive but who have been diagnosed as both dying and terminally ill; some of these patients are imminently ill. As the dietitian, you can be an integral member of the health care team helping both the dying patient and the patient's family live until death occurs.

Dying is generally understood to mean the progressive failure of body systems to retain normal functioning, thereby limiting the life span. A terminal illness is an illness that is irreversible and will progress to death because treatments cannot influence it. Because it is difficult to diagnose when a patient is terminally ill and when death is anticipated, imminently ill is generally understood to mean that death can be expected to occur within a few hours or, at most, a few days.

CAUSES OF DEATH

Today, about three of every four people in our society die in institutions. Common causes of death in children include accidents, malignancy (brain tumors and leukemia), birth defects, and pneumonia. In older adults (over 60 years of age), degenerative diseases are the most frequent cause of death; they include cardiovascular and cerebrovascular diseases, malignancy, and respiratory diseases. Most causes of death have a nutritional component. The most common cause of death in patients admitted to palliative care units is cancer.[1]

DIFFICULTIES IN DEALING WITH DEATH AND DYING

Cultural Changes

Dealing with death is difficult for a variety of reasons. One reason is that we are shielded from death. Our materialistic and affluent culture has ignored death by emphasizing the enjoyment of living. At the beginning of the twentieth century, we were an agrarian society. The events of life — birth, life, and death — were shared by the family and community.[2] Death could hardly be ignored. When Americans moved from the country to the city, we were exposed less and less to the birth and death portions of the life cycle. Today, many people will go to any extreme to avoid exposure to death. It is almost as if they feel that if they cannot see death, they can deny that it occurs. In fact, modern mass communication and entertainment media have made death so commonplace that it has become unreal and unaffecting to many. Clinical dietitians, however, are routinely faced with death; they cannot hide from it and are in an integral position to help others deal squarely with it by providing individualized care and support.

The move from rural to urban life brought other changes, including a decrease in the size of the nuclear family and a breakup of the extended family. These trends have not only helped shield us from death and dying, but have also resulted in less family support to comfort us when we grieve.

Separation of the aged and ill from the midst of society is another reason why we have trouble dealing with death. Elderly or ill persons are frequently moved from their homes to nursing homes or hospitals. For the family of an aged or ill person, this move may hide the dying process, but for the elderly or ill patient, death and dying too often become a lonely experience. The dietitian working in a variety of health care settings is often in a position to alleviate this loneliness by advocating for the patient's needs and best interests.

Many people believe that the secularization of our culture has resulted in the loss of religious answers to questions of life and death. This loss has made it more difficult to cope with the grief process. However, today's churches and synagogues seem to be increasing their involvement in ethical issues that affect death and dying.

Technology in medicine has advanced greatly over the last 100 years. Advanced technology often creates the illusion that humans are in control of death and can forestall the inevitable sadness of ultimate separation. Indeed, modern medicine has found cures for diseases that were once thought incurable. And for patients who have diseases that remain incurable even today, the length of life can be extended considerably. Indeed, through use of aggressive nutritional support, it is possible to keep a patient alive longer than meaningful life can be maintained. An overreliance on medical technology makes it difficult to face death as an inevitable part of life. Because nutrition and feeding issues are at the crux of some ethical questions concerning the care of patients, including those who are terminally ill, the expertise and leadership of the dietitian in exploring ethical issues are critical. The dietitian has a crucial role in advocating for the patient's best interests.

Denial by Health Care Professionals

Often health care professionals, including dietitians, deny death as much as lay people. Evidence of this is easily seen in our avoidance of the dying patient's room, in not telling the patient or family the truth about terminal illness, and in not taking the time to listen to the life story of a dying patient.

To help the dying, we as health professionals must first acknowledge our own mortality. Only then can we avoid rejecting dying patients or, at the other extreme, fusing with them. It is often very easy to become too attached to patients, especially those who are unassuming and whose plight in life seems terribly unfair. Too much attachment causes us to suffer with the patient, often to the point that we become overwhelmed, thereby becoming useless as helping professionals.

Denial in the Elderly versus the Younger Person

The elderly and the young cope with illness and the dying process somewhat differently. Some frequent but not universal differences are as follows:[3]

- The elderly spend more time thinking about death; they have rehearsed death and have a lifetime of coping mechanisms upon which to call. Young people often have limited experiences or thoughts about death.

- The elderly often state that they are not afraid to die; many young people state that they are afraid to die, yet many others, especially the very young, indicate no or little fear of death.

- The elderly view death more calmly and peacefully than the young.

- The elderly tend to espouse more traditional religious feelings and beliefs; the young often cannot identify what beliefs they hold sacred.

- The elderly think about the last opportunity to see loved ones, bringing business affairs to completion, and reminiscing about life; the young tend to deal primarily with the experiences of the present.

- The elderly are less concerned about cessation of experiences; cessation of experiences is a great sorrow to most young people.

- The elderly value the quality of the remaining time more than its quantity, often foregoing therapy in the last few months of life that may make them uncomfortable. Younger persons often endure almost intolerable therapy and side effects to buy a few more days of life.

HONESTY AND HOPE: ARE THEY COMPATIBLE?

"Truth and hope are not mutually exclusive, and the informed patient is frequently better able to fight for his life because he knows the real battlefield. Surely most of us wish to take some responsibility for our dying as well as for our living!"[4]

Telling patients that they are terminally ill is not an easy task.[5] Rarely, if ever, should the dietitian be the health care professional or person who tells patients that they are dying. The reasons are obvious. Generally, dietitians do not have the medical competence to provide an accurate description of the disease process and possible therapies. Nor do they have the psychosocial knowledge required to deal with patients' feelings and actions that are evoked when they learn unpleasant news. Similarly, most dietitians have not established the rapport necessary to be able to tell patients what they need and want to know because they do not make the frequency of visits that doctors and nurses make. And lastly, dietitians generally do not have the latest information regarding the patients' situations and prognoses.

Many times, however, after the doctor or nurse has told the patient and family the "bad news" — news the patient or family may want to deny — the patient or family may query the dietitian regarding what the doctor or nurse said. This may be done in an attempt to obtain a different, more hopeful answer or to blame the doctor or nurse for the bad news delivered. Or the query may simply and importantly be one that seeks confirmation of the news.

As health professionals, we must grant patients and their families the privilege of "hope." Even to the end, most patients and their families hope for the discovery of a cure. Some patients may attempt unorthodox therapies, such as laetrile, as a final hope. If the patient or family asks you about laetrile and the diet as adjunct therapy, respond with truthful answers to the patient's questions. After the pros and cons of these cancer therapies are identified, the choice of the patient should be honored. Although the weight of evidence may be strongly against unorthodox medical therapies, it would be wrong of health care providers to try forcibly to take away this hope.

Health care professionals, including the dietitian, should encourage the deeper hopes — for example, the hope of reconciliation of estranged persons, the hope of a love to be returned, the hope of a peace restored, the hope of a beautiful sunset. "Still deeper is the hope that in the end we may be at peace with ourselves and our God or sense of life's purpose."[6]

Dying patients have many needs, and they express their needs in varied ways. Perhaps one of the greatest needs is to talk and to tell one's story. Dietitians and other health care professionals need to learn to listen honestly, to listen more than to talk, and to develop patients' trust so that they will choose us to receive their story.

OPPORTUNITIES FOR DIETITIANS

The provision of palliative nutritional care to terminally ill patients and their families represents an entrepreneurial opportunity for dietitians and a benefit to health care institutions. The need for home nutrition services, day care nutrition services, and long-term care nutrition services is growing rapidly. The diagnosis-related group (DRG) reimbursement system, the hospice option in Medicare and Medicaid, and the emergence of prepaid insurance plans, such as health maintenance organizations (HMOs) and preferred provider organizations (PPOs), have changed patterns of patient care and reimbursement. Patients are staying for fewer days in the hospital, and home and nursing home care for rehabilitation or terminal care is increasing. Reduced hospital staffs are frequently unable to render all the services they once provided or desire to provide.

These trends increase the likelihood that the entrepreneurial dietitian can successfully sell nutritional services to health care institutions and programs that care for terminally ill patients. The palliative care and hospice movement in the 1960s in England and the 1970s in the United States and Canada has brought changes to traditional health care which was sorely in need of the caring philosophy that had been set aside. Dietitians have been involved in tangential ways since the beginning of palliative care in the United States, but only recently has the importance of their services been recognized. There is an increased possibility for palliative nutritional services if dietitians identify the needs and position themselves in the right spots at the right time.

Caring for the terminally ill, as in the palliative care movement in health care today, is a new area for dietetics practice. It can be an especially rewarding area, particularly for those professionals who are sensitive to palliative care and bereavement issues and who can think critically about ethical issues. To enable dietetic professionals to meet these needs, a shift in nutrition education toward preparing students for more diversified and less traditional positions is needed.

NOTES

1. Vincent Mor and Susan Masterson-Allen, *Hospice Care Systems: Structure, Process, Costs, and Outcomes* (New York: Springer, 1987), 21–22.

2. Balfour M. Mount, "Death—A Fact of Life?," *Crux* (Toronto) XI (1974): 6.

3. Nancy L. Bohnet, "The Dying Elderly" in *Nursing Care of the Terminally Ill*, ed. Madalon O'Rawe Amenta and Nancy L. Bohnet, (Boston: Little, Brown & Co., 1986), 227–233.

4. Cicely M. Saunders, *The Management of Terminal Disease* (London: Edward Arnold Ltd., 1978), 6.

5. Ann G. Blues, "Honesty Tempered with Hope" in *Hospice and Palliative Nursing Care*, ed. Ann G. Blues and Joyce V. Zerwekh (Orlando, Fla.: Grune & Stratton, 1984), 11.

6. Ibid., 16.

Chapter 2

The Dying Process: Physiological and Psychological Changes

Throughout every moment of our being, we are living and we are dying. Terminally ill patients and their families often ask health care professionals to help them live as fully as possible until they die. As a member of the health care team, the dietitian can contribute to the achievement of a comfortable and dignified death. In order to do so, it is essential to understand the process of dying, including the physiological and psychological changes that occur.

PHYSIOLOGICAL CHANGES

The physiological changes that occur during the dying process are influenced by the patient's age, diagnosis, and physical condition. Many terminally ill patients are older adults, diagnosed with cancer, who have lost considerable weight due to anorexia. These physiological changes and some additional predictable changes that occur in most terminally ill patients as death nears are discussed in this section.

Aging

According to Paola S. Timiras,[1] biologists define aging as the sum total of all changes that occur in a living organism with the passage of time and that lead to functional impairment and death. Approximately 75 percent of terminally ill patients are over the age of 55 years. The average age of terminally ill patients, however, may decrease as more and more relatively young patients with acquired immune deficiency syndrome (AIDS) elect palliative care. The physiological changes that occur with the aging process influence the nutritional care of patients by affecting their self-esteem, physical activity, appetite, and nutrient utilization (Exhibit 2-1).[2-5]

Exhibit 2-1 Physiological Changes That Occur with the Aging Process

Physical Appearance
Graying of hair
Wrinkling and irregular pigmentation of skin
Changes in external dimensions
Cardiovascular System
Bradycardia
Decrease in heart size
Fall in cardiac index
Respiratory System
Decrease in maximum breathing capacity and vital capacity
Decrease in maximum work rate of respiratory muscles
Decrease in maximum oxygen uptake
Musculoskeletal System
Decrease in muscle mass
Decrease in basal metabolic rate caused by the decrease in metabolizing tissue, decrease in
    body surface, and changes in body composition, with no difference in ability of the
    thyroid gland to produce or release thyroxine
Increase in muscular tremors
Labored movement with gait becoming shuffle or totter
Central Nervous System
Decrease in total number of brain cells
Decrease in cerebral oxygen consumption
Atrophy of spine that may result in loss in height
Decline in nerve conduction velocity
Increase in incidence of depression
Digestive System
Loss of teeth
Decrease in production of saliva and hydrochloric acid
Decrease in esophageal peristalsis and increase in esophageal reflux
Decrease in digestive enzyme secretion
Decrease in gastrointestinal motility and increase in constipation
Decrease in size and weight of liver and pancreas
Anorexia
Excretory System
Decrease in renal function and tubular excretory capacity
Decrease in renal blood flow
Decrease in glomerular filtration rate
Decrease in number of nephrons
Reproductive System
Loss of reproductive ability in women with menopause, and atrophy of uterus and ovaries
Decrease in sex drive in men after climacteric, and increase in size of prostate gland
Immune System
Rise in autoimmune titers
Fall in isoimmune titers
Endocrine System
Decrease in carbohydrate tolerance with glucose tolerance testing
Change in secretion of thyroid and adrenal glands may occur in some people

Exhibit 2-1 *continued*

> **Special Sense System**
>   Decrease in taste and smell acuity
>   Loss of hearing for higher tones
>   Increase in density, dehydration, muscle weakness, and hardening of the lens of the eye
> **Thermoregulation**
>   Change in body temperature if heat output changes or heat dissipating mechanisms decrease
> **No or Little Effect on the Following Parameters**
>   Blood acid-base and electrolyte balance
>   Blood glucose concentration
>   Osmotic pressure
>
> If these homeostatic parameters are displaced in the elderly person, the rates at which readjustments return to normal are slower than in the younger person.

Some investigators hypothesize that death can result from aging itself, rather than from some identifiable disease.[6] Unlike the marvelous "one-hoss shay," however, we do not fall apart all at once.[7] As the body's homeostasis is challenged more and more, specific organ systems are affected. With advanced age and disease, recovery becomes less likely.[8]

Malignancy

Usually, the failure of body systems that causes death results from disease and trauma. The most common cause of death in terminally ill patients is cancer. Exhibit 2-2 summarizes the systemic changes that occur in patients with terminal cancer.[9]

Exhibit 2-2 Systemic Changes Associated with Terminal Cancer

> **Cachexia:** loss of weight, body fat, protein, and carbohydrate; increased basal metabolic rate; abnormal iron metabolism; weakness; changes in drug metabolism
> **Malabsorption:** villous atrophy, impaired absorption of essential nutrients, vitamin and mineral deficiencies resulting in modified drug absorption and efficacy
> **Renal impairment:** elevated blood urea and serum creatinine levels, delayed drug excretion, uremia with poor renal perfusion
> **Hepatic failure:** jaundice, pruritus, nausea and vomiting, anorexia, decreased protein synthesis, hypoalbuminemia with resultant peripheral edema, alteration in drug metabolism, decreased blood coagulation, hepatic enlargement, pain
> **Hematological problems:** anemia, coagulation abnormalities
> **Hypercalcemia:** confusion, abdominal pain, restlessness, irritability, drowsiness, coma
> **Hyperuricemia:** painful gout
> **Peripheral Edema**
> **Excessive Secretion of Adrenocorticotropic Hormone:** Cushing's syndrome
> **Excessive Secretion of Antidiuretic Hormone:** fluid and electrolyte abnormalities, including water intoxication and low serum sodium, weakness, confusion, convulsions, coma
> **Infection and Depressed Immune Response**

Starvation

Starvation, due either to lack of food or the ravages of illness, such as a malignancy, reduces total cell mass and causes loss of body weight. The decrease in total cell mass is accompanied by an increase in total body water, which is produced by a decrease in intracellular water and an increase in extracellular water. Fat and skeletal muscle loss occurs after the initial loss of labile glycogen and protein stores. Along with loss of fat and protein, alterations in metabolism occur as the body metabolizes ketones derived from proteins and lipids. This alteration causes sodium retention, fluid conservation, and major shifts in intracellular fluids that result in the anasarca state frequently seen in starvation.[10]

Terminally ill patients often fear changes associated with illness more than death itself. Loss of body functions is usually progressive, but losses may also occur suddenly. Do not take for granted that the patient can walk, eat, breathe, sleep, or go to the bathroom without help. By questioning the patient and family, you may find that the patient has lost 50 pounds or more during the past year. Muscle and fat loss, loss of hair, and other external changes may greatly bother the patient and family, especially if the changes have occurred quickly.

Final Cause of Death

Regardless of the underlying pathology, it is cardiopulmonary failure that is the final cause of death. Therefore, the best indicators of imminent death are cardiac and respiratory signs.

The onset of circulatory failure may be gradual or sudden. Gradual decompensation and hypovolemia frequently occur before death. When the functioning of the circulatory system is compromised, less blood is available to the tissues, a drop in blood pressure is noted, tachycardia and irregular pulse result, impaired mentation due to diminished blood to the brain is common, and the extremities become cool and cyanotic. At the same time, reduced urinary output, chest pain, and edema in the lungs and periphery may be noted. Sudden circulatory failure may be due to a myocardial infarction or massive blood loss.

Pulmonary failure, as may circulatory failure, may be gradual or sudden in onset. Causes of pulmonary failure include pneumonia, emboli, effusion or edema, obstruction, and obstructive lung disease. Depression of the respiratory center in the brain can also occur secondary to medication usage, but it is more likely to be caused by central nervous system failure due to disease. Pulmonary failure is characterized by hypoxia and hypercapnia that result in mental confusion or slowness, apprehension, and eventually coma. The patient may have irregular and rapid breathing and an excessive accumulation of pulmonary secretions that can result in choking and gurgling sounds, which can greatly distress the patient and family.

Circulatory and pulmonary failure can be expertly handled with oxygen and medications so that the patient and family need not suffer when death approaches.

Predictable Changes As Death Approaches

The major signs and symptoms in the final days and hours of life have been eloquently identified and discussed by Joyce V. Zerwekh.[11] These signs and symptoms include

- cessation of eating and drinking
- oliguria and incontinence
- difficulty in breathing
- cyanosis
- decreased mental alertness
- changes in vital signs

Although these signs and symptoms are highly variable, when they are recognized, preparations can be made to ensure comfort at the end of life.

Cessation of Eating and Drinking

When patients stop eating and drinking, it is correct to assume that life will soon cease. There may be several reasons why persons stop eating and drinking. Sometimes they simply have no energy left or have no desire to eat. At other times, their disease may prevent them from swallowing or digesting food. Patients usually stop eating solid foods before they stop drinking fluids. Before death, the intake of liquids usually dwindles to occasional sips.

Family members often worry that lack of food and fluid intake is painful to the patient. To the contrary, dehydration tends to have an euphoric effect. The most commonly noted difficulty with cessation of eating and drinking is dryness of the mouth and lips.[12] Oral dryness can be alleviated by sucking on small ice chips, frequent cleansing of the mouth, giving sips of fluid if tolerated, and applying oil to the lips. As death becomes imminent, it is unkind and useless to force food or fluid on a patient.

Oliguria and Incontinence

Because patients generally drink fluids poorly for several days before death, urine output can be expected to decrease in volume, but increase in concentration, thereby turning the color of urine quite dark.

Incontinence frequently occurs before death because of the general fatigue, muscle weakness, and decreased mental acuity that often precede death. Depending on the amount of fluid consumed, the patient may be incontinent of large or small volumes of urine. In either case, bedding needs to be changed frequently and the lower part of the body bathed as quickly as possible so that skin irritation does not occur. It may be necessary to insert a retention catheter into the bladder to prevent repeated wetness and skin breakdown. Death usually occurs within 48 to 72 hours after urine output ceases.

Difficulty in Breathing

Before death, most patients have some difficulty breathing. The possible causes of breathing problems are numerous and include disease, pneumonia, and fluid accumulation in the lungs because of circulation problems. When breathing problems occur, treatment should be specific to the cause. Sometimes propping the patient up, moving him or her to a hospital bed with a raised head, giving oxygen, or administering sedatives, such as Benadryl or Vistaril, and narcotics are helpful treatments.

Probably the most disconcerting breathing problem to family members is the "death rattle." This sound is caused by the passage of breath through pharyngeal and pulmonary secretions that accumulate because the patient is unable to cough up sputum or swallow saliva that lodges at the back of the throat. The sound is loud, coarse, and bubbling. Because imminently ill patients with breathing difficulties are usually somewhat unconscious, they do not generally hear the sound. The condition needs to be alleviated, however, because the family is often very distraught, and those patients who do hear it may become apprehensive. Treatment is simple; atropine is administered to dry the secretions. If the patient is apprehensive, Benadryl or Vistaril is warranted.

Cyanosis

Cyanosis, progressive coldness, and purple discoloration in patients' arms and legs are signs of slowed circulation caused by the heart putting out less and less blood. These typical findings begin in the feet and proceed to the legs, then the hands, and on to the groin. The purple discoloration is due to the increased concentration of reduced hemoglobin in the body. Zerwekh notes that "the color and temperature of extremities is one of the most useful indicators that the end of life is approaching."[13]

Decreased Mental Alertness

As the general circulation slows, so does the amount of blood reaching the brain, lungs, liver, and kidneys. Decreased brain perfusion, along with an imbalance of oxygen, carbon dioxide, and other chemicals in the blood, usually results first in sleepiness and apathy and then disorientation and confusion. Restlessness follows and finally there is a decreased level of consciousness progressing to coma and death. Additionally, as death draws near, a patient's energy level is diminished. Even the simplest activities of everyday living can tire the patient greatly. Comatose patients cannot control any body functions or make their body respond as desired. They may, however, be able to hear and comprehend what is going on around them, which is an important consideration for all practitioners when speaking to the patient or to others in the patient's presence.

Sleepiness and apathy are conditions that should be allowed to occur naturally. Disorientation can best be relieved by talking calmly and honestly with the patient. Medications can be helpful in controlling restlessness; Benadryl and Vistaril are especially effective. It is critically important to ensure that the restless patient is kept safe from falls or self-inflicted trauma. The comatose patient should be made physically comfortable and should not be ignored.

Changes in Vital Signs

Changes in vital signs close to the time of death typically include a decrease in body temperature, an increase in rate and irregularity of the pulse, a rise and then a decrease in respirations with an increase in the number and length of periods of apnea, and a fall in blood pressure. These changes in vital signs are an indication that the time has come to summon family members or others who have requested to be present at the time of death. When the extremities become cold and cyanotic, the breathing irregular with periods of apnea, and the pulse and blood pressure weak or unpalpable, death can usually be expected within an hour. Immediately before death, incontinence of bladder and bowel often occurs. At the time of death, eyelids may remain slightly open and the jaw usually relaxes with the mouth open. Death is defined as the last inhalation.

PSYCHOLOGICAL CHANGES

It is important for the dietitian to understand the psychological changes that commonly occur in patients and their families upon the diagnosis of terminal illness and during the process of dying. Although the psychological makeup and adaptive characteristics of patients and families vary, do not underestimate the importance of these psychological changes or fail to appreciate their interaction with the physical process of dying.

Grief, Loss, and Coping

Grief is defined as "deep sorrow or mental distress caused by loss, remorse, or affliction."[14] Mourning is the process of experiencing grief. Bereavement, which subsumes grief and mourning, is the complex series of reactions following death.

The time after death is usually thought of as the major time of grief, mourning, and bereavement. For terminally ill patients and their families, however, grief and mourning occur before death and begin when the patient and family learn about the illness and understand that length of life is limited. Preparatory grief is felt by the dying person who mourns the loss of a potentially long future. Anticipatory grief is grief felt by the family members who experience the dying of a loved one.

The goal in working through grief is emancipation from the deceased person and the formation of new relationships. If grief work is not accomplished, emancipation cannot occur, and the survivor will remain suspended in unresolved grief.[15] Bereavement is a time of risk, often lasting 1 to 3 years or longer.

Grief is a normal reaction to a loss. Loss is no stranger to any of us. We cope with loss constantly, as in these situations.

- the loss of grade-school friends when a family moves out of state
- the loss of a special locket given by a loving grandmother
- the loss of a home to fire
- the loss of a job or expected promotion
- the loss of a son or daughter to college
- the loss of independence

The way we tend to cope with a major loss, such as our own death or the death of a close friend or family member, will generally be similar to the way in which we have coped with smaller losses throughout our lives. Coping skills, as are other skills, are affected by a person's maturity, intelligence, and strategies learned from dealing with other losses.[16] Experiences with past losses do not necessarily decrease the pain of a loss, but can assure us that pain does subside in time.

Successful bereavement requires the completion of four tasks. A return to good health and well-being requires that bereaved persons complete each task in their own time and way. These four tasks, frequently referred to as "grief work," are:[17]

1. Accept the reality of the loss.
2. Experience the pain of grief.
3. Adjust to an environment where the deceased person is missing.
4. Withdraw emotional energy and reinvest it in another relationship.

Grief is not solely a negative experience. "There are possibilities in the experience of grief for growth, meaningful attachments, and joyous affirmation in living. When one is open to the suffering that is grief, then one can know the joy that is life."[18]

Reactions to Loss and Grief in Adults

Physiological Reactions

Grief produces changes in the endocrine, immune, cardiovascular, and nervous systems through mechanisms that are only poorly understood at present. Therese A. Rando identified these psychophysiological reactions to loss:[19]

- anorexia
- gastrointestinal disturbances
- weight change
- inability to sleep
- crying
- tendency to sigh
- lack of strength
- physical exhaustion
- feeling of emptiness and heaviness
- feeling of "something stuck in the throat"
- heart palpitations and other indications of anxiety
- nervousness and tension, an inability to sit still
- loss of sexual desire
- psychomotor retardation
- decreased sensory acuity
- shortness of breath

Bereavement involves several stages—shock, pain, adjustment, and acceptance. During the initial shock stage of bereavement, crying, sighing, chest pains, tightness in the throat or chest, and dry mouth are frequent reactions. In the pain stage of bereavement that follows, the bereaved person may occasionally hallucinate and see or feel the deceased person's presence. Anxiety and depression are common, as are weakness and fatigue, insomnia, eating disturbances, absentmindedness, and hyperactivity. The adjustment and acceptance stages are marked by a decrease in these symptoms. When ultimate acceptance is reached, these symptoms are rare.

Grief reactions can produce physical illness. In 1944, Erich Lindemann studied 41 colitis patients and found that over 80 percent had developed colitis shortly after the loss of a close person.[20] Colin Murray Parkes in 1964 also found a close association between anxiety and grief and such somatic symptoms as headache, digestive upsets, and rheumatism in middle-aged widows and widowers.[21] In 1972, Parkes further found that the death rate for widowers rose 40 percent over the expected rate for married men of the same age.[22] The major portion of this increase was due to heart disease, especially coronary thrombosis and arteriosclerotic heart disease. More recently, Steven Schleifer and colleagues found a decreased cellular immunity in bereaved persons.[23] They established that the responses of the B- and T-lymphocytes may be diminished even though there may not be fewer lymphocytes.

Emotional and Psychological Reactions

"It has been said that when one loses a child one loses one's future, and when one loses a parent one loses one's past, but when the loss is the spouse, one seems to lose the present."[24] The loss of a child is one of life's greatest sorrows, and the customs in our culture have not helped parents deal openly with such a loss. Although mothers of a lost child are allowed to cry and mourn freely, fathers are expected to suppress all outward signs of grief and remain stoic, silent, and subdued. Men are expected to go to work as usual and answer such questions as "How's your wife taking the loss?" Rarely are fathers of a deceased child asked how they themselves are bearing the loss. Because fathers are expected to remain constantly in control, men generally display less emotion than women and may deny their own feelings. Fortunately, societal attitudes concerning the expression of grief by men are changing. Self-help groups help parents and surviving children deal with the death of a child. Supportive networks for bereaved parents are essential, as is the need to change the impression that "real men never cry."

Widowers take longer to recover than women after the death of a spouse despite the appearance that men are better adjusted. By returning to work, hobbies, or social events soon after the death of a spouse, it may appear that widowers adjust easily. However, men usually do not work through their attachments or examine their feelings as soon after death as women and therefore complete adjustment is usually slower. Holidays, particularly Christmas, are trying times for widows as well as widowers.

Bereaved persons experience significant emotional and psychological reactions. In 1970, Parkes reported that memories of the deceased may be so clear at times that survivors think they actually see the deceased, hear the deceased speak, and sense the deceased to be physically near.[25] J.J. Schwab in 1976 noted that unresolved grief can result in conversion reactions in which the survivor develops symptoms similar to those of the deceased.[26] A preoccupation with objects and places associated with the deceased person can cause the survivor to gaze constantly at certain objects or to avoid those objects or places that evoke memories of the deceased. Over about a year, the grief that these items or places evoke gradually subsides in intensity.

One frequent response to grief is increased use of tobacco, alcohol, and drugs by the bereaved person.[27,28] Additionally, there appears to be a two-fold to three-fold increase in mental disorders among those persons who have experienced early childhood bereavement.[29]

Social Reactions

Mourning brings a general restlessness that may drive the mourner to a constant flurry of activity in order to keep from being alone or from having time to think. Misguided and frenzied activity can be a way of avoiding dealing with painful thoughts and emotions.

Delinquency can be an unfortunate reaction to grief. In 1965, Shoor and Speed found that juvenile delinquency can occur as an unresolved grief reaction to a family death.[30] Often such an incident is the first antisocial behavior ever exhibited by the juvenile; it usually appears suddenly, and with counseling through the bereavement process, most of the behavior problems disappear.

A long-lasting terminal illness of a child can put great strain on a marriage. Harriet Sarnoff Schiff estimates that as many as 90 percent of bereaved couples have serious marital difficulties after a child's death.[31] Marital problems can revolve around methods of coping (such as drinking or staying up all night), guilt (blaming each other or self for a loss), fatigue (resulting in loss of leisure time, sex, and affection), or financial problems (often due to a long expensive illness). The longer these unresolved problems continue, the greater the potential for divorce. However, if both parents have had the opportunity to care for the dying child together, they are less likely to grow apart. Marriages that survive the loss of a child tend to be highly stable.

Self-help groups and bereavement programs can help bereaved families to acknowledge that everyone grieves at a different rate and at a different time, but that mutual support is needed by everyone at this very difficult time. To experience a second loss — that of a marriage partner — due to lack of psychological support during the grief time is a great burden.

During the time of grieving, women will often question their abilities as mothers and wives. Support from their husbands, families, and others is critical. Husbands often feel similar self-doubts, but may find themselves less able to express them. Fathers who have not had experiences in physically caring for a terminally ill child may not be able to experience anticipatory grief throughout the child's illness. These fathers may withdraw from the situation and fear the death more than the mothers who have been the primary caregivers and who may even begin to view death as a welcomed relief. Death comes as a greater trauma to these fathers, and grief work is usually harder. The strain of a child's death often goes unrelieved. The longer these unresolved feelings smoulder, the greater the potential for grief to become pathological.

Parkes, at St. Christopher's Hospice in 1978, found the following persons to be at highest risk for abnormal grief response during bereavement:[32]

- people of low socioeconomic status

- housewives or those without employment outside the home

- parents with young children at home; children are also at risk

- those without a supportive family or those with a family that actively discourages the expression of grief

- those who showed a strong tendency to cling to the patient or others before death and/or to pine intensely after death

- those who express strong feelings of anger or bitterness before or after the patient's death

- those who express strong feelings of self-reproach

Persons who experience a tendency toward suicide or mental illness in the past are also at special risk during bereavement for abnormal grief reactions.

Cognitive Development in Children and Their Grief Reactions

Jean Piaget's schema of cognitive development in children indicates that (1) children's ideas about death are influenced by family, society, age, and cognitive development, and (2) their cognitive development must be considered when explaining death to children.[33] Understanding a child's cognitive development will help dietitians anticipate common expressions of grief behavior in children.

Toddlers (Age Birth–3 Years)

Death can be devastating to toddlers for two reasons: one, they cannot choose words to express what they comprehend, which may be deeper than their ability to speak and two, adults must use simple words that children will understand, but may have trouble assessing the actual comprehension of toddlers. Children as young as age 3 can grasp the idea of death.[34] When explaining death to toddlers, it is best to base explanations on tangible experiences, such as the death of an animal or insect that the child has seen.

Separation and abandonment are the most important issues for the toddler. Because these children focus on their own needs, they need to know that someone will be there to take care of them. Therefore, the goal for toddlers is to maintain routines and familiar people and events before and after death.

Preschoolers (Age 3–5 Years)

The preschooler is curious and frequently asks questions about death, coffins, and burial, such as "How will she breathe under the ground?, Will she be afraid of the dark?, Can we give her a banana to eat?" Preschool children see death as reversible. They do not think everyone dies, and they do not think that they can die. Although perhaps not appearing to be troubled by the death of a parent or sibling, the preschooler often experiences separation anxiety. This is characterized by changes in behavior, reverting to younger age behaviors, and repeated questioning when the person will return. Separation is the key issue for these children; therefore, they need to be told over and over again that they are important, loved, and will not be abandoned.

Preschool children must also be told, generally many times, that they in no way caused the death of the parent, sibling, or friend. Such words as "passed away," "asleep," and "have gone on a long trip" have confusing and frightening meanings to children and therefore should not be used to explain death. Although difficult to explain, the correct words—"death," "dead," and "died"—should be used. As with the toddler, the goal for the preschooler is to maintain routines and familiar people and events before and after death.

School-Aged Children (Age 6–12 Years)

School-aged children have a general understanding of the concept of death although they often see death as magic. They understand that death is final, and they usually want open, honest answers to frank questions. They ask about what happens to a dead body and what caused the death, what happens after death, what hurts, and why. They want to know if illness and death will happen to them and to everyone they love.

Grieving parents should show honest emotion in front of their children. If children see their parent cry at suffering a loss, they learn that it is okay for them too to feel sorrow and to cry. For many children, tears are the beginning of relief. It is confusing and harmful to children to see a composed parent who never expresses grief. Children who never see others grieve may wonder how something that could make themselves hurt so much could not affect others.

These children may experience guilt because they often think that they may have caused the illness or death of another person, and they need reassurance that they did not nor could have caused or prevented illness and death. The school-aged child needs to be relieved of the fear that mutilation and violence await everyone and that death is always painful.

Because children under age 5 years do not understand death as permanent, they cannot really participate in decisions affecting their own care if they are terminally ill. After age 5, however, children can understand death as permanent, and if they are terminally ill, they should be involved in decisions about their care, such as whether or not to stop therapy and how they want to enjoy their final days.

Adolescents

Adolescents are moving between childhood and adulthood, dependence and independence. They understand the reality and finality of death. They often struggle, however, with the religious and philosophical issues that make death hard to accept. As they seek out their future, they see death as an enemy. Adolescents may deny death and repress their anxiety about it by trying to act in grown-up ways that they have seen in the past.

In dealing with an adolescent about death, health care professionals must be honest, tolerant, and perceptive. Adolescents, as well as children of all ages, need reassurance about their own good health and that of those they love. Grieving adults should share their feelings, such as hurt and anger, with children of all ages, but should do so without overwhelming the child with added burdens. After a discussion of the biological, physiological, and psychological aspects of death with the adolescent, spiritual or philosophical explanations are best discussed. Leaving this discussion to the last is usually best because it is abstract and hard to understand. Adolescents at times will surprisingly display great wisdom interspersed with childish acts. Adults can often learn a great deal from adolescents when both try to work together.

Expression of Grief Behavior in Children

Children express themselves through behavior. By acting out their feelings, children relieve their emotional burdens. Regression is common in the young child. Under stress, many children may begin bed-wetting or thumb-sucking, may refuse to eat or feed themselves, and may request baby bottles. School-aged children may begin to fear school or sleeping alone. The adolescent may withdraw, cease eating or overeat, deny the illness, and refuse therapy. Children of all ages may throw temper tantrums or exhibit discipline problems. Therapeutic play, through use of dolls, clay models, or drawings, can help children work through their fears and sadness. Older school-aged children and adolescents are often aided by another person who can help them articulate the diverse and often conflicting feelings that they find difficult to express.

Elisabeth Kubler-Ross has shown that the drawings of terminally ill children, even by very young children, can reveal the child's inner knowledge in symbolic form.[35] For example, children who know their parents do not wish to talk about the child's cancer may draw their parents without mouths. Those who feel abandoned by their parents or schoolmates may draw themselves in a box away from others in the picture.

In a desire to protect terminally ill children from the reality of their condition, parents and health care professionals can actually increase the children's burdens. When the topic is avoided, children must pretend ignorance. Parents are well advised to take clues from children, telling them what they want to know and answering questions on their level. Sometimes terminally ill children do not wish to speak of death for they are concerned not only with dying but with living, and like the adult who is terminally ill, they wish to live as fully as possible until they die. These wishes too should be acknowledged and obeyed.

In trying to meet the needs of the terminally ill child, the needs of siblings may be ignored. Life becomes quite rough for the siblings of a dying child. Their own relationships with their parents are disrupted, as is their normal routine. They often come home to an empty house if the sick child is hospitalized. Too, they experience sadness that brother or sister is dying, anger at being neglected, fear of their own dying, jealousy at the attention the sick child is receiving, and guilt because of their own good health.[36]

Despite the fact that as children we all had angry thoughts about our siblings at times, when children experience the actual loss of a sibling, they feel great suffering. Sibling grief reactions include depression, anxiety, trouble at school, stomachaches, and headaches. Parents and teachers should not label children "abnormal" who have these grief reactions, but instead should expect and see these reactions as self-limiting over time, provided the children are able to express and resolve their grief.

Such children can be helped to cope effectively and even grow, especially in self-confidence, if they are given the opportunity to participate in the care of the dying child. Ida M. Martinson notes that children who have been involved in home care as a sibling dies have a healthier bereavement course than children who are not involved in the care of a dying sibling.[37] As much as possible, siblings need to be included in family discussions about the diagnosis, prognosis, and treatment of their dying brother or sister. Home care provides siblings with more opportunity for caring for the dying child than does hospital care.

When dying children are hospitalized for a long time, siblings are likely to grow apart. All siblings should be warned that an ill brother or sister is likely to experience physical changes, such as hair loss, weight gain or loss, and pain if they are hospitalized for therapy, but that the pain can be controlled with help from medications, the family, and the health care team. Avoiding sibling resentment throughout the dying sibling's illness is difficult, but can be minimized if the situation is explained to healthy children, if they are also given time alone with parents, and if they can participate in caring for the ill brother or sister. Openness and honesty, albeit difficult, is the key to successful sibling coping.

At the same time that surviving children are feeling sorrow because a sibling has died, they may also be feeling relief, hoping that their parents will have more time for them. These contradictory thoughts are confusing to children. Unfortunately, surviving children may not receive the love and time that they need after the death of a sibling because the parents continue to be lost in their own grief and are unable to comfort them. Grieving parents frequently need to be reminded to view living children not as a burden, but as fellow grievers whose experiences, questions, and understandings parallel those of the parents and can be a source of comfort when the grieving process is shared.

A FEW CLOSING THOUGHTS

The thoughts of Robert Buckingham, a highly known researcher in caring for terminally ill patients and their families, provide an appropriate conclusion to the psychological aspects of the dying process. Additionally, they provide direction to health care practitioners who care for terminally ill patients and their families.

Knowing and understanding that a loved person is dead is not the same as accepting it.[38]

Successful resolution of the mourning process implies that the deceased will remain a living memory without the pain that originally accompanied the grief reaction.[39]

Parents should recognize the fact that in order for a child to mourn the dead parent, he not only needs his own recollections of that parent; but he also requires the surviving parent's help in confirming the objective truths of his memories, of both positive and negative aspects of the dead parent's personality.[40]

The death of a parent marks the end of one's oldest relationship and affects one's relationships with survivors.[41]

Grief cannot be eliminated, any more than death can be eliminated, but it can be softened and resolved with compassionate, knowledgeable care.[42]

NOTES

1. Paola S. Timiras, *Developmental Physiology and Aging* (New York: Macmillan Publishing Co., Inc., 1972), 411–428.

2. Donald M. Watkin, "The Physiology of Aging," *American Journal of Clinical Nutrition* 36 (1982): 750–758.

3. Paola S. Timiras, "Biological Perspectives on Aging," *American Scientist* 66 (1978): 605–613.

4. Trevor H. Howell, *A Student's Guide to Geriatrics*, (Springfield, Ill.: Charles C Thomas, Pub. 1970), 25–45.

5. Marvin M. Schuster, "Disorders of the Aging GI System," *Hospital Practice* 11, no. 9 (September 1976): 95–103.

6. Robert R. Kohn, "Causes of Death in Very Old People," *Journal of the American Medical Association* 247 (May 28, 1982): 2793–2797.

7. James F. Fries, "Aging, Natural Death and the Compression of Morbidity," *New England Journal of Medicine* 303 (1980): 130–135.

8. Donald T. Watts and Christine K. Cassel, "Extraordinary Nutritional Support: A Case Study and Ethical Analysis," *Journal of the American Geriatrics Society* 32, no. 3 (March 1984): 237–241.

9. K.C. Calman, "Physical Aspects," in *The Management of Terminal Disease*, ed. Cicely M. Saunders (London: Edward Arnold Ltd., 1978), 39–43.

10. Lon O. Crosby, "Nutritional Care," in *Clinical Care of the Terminal Cancer Patient*, ed. Barrie R. Cassileth and Peter A. Cassileth (Philadelphia: Lea & Febiger, 1982), 137–150.

11. Joyce V. Zerwekh, "The Last Few Days," in *Hospice and Palliative Nursing Care*, ed. Ann G. Blues and Joyce V. Zerwekh (Orlando, Fla.: Grune & Stratton, 1984), 177–197.

12. Joyce V. Zerwekh, "The Dehydration Question," *Nursing '83* 13 (1983): 47–51.

13. Zerwekh, "The Last Few Days," 183.

14. Funk & Wagnalls Company, Inc., *Standard College Dictionary* (New York: Harcourt, Brace & World, Inc., 1963), 590.

15. Erich Lindemann, "The Symptomatology and Management of Acute Grief," *American Journal of Psychiatry* 101 (1944): 141–148.

16. Therese A. Rando, *Grief, Dying, and Death: Clinical Interventions for Caregivers* (Champaign, Ill.: Research Press Company, 1984), 228–229.

17. James William Worden, *Grief Counseling and Grief Therapy* (New York: Springer, 1982), 11–16.

18. Patricia Murphy, "Studies of Loss and Grief: Tragic Opportunities for Growth," *American Journal of Hospice Care* 2 (1985): 10.

19. Rando, *Grief, Dying, and Death*, 227–250.

20. Lindemann, "Symptomatology and Management of Acute Grief," 141–148.

21. Colin Murray Parkes, "Effects of Bereavement on Physical and Mental Health — A Study of the Medical Records of Widows," *British Medical Journal* 11 (1964): 275–279.

22. Colin Murray Parkes, *Bereavement Studies of Grief in Adult Life* (New York: International Universities Press, Inc., 1972), 14–28.

23. Steven J. Schleifer, Steven E. Keller, Maria Camerino, et al., "Suppression of Lymphocyte Stimulation Following Bereavement," *Journal of the American Medical Association* 250 (1983): 374.

24. Robert W. Buckingham, *The Complete Hospice Guide* (New York: Harper & Row, 1983), 134.

25. Colin Murray Parkes, "The First Year of Bereavement," *Psychiatry* 33 (1970): 444–467.

26. J.J. Schwab, "Therapeutic Interventions" (Paper presented at Kent School of Social Work Conference on Death and Grief, Louisville, Kentucky, 1 April 1976.).

27. Marian Osterweis, Fredric Soloman, and Morris Green, eds., *Bereavement Reactions, Consequences, and Care* (Washington, D.C.: National Academy Press, 1984), 15–44.

28. M. Chenard, *Coping with Grief* (Convent Station, N.J.: KaKouna Press, 1981), 16.

29. N. Brozan, "Helping Bereaved Children," *New York Times*, 28 January 1985: p. B-7.

30. M. Shoor and M.H. Speed, "Death, Delinquency and the Mourning Process," in *Death and Identity*, ed. Robert Lester Fulton (New York: Wiley & Sons, 1965), 44–56.

31. Harriet Sarnoff Schiff, *The Bereaved Parent* (New York: Penguin Books, 1978), 57.

32. Colin Murray Parkes, "Psychological Aspects," in *The Management of Terminal Disease*, ed.

Cicely M. Saunders (London: Edward Arnold Ltd., 1978), 58.

33. John H. Flavell, *The Developmental Psychology of Jean Piaget* (New York: Van Nostrand Reinhold Co., 1963), 15–40.

34. Myra Bluebond-Langner, *The Private World of Dying Children* (Princeton, N.J.: Princeton University Press, 1978), 166–197.

35. Elisabeth Kubler-Ross, *On Death and Dying* (New York, MacMillan Company, 1969), 178–179.

36. Ida Marie Martinson, *Home Care for the Dying Child: Professional and Family Perspectives* (New York: Appleton & Lange, 1976), 86.

37. Ida Marie Martinson, "Home Care for Children Dying of Cancer," *Pediatrics* 62 (1978): 106–113.

38. Robert W. Buckingham, *The Complete Hospice Guide* (New York: Harper & Row, 1983), 125.

39. Ibid., 125.

40. Ibid., 129.

41. Ibid., 134.

42. Ibid., 143.

SUGGESTED READINGS FOR CHILDREN

Arnold, Joan Hagan, and Gemma, Penelope Buschman. *A Child Dies: A Portrait of Family Grief.* Rockville, Md.: Aspen Publishers, Inc., 1983 (160 pages).

Dodge, Nancy. *Thumpy's Story . . . A Book for Children about Death and Grief.* Springfield, Ill.: Prairie Lark Press, P.O. Box 699-B, 1984.

Gaes, Jason. *My Book for Kids with Cancer.* Aberdeen, S.D.: Melius & Peterson Publishing, 1987.

Grollman, Earl, and Grollman, Sharon. *Talking About Death.* Polson, Mont.: Creative Children, Inc., 1985 (21 pages).

Grollman, Earl, and Grollman, Sharon. *Talking About Serious Illness.* Polson, Mont.: Creative Children, Inc., 1985 (30 pages).

Grollman, Earl, and Grollman, Sharon. *Talking About Suicide.* Polson, Mont.: Creative Children, Inc., 1985 (24 pages).

Sanford, Doris. *It Must Hurt A Lot.* Portland, Ore.: Multnomah Press, 1985 (32 pages).

SUGGESTED READINGS

Hymovich, Debra P. "Child and Family Teaching: Special Needs and Approaches." *The Hospice Journal* 2, no. 1 (Spring 1986): 103-120.

Taylor, Lendel Mark. "Hospice Care and Children." *American Journal of Hospice Care* 3, no. 4 (July/August 1986): 26-28.

Chapter 3

An Introduction to Palliative Care

The palliative care movement is based on the long-held recognition but only recent practice that only by honestly facing the problems surrounding death can the fear of death be eliminated and the problems of dying be overcome. The underpinning of the movement is the recognition "that by controlling pain, relieving unpleasant symptoms and providing strong emotional support, death could be natural and dignified instead of a daunting and dehumanizing process."[1]

The purpose of this chapter is to create a picture of palliative care today by presenting its definition, history, philosophy, objectives, standards of care, types of programs, and financial and reimbursement characteristics. With this knowledge, the role of the dietitian in palliative care programs can be more fully understood and appreciated.

WHAT IS PALLIATIVE CARE?

There comes that time in the lives of many patients when medically we must turn from the goal of arresting disease (*curative care*) to the goal of relief of symptoms (*palliative care*). This time usually comes when the patient is diagnosed to have a terminal disease. A disease is defined as terminal when it has progressed beyond the point at which care for the purpose of disease remission is of any value. The length of this condition is difficult to determine and is highly variable, lasting only days in some patients to weeks or months and possibly years in others. Palliative care advocates that, when the quantity of life can no longer be increased, the quality of life must be maximized.

Palliative care is as aggressive as curative care. It is "neither the absence of care nor the provision of passive care. It is active intervention of a specific, goal-oriented kind."[2] Palliative care programs have erased the sad and erroneous words —"there is nothing more to be done"— by addressing the problems of pain, loneliness, and loss of control that are common in dying patients. The aim of these programs is to help the patient and family concentrate on matters of living. Recognizing that human beings are a composite of physical, social, psychological, and spiritual elements, palliative care is interdisciplinary in nature. Because patients are generally surrounded by family and others, palliative care programs identify the patient and the family members as the unit of care.

WHEN IS PALLIATIVE CARE APPROPRIATE?

When is palliative care appropriate? Who should receive palliative care instead of curative care?

These hard questions have no simple answers because it is impossible to apply the word "incurable" with certainty and because it is hard to know when curative treatment is no longer effective. Ann G. Blues suggests that we answer the following six questions in the affirmative before foregoing curative treatment in lieu of palliative care:[3]

1. Has every possible conventional curative therapy been used in an effort to eradicate or control the disease?
2. Are symptoms that indicate a terminal stage actually related to the progressive disease and not to other conditions that are not terminal?
3. Can palliative care relieve symptoms so as to add substantially to the patient's quality of life?
4. Are the patient and his or her family informed and active participants in the decisions that are being made regarding choice of treatment?
5. Has a complete assessment been performed by a physician and a multidisciplinary team in order to document the course of the disease and the patient's specific problems?
6. Does the assessment include attention to the patient's psychological, spiritual, and social needs?

Only when these questions are answered in the affirmative can appropriate palliative care be planned. Further, what is appropriate care can only be competently answered by the joint consensus of the patient, family, physician, and interdisciplinary team.[4]

Much to the good, medical advances have lengthened the time between the diagnosis of a fatal illness, such as malignancy, and death. However, as a result, patients now have more time to develop unrelenting pain, fear, unwanted dependency, and feelings of dehumanization.[5] Because palliative care programs deal with these problems aggressively, it is not uncommon for patients, after a period of individualized palliative care, to appear stronger. Renewed vigor may trigger the desire of patients, their families, or health care team members to reinstate aggressive curative measures. Regardless of what patients choose, they should be given the option to move freely if desired between the "cure" and "care" systems.[6]

HISTORY OF PALLIATIVE CARE

Palliative care is a concept that embodies the centuries-old practice of mutual caring for one another.[7] In the early Greek and Roman eras, such kindness and generosity was usually shown to travelers.

The Earliest Beginnings

The ancient Greeks and Romans believed that to care for strangers would bring blessings from the gods. In Greece, travelers were believed to be under the protection of Zeus Xenios. In Rome, the special bond between host and guest became a contract blessed by Jupiter Hospitalis. In both ancient Greece and Rome, healing sanctuaries known as aesculapia grew up around temples. The Greeks and Romans felt it to be a privilege to help their fellow citizens along the highway of life.[8]

In late Roman and early Christian times, places to shelter pilgrims, the poor and the sick for social and humanitarian reasons sprang up and were called xenodochia. The Decree of Constantinople, 335 A.D., closed the remaining aesculapia and built Christian hospitals and Christian xenodochia. These Christian shelters were self-sustained communities staffed by ordained deaconesses who supplied acute, ambulatory, and long-term care. Poor wayfarers, the sick and dying, women in labor, orphans, and religious pilgrims were cared for in these shelters.[9,10]

The Middle Ages

During the Middle Ages, the words "hospital," "hostel," and "hospice" were used interchangeably, each having a Latin root, "hospes," meaning both host and guest. It was not until the functions and purposes of each facility became more specialized in later years that the terms began to have distinct and separate meanings. During the Crusades, travelers' rests or "hospitia" in which clerics provided food, temporary shelter, and sick care to pilgrims, sprang up adjacent to monasteries. The Knights of Hospitallers of the Order of St. John of Jerusalem in the twelfth century offered aid to religious pilgrims and the sick throughout Europe. Their holdings included active hospices in England, Germany, Italy, Cyprus, and Rhodes.

In the medieval world view, life was not separate from dying. Therefore, pilgrims, travelers, and the dying were housed together, for all were on a journey and needed a place to stop for comfort. What happened to the soul, mind, and spirit was at least as important, if not more so, than what happened to the body. Dying persons were viewed as special because their existence was moving on to a higher plane that each person should desire.[11,12]

As medical practice evolved in sophistication, the "caring" component seemed to lose ground to "curing." Anatomy and surgery developed in the fifteenth century. As physicians moved into hospitals and emphasized the curative and acute physical problems of the sick, monks and nuns remained in their cloisters and cared for those people whom physicians could not heal — the disabled, the chronically ill, and the terminal patients.

The Recent Past

During the 1800s and 1900s as great advances in medical practice occurred, hospitals began to look and feel more like laboratories. Hospitals became well equipped to aid in an acute, life-threatening situation, but seldom seemed able to offer comfort to travelers near their journey's end. In addition, the responsibility of caring for the sick and dying became less a private or religious function and more a public and governmental function.[13]

Era of Modern Palliative Care

Modern palliative care had its beginnings in the 1950s due in large part to the work and inspiration of two women, Cicely Saunders in England and Elisabeth Kubler-Ross in the United States. Cicely Saunders, a physician, former nurse, and social worker, in turn attributes her inspiration to one of her terminally ill patients, David Tasma, an agnostic Jew who had escaped from the Warsaw ghetto in World War II. Through David, this devoutly religious woman came to realize the vast and acute need for alleviating the suffering of the terminally ill. She devoted herself to the task of identifying how to help people die peacefully and with a sense of meaning and purpose about their lives. She and David dreamed of a place, a haven, where the needs of the dying could be met. When David died in 1948 he left 500 pounds British sterling to Dr. Saunders, saying, "I'll be a window in your Home."[14]

St. Christopher's Hospice in Sydenham (near London), England, opened in 1976 and is the result of the dreams and hard work of Dr. Saunders, David, and many others. St. Christopher's was planned to combine the old concept of hospitality and care with the modern skills of a hospital. Through her work at St. Christopher's, Dr. Saunders refined the ideas and protocols that have become the cornerstone for modern-day palliative care. She identified the following five basic elements of a model palliative care program:

1. management of the patient's care by a skilled, interdisciplinary team whose members communicate regularly with one another

2. effective control of the common symptoms of terminal disease, especially pain in all its aspects

3. recognition of the patient and family as a single unit of care

4. an active home care program

5. an active program of bereavement follow-up for the family after the death of the patient[15]

At the same time as Dr. Saunders was formulating a practical philosophy of caring for terminally ill patients, Dr. Elisabeth Kubler-Ross, a Swiss-born psychiatrist at the University of Chicago Medical School, began working with dying patients. Her observations provided a powerful impetus to the development of palliative care programs in the United States. First, she observed that health care providers, patients, and their families knew little about the dying process. She further noticed that dying patients were generally quite willing to talk about their plight and were eager to be heard despite their physicians' doubt. Third, she observed that doctors and nurses decreased their contacts with patients once a terminal diagnosis was made. And last, she found that at the time when dying patients needed more attention and support, they often received less of it.

Expanding her research, Dr. Kubler-Ross developed a framework describing the transitional stages of dying. Her formulated theories were first published in her best-selling book *On Death and Dying*[16] in 1969, which shattered the taboo of not discussing the subject openly and publicly (see Chapter 13). Although other writers[17] have criticized the transitional stages and some[18] have refined them, Dr. Kubler-Ross never claimed that all the stages must be passed through by every patient in a consistent manner. Because palliative care programs deal primarily with cancer patients whose disease is irregular and unpredictable, the stages may not be easily identified. Dr. Kubler-Ross taught that coping with loss and death can only begin in a climate that encourages open communication and acceptance of and by the patient, family, and health care team.

TYPES OF PALLIATIVE CARE PROGRAMS

Together, Drs. Saunders and Kubler-Ross raised the consciousness of many health professionals and public citizens and spurred the modern-day development of palliative care. The first palliative care program in the United States was incorporated in November 1971 as Hospice, Inc. in New Haven, Connecticut. In mid-1974, Hospice, Inc. began serving patients with a community-based home care program and a bereavement program. Still later, Hospice, Inc. became the Connecticut Hospice, Inc., and in the fall of 1979 it opened a 44-bed inpatient facility to augment its home care program. By the late 1970s Connecticut Hospice,

Inc. had become the leader in palliative care program development in the United States. It had, among other endeavors,

- served as a clearinghouse for hospice information in the United States
- coordinated and sponsored the National Symposia on Hospice Care
- contracted with the Department of Health, Education, and Welfare and the National Cancer Institute to study the provision and utilization of hospice services
- held dialogues with governmental officials regarding the need to license and accredit hospice programs
- developed national standards of hospice care
- patented the term "hospice" as a nationally registered service mark (1978); ownership was subsequently transferred to National Hospice Organization (NHO), a nonprofit organization incorporated in Washington, D.C.

In recent years, palliative care activity and innovation flourished in communities from the East to the West Coast and from the North to the South. In just 11 years the number of hospices in the United States increased from one in 1974 to over 1,700 in 1985.[19] Reflecting the nature of the pluralistic society in twentieth-century United States, there are many types of palliative care programs. Madalon O'Rawe Amenta classifies program models into five types: (1) acute care hospital-based, (2) long-term care facility-based, (3) community-based comprehensive home health agency, (4) community-based independent, and (5) volunteer programs.[20]

Acute Care Hospital-Based Programs

Acute care hospital-based programs usually are run in discrete hospital units containing one to ten beds with specially trained staff and a high nurse-to-patient ratio. Other hospitals may not have a designated palliative care unit or specially designated team, but identify patients in units who receive palliative care. Still other hospitals use the scatter-bed model with a specially trained team that floats within the hospital and provides consultation to the unit staff who care directly for the patient. Parkwood Community Hospital Hospice Program (now Nu Med Medical Center) in Canoga Park, California (near Los Angeles) was the first inpatient hospital palliative care unit in the United States in 1978.

The strengths of acute care hospital-based palliative care programs include the administrative expertise and financial stability of the parent institution and a large physician referral base. Problems include a tendency toward less specialized palliative care and toward more conventional care with loss of institutional autonomy. Too, patients unable to pay might not be admitted to the program.[21]

Long-Term Care Facility-Based Programs

Long-term care facility-based programs are found in skilled nursing facilities with dedicated palliative care beds. This type of program may or may not have specially trained staff. Arrangements for home care follow-up are usually accomplished through home health care agencies or other palliative care programs. The strengths and weaknesses of this type program are the same as for hospital-based programs.

Community-Based Comprehensive Home Health Agency Programs

Community-based comprehensive home health agency programs either hire a palliative care team to provide care, or nursing staff members at the home health agency are assigned to families with terminally ill patients as part of their generalized caseload. Staff burnout in these programs is common due to the frequently limited education of home health agency staff members on palliative care techniques and the large and diversified caseload to which they are assigned. Budgetary constraints in under-funded home health agency programs limit the type and amount of palliative care that can be provided. When palliative care team professionals are hired for these programs, they frequently have little or no control over agency program policies, and are thereby limited in providing some aspects of care not commonly practiced in home health agency programs. When over-stretched program administrators do not fully understand or appreciate what palliative care entails, internal politics can develop, which ultimately result in less-than-the-best care that is rendered to terminally ill patients and their families.

Community-Based Independent Programs

Community-based independent programs, in contrast, have specially trained staff who provide palliative home care and/or inpatient care within their own free-standing inpatient facility. The free-standing facility typically has home-like patient rooms and family rooms for the terminally ill patient and family to socialize. A kitchen is usually also available. Unrestricted visiting hours and the presence of children and pets make the free-standing palliative care facility a comfortable place to receive care. In this inpatient facility, family members are encouraged to give the patient as much care as they desire including baths and medications. Family members often sleep in the patient's room or in other designated rooms if available. The staff of these community-based independent programs may provide palliative care to terminally ill patients and their families living in their own homes or may contract with comprehensive home health agencies to provide some direct patient services to home care patients. For these and many other reasons, paid staff in the free-standing facilities report significantly less burnout and a greater sense of accomplishment than workers in hospital-based and home health agency-based programs.[22]

The first free-standing facility in the United States was the Hillhaven Hospice at Tucson, Arizona, occupied in 1977. Community-based independent programs should prosper if they demonstrate high quality patient care and administrative excellence.[23] The newest facilities, which are currently being developed, include day care centers with or without inpatient beds and with or without home care programs.

Volunteer Programs

Volunteer programs are often grassroots efforts with extensive community support and local community boards. Most volunteer programs employ at least one full-time and one part-time employee and 35 to 100 volunteers. The delivery of care to patients is usually coordinated through hospitals and home health care agencies. Unfortunately, administrative knowledge and experience tend to be lacking in volunteer programs, and they generally enjoy less support from the medical community than other programs. Program failure often results from inadequate funding through donations and gifts, contractual problems with hospitals or other agencies, and strict accreditation requirements which inexperienced administrators may not know how to meet. Many volunteer programs are disappearing or merging into other pre-existing models.[24]

Since the inception of palliative care programs in this country, much thought and discussion has centered around the question: Is palliative care and hospice a program or a facility? Sometimes the answer is not readily apparent. Both are a philosophy around which has developed a program of care that is compassionate and competent. Palliative care can be delivered in a multitude of settings, often in buildings that carry the name "hospice" or "palliative care center." As their shared philosophy becomes more and more integrated into hospital and other health care services, fewer buildings may bear their names, and palliative care or hospice as a program separate from other traditional hospital and health care programs may cease to be necessary.

HOW TO SET UP A PALLIATIVE CARE PROGRAM

Often, the success of the beginning efforts of a palliative care program is determined by the type, number, and quality of professionals and interested lay volunteers involved in the conceptualization and development phases. Because we as dietitians work with a variety of terminally ill patients in many types of health care programs — hospital, nursing home, convalescent center, and home care —

our profession is an ideal one to be involved in the development of a palliative care program.

The Planning Committee

The first step in setting up a palliative care program is to establish a planning committee. Alma Stanford and Joyce V. Zerwekh succinctly state the goal of the planning committee in the form of a question: "What can we do together to address the needs of the terminally ill in our institution and community more effectively?"[25] This goal embodies the philosophy of collaboration that is needed in developing any new program that will affect many people.

To develop a community-based program, the planning committee should include both professionals, such as nurses, physicians, clergy, and social workers, and interested business persons and lay leaders. The planning committee interested in beginning a hospital-based program should also include persons in power within the hospital system. Top administrative and medical staff, including department heads, should be involved in the planning process. Without collaboration, an undesirable competitiveness— the "we versus they" mentality—can easily develop, and the planning of a program may never come to fruition.

The initial task of the planning committee is self-education. Each planning committee member must become well versed in palliative care literature. Visiting other programs that exemplify a variety of models and settings is useful. Keeping in close touch with the National Hospice Organization and local, regional, and state hospice associations is also essential.

After self-education, the next task is to conduct an assessment of the needs and resources of the community. The dietitian's familiarity with major community resources can be invaluable to the planning committee in conducting this assessment. In a needs assessment the committee is seeking answers to these questions.

- What is the overall incidence of death in the community?
- What is the incidence of death from cancer?
- How many terminally ill patients are cared for by local hospitals, nursing homes, and convalescent centers?
- How many terminally ill patients are cared for in the home?
- How many terminally ill patients must be cared for outside the community because local services are inadequate?
- Are there other palliative care programs existing in the community or nearby locale?
- What local resources are currently available to help the terminally ill patient and family? Are these resources used by the terminally ill?

- If a palliative care program were to be developed, what type of services are available in the community that could be offered to terminally ill patients? Are these services—the local affiliate of the American Cancer Society, Visiting Nurse Association, Department of Public Health, agencies providing child care, Meals on Wheels food delivery, congregate feeding centers, food pantries, drug stores with delivery services and price discounts to elderly or needy patients, Candlelighters, homemaker services, and grocery stores with home delivery—available and can they be used by terminally ill patients?

- Would support be available from professionals, such as clergy, social workers, gerontologists, family counselors, nurses, dietitians, occupational therapists, physical therapists, physicians, pharmacists, psychiatrists, and psychologists?

One goal of a hospital-based program should be to integrate the palliative care concept into daily medical and nursing practice throughout the hospital. In order to achieve this goal, special consideration will need to be paid to current hospital practice. How will palliative care impinge on current hospital practice, and how will hospital practice impinge on palliative care? If a hospital-based program is being anticipated, such additional questions as the following need to be addressed by the planning committee:

- How many terminally ill patients does the hospital serve?
- What is the annual hospital mortality rate?
- What are the usual causes of death?
- On what unit(s) or in what area(s) of the hospital do patients usually die?
- Does the hospital staff see a need for a palliative care program?
- What does the hospital staff see as their needs and the needs of their patients?
- What are the staff's expectations?
- What departments and units (and individual staff members) exist in the hospital that are offering components of palliative care, such as bereavement counseling, home care nursing, palliative physical care, and pastoral care?
- How will lines of authority and a board of directors or an advisory board be created? If an advisory board is created, who should comprise the membership? What will be the responsibilities of the board?

As the planning committee proceeds in its deliberations, never far from consideration should be these questions.

- Why do we want to establish a palliative care program?
- What services can we provide that are not already adequately provided?

- Where will we obtain funding?
- How will we advertise and promote our program?

The planning committee will need to determine what target patient population will be served by the program. Palliative care programs generally provide care to terminally ill patients with lingering illnesses that have a somewhat predictable course of progression. Persons who rapidly and unexpectedly die in the emergency room, obstetrics department, and intensive care unit should not be considered potential targets for palliative care. Although cancer patients comprise the largest group of patients receiving palliative care in the United States, it is incorrect to assume that patients with other illnesses do not need the same services. Dying patients with pulmonary, cardiovascular, neurological, immunodeficient, and renal diseases are often in need of palliative care. Too, because dying and terminal illnesses transcend age barriers, palliative care should be available to persons regardless of age. Many programs do not take infants, children, or even adolescents into their care, although the number of programs serving these sectors of the population is increasing.

Educating the community and hospital employees about the plans for a palliative care program is another task of the planning committee. Community education can be done in several ways—through public relations efforts, mass media public service announcements, a community-wide "kick-off gala," and other innovative methods. When deciding on whom to educate in the hospital-based program and when to educate them, it is usually wisest to focus educational efforts first on those key policy-making persons, then on the entire hospital staff through disseminating basic information hospital-wide, and finally following up with more specific, indepth informational sessions with individual departments and units.

Philosophy Statement

Writing a statement of philosophy is a critical step in the conceptualization and development of a palliative care program. Developing such a statement helps members of the planning committee explore their own feelings about death and their expectations for the palliative care program. A well-formulated statement of philosophy will help keep the planning committee unified and in agreement regarding its mission. Furthermore, it will help prevent confusion as it undertakes its decision-making tasks. When developed as a group, the underlying premises and meaning of the philosophy are understood because they have been thoroughly explored and examined. Lastly, a statement of philosophy is a useful document for educating the public and others about the program.[26]

When writing a statement of philosophy for a hospital-based palliative care program, the hospital's philosophy of care needs to be considered. Sometimes, the hospital philosophy indicates that it is committed only to acute curative medical care. This philosophy is inconsistent with the palliative care philosophy and therefore may be a roadblock for palliative care programs in that institution. In contrast, the hospital philosophy may complement the palliative care philosophy if it has a stated commitment to the care of the dying and to broad family and community service.

The National Hospice Organization (NHO) issued a philosophy of hospice care that is used nationally as a guide for individual programs. The philosophy, revised in 1981, reads as follows:

> Hospice affirms life. Hospice exists to provide support and care for persons in the last phases of incurable disease so that they might live as fully and comfortably as possible. Hospice recognizes dying as a normal process whether or not resulting from disease. Hospice neither hastens nor postpones death. Hospice exists in the hope and belief that through appropriate care and the promotion of a caring community sensitive to their needs, patients and families may be free to attain a degree of mental and spiritual preparation for death that is satisfactory to them.[27]

Program Description

After the statement of philosophy is developed, a program description is written that describes the services offered by the program. Usually the description lists the health care team members involved in the program with phrases, such as physician-directed, nurse-coordinated, and interdisciplinary team-utilized. A further statement is usually included to indicate that the patient's personal physician is in charge of the patient's care but that the program has a physician who can assist the patient and patient's physician as needed. Most program descriptions also acknowledge that the patient and family are considered to be the unit of care and that the family is encouraged but not required to be an integral part of the health care team.

Also included in the program description are those services provided by the program, which may include part or all of the following: home care, inhospital care, day care, coordination with existing community resources, and bereavement care. The program's policy outlining who can be admitted to the program and any restrictions based on such factors as age, ability to pay, race, and ethnic origin is also stated. Finally, the pledge that palliative care services are available 24 hours a day and 7 days a week is generally made in the program description.

The program description of the Hospice at Riverside in Columbus, Ohio, is shown below.

> Hospice at Riverside provides a coordinated, individualized program of home care, inpatient care, day hospice, and bereavement follow-up to help patients and families cope with a terminal illness. This comprehen-

sive program is administered out of Kobacker House, a free-standing facility.

A medically directed team of nurses, social workers, chaplains, psychologists, nutritionists, pharmacists, therapists, home health aides and volunteers works closely with the patient, family and attending physician to develop a plan of care that provides physical, emotional, social and spiritual support twenty four hours a day, seven days a week. The focus of the program is care at home. However, the inpatient bedrooms at Kobacker House are made available on a short-term basis for respite care and/or pain and symptom management when needed. Day hospice facilities provide a unique opportunity for people with terminal illness to get daytime care and fellowship while families continue working and meeting personal obligations.

Service is provided regardless of the individual's ability to pay. Those who are eligible for admission to the program meet the following criteria. They must:

1. reside in Franklin or southern Delaware counties
2. have a terminal illness with a life expectancy of six months or less and are no longer undergoing curative treatment
3. have an attending physician who approves of the referral and agrees with the hospice principles of care
4. have a family or supportive network that can arrange for a 24 hour caregiver when needed

Support groups and community education in the areas of grief and loss, palliative care and the care of the dying are also provided. Hospice at Riverside is certified by Medicare as a hospice provider and is accredited by the Joint Commission on Accreditation of Healthcare Organizations.[28]

Admission criteria to a palliative care program reflect the program's description. General admission criteria usually include those listed in Exhibit 3-1.[29-31]

Goals and Objectives

Goals and objectives of the program are derived from the statement of philosophy and the program description. Goal statements usually include information about services offered, fiscal security and reimbursement issues, certification, licensure, research, and evaluation. Along with these goals, an estimate of the personnel, resources, and time necessary to accomplish them should be stated. The

Exhibit 3-1 General Admission Criteria to Palliative Care Programs

---

1. The patient has a diagnosis of terminal illness, the disease is specified as progressive and causing death, the stage of the patient's disease is identified, and the method of determination is stated.
2. A determination has been made that cure is no longer considered a realistic outcome of care.
3. The patient has a limited life expectancy (usually less than 6 months prognosis).
4. The patient, family, physician, and hospice program determine and document that the patient and family need skilled intervention.
5. A primary caregiver is present in the home when home care is planned.
6. The patient and family consent to palliative treatment.
7. The patient's physician or other designated physician consents to palliative treatment and supports the tenets of palliative care.
8. The availability of program staff to care for the patient is stated as a requirement; the program provides the patient and family with guidelines that identify the referral services that the program can make available to the patient and family.
9. The program and family (or other caregivers) agree on the expectations of the family and caregivers in giving care to the patient.
10. The program and family (or caregivers) agree on the role that the program staff will play in caring for the patient and family (or caregivers).
11. The patient and family live within a certain distance or travel time from the program site.
12. An acceptable age of the patient may be indicated, such as a minimum or maximum age requirement.
13. Limits on patient eligibility may be stated; ineligible patients may include those who are comatose, have a prognosis of less than 2 days, or have a language barrier that does not permit communication with staff.
14. A statement may be made that there is no discrimination due to race, color, religion, sex, national origin, and ability to pay.

---

principles outlined by the NHO in its standards document[32] should be incorporated into the goals of a program. Jack McKay Zimmerman, medical director of Church Hospital Home Care/Hospice Care Program in Baltimore, suggests the program goals listed in Exhibit 3-2 for care of terminally ill patients, regardless of the type of program.[33]

Objectives (both long term and short term) are next written to clarify the program's goals and make them operational on a day-to-day basis. For example, choosing the second goal in Exhibit 3-2 — provide, for the patient and his or her family, appropriate understanding of the nature of the patient's situation and psychological support to both in dealing with the illness and with impending death — a secondary goal and its corresponding objectives can be written as follows:

Secondary goal: To develop and maintain a bereavement component of the palliative care program.

Exhibit 3-2   Goals of Palliative Care Programs

---

1. Provide the finest available medical care for the patient's medical problems.
2. Provide, for the patient and his family, appropriate understanding of the nature of the patient's situation and psychological support to both in dealing with the illness and with impending death.
3. Provide appropriate spiritual support to the patient and family in dealing with the philosophic and religious aspects of the illness and impending death.
4. Provide assistance to the patient and family in dealing with interpersonal social and financial problems.
5. Render patient care in the optimal setting for the particular circumstances.
6. Provide certain valuable program characteristics, such as continuity, comprehensiveness, and adaptability to individual circumstances.
7. Provide a setting for research into the care of the terminally ill.
8. Provide for ongoing education in the care of the terminally ill.
9. Have a positive impact on the remainder of the health care system.
10. Be financially feasible.

Source: Reproduced with permission from *Hospice: Complete Care for the Terminally Ill* by Jack McKay Zimmerman, copyright 1981, Urban & Schwarzenberg, Baltimore - Munich.

Objectives

1. Coordinate with the hospital pastoral counseling program in developing a bereavement component that is compatible and consistent with the hospital program.
2. Hire a bereavement coordinator.
3. Develop a system for coordinating the bereavement plans for bereaved families by assigning an interdisciplinary team member to each family.
4. Expand educational programs in bereavement training for interdisciplinary team members.
5. Provide quarterly bereavement gatherings for families of deceased patients.
6. Create a bereavement handbook.
7. Conduct research related to the interdisciplinary team approach to bereavement care.

All in all, the development and implementation of an in-hospital palliative care program usually takes a minimum of 6 months, whereas the development of a community-based program usually takes at least 12 months. Making the decision about when to start providing patient services is difficult. To start services before team education and training are complete can be disastrous. Frustration, feelings of helplessness, and misinterpretation of expected roles and functions can wreak havoc on a developing program. Waiting until everyone is fully educated and trained, on the other hand, can take a very long time, and previously gained momentum can be lost. Waiting for the perfect program will undoubtedly result in no program at all.

Standards of Palliative Care

In this ever-changing world of health care, standards are necessary to govern day-to-day practice and ensure the future of care for terminally ill patients and their families. Standards are necessary regardless of the type of palliative care program. In 1979, the NHO Standards and Accreditation Committee published *Standards of a Hospice Care Program* which was subsequently ratified by the NHO membership. It was the Standards and Accreditation Committee's mandate "to identify those standards which are intrinsic to all forms of Hospice care . . . . to establish criteria which outline acceptable limits for Hospice care. . . . [and] to create and implement mechanisms."[34] The Committee's activities were to be carried out under the direction of the NHO board of directors and in response to input from the NHO membership at large.

Another document, the *Hospice Standards Manual*, published by the Joint Commission on Accreditation of Healthcare Organizations, provides the basis upon which a hospice program is evaluated when a Joint Commission survey is conducted for accreditation purposes. The *Manual* is the most comprehensive and thorough document published for what constitutes an acceptable hospice program. The Joint Commission surveys are conducted by consultant surveyors who are actively involved in some aspect of hospice work. The survey requires written documentation of compliance, on-site observations by Joint Commission surveyors, and public information interviews with consumer representatives, including staff of the program. The on-site survey lasts 1–3 days, after which the decision to accredit or not to accredit is made. The program director has appropriate recourse if the accreditation is not favorable.

Ongoing Palliative Care Program Committees

Several program committees, organized around tasks to be performed, operate simultaneously for the purposes of program development, continuation, and evaluation. The professional expertise of dietitians qualifies us to serve on several program committees, including the following:

- patient care committee
- intake and admissions committee
- finance development committee

- public relations committee
- bereavement committee
- ethics committee
- counseling–spiritual concerns committee
- education and training committee
- volunteer committee
- research and evaluation committee
- quality assurance committee

The patient care committee, ethics committee, and quality assurance committee are the committees on which the dietitian can have major impact.

Frequently, the dietitian has the opportunity to be involved in the development and the ongoing activities of palliative care programs. If you are not privileged to be involved in the initial planning deliberations, you should participate in inservice education programs during which the statement of philosophy, program description, goals, objectives, standards, and the policies and procedures are discussed. You should be made aware of the activities of the program before working with the team and should be kept up-to-date as goals are accomplished or revised as needed. Attending staff meetings provides you with a means to learn about how the program functions administratively.

If a program has already been developed and you have not been involved in its inception, you may have to do a selling job in order to be included on the interdisciplinary team. In order to explore in a nonthreatening way what dietitians can do for terminally ill patients and their families, you may wish to present a relevant nutrition topic at weekly interdisciplinary team meetings. Presentation of a 5-minute topic, such as those identified in Exhibit 3-3, is an informative and practical method of educating the team and becoming involved in palliative care in three ways: (1) The talks give the team members information about what the dietitian can do for patients and in so doing can help formulate the role and responsibilities of the dietitian in palliative care programs, (2) the talks prepare the team to answer some of the questions on nutrition that they will be frequently asked by patients and families, and (3) the talks promote the acceptance of the dietitian as a participating and valued member of the interdisciplinary team.

In addition, to identify the dietitian's expertise and encourage your inclusion on interdisciplinary care teams, volunteer your expertise in developing policies and procedures related to the actual mechanism of feeding patients. Dietitians have expertise critical to the establishment of a successful inhouse program. Sometimes we must encourage program planners to utilize our expertise by actually providing the planners with a listing of food service/nutrition services that an inhouse or outpatient/home care or off-campus institution program will need.

Exhibit 3-3   Suggested Topics for Mini-Lectures

- "Chicken Soup and Things" — the meaning of food to the ill patient versus the well individual
- "Let Them Eat Cake" — the philosophy of feeding terminally ill patients
- "Dehydration: Is it an Uncomfortable Death?"
- "Death of a Government Hostage" — dealing with the guilt imposed by the dietary recommendations of the National Cancer Institute
- "Dying: A Time for Hot Dogs and Salt Shakers" — dietary modifications in terminally ill patients with cardiovascular disease
- "Stimulating the Stomach with Steroids" — the pros and cons of steroid use in dying patients
- "Milk and the Endocrine System" — why diet fails to correct hypercalcemia
- "Foods: The Hiccough Producers"
- "Foods: The Odor and Gas Producers"
- "Foods: The Constipators"
- "Foods: The Rotor-Rooters"

RESISTANCE TO PALLIATIVE CARE

The palliative care movement has its critics. For example, "right to life" supporters may view palliative care programs to be a misguided attempt to control population growth. Some civil rights activists warn that palliative care programs force death when life could be maintained by technical means. Other critics fear that ultimately the nonproductive members of society, such as the elderly, the mentally ill or retarded, and the physically impaired, may be denied basic health and other types of services. Too, advocates of nontraditional or unproven methods of medical therapies may view palliative care as infringing on their rights to sell products or services. A compassionate and competent palliative care program can rebuff these criticisms.

HOSPICE FINANCING AND REIMBURSEMENT

Financing of palliative care in the United States is in flux and will undoubtedly remain so as long as health care expenditures comprise a large portion of the federal government's budget. Mary Cummings attributes much of the problem in understanding the financial status of palliative care programs in the United States to palliative care programs themselves. She laments the nonstandardized accounting and reporting systems using incomplete data, wide variability in program content and intensity, flawed research designs and estimating methods, and lack of documentation of total costs of patient care per illness that make definitive discussion of palliative care financing very difficult.[35]

Nationwide studies of palliative care financing and costs include the 1979 U.S. General Accounting Office project,[36] the Joint Commission on Accreditation of Hospitals project,[37] the National Hospice Study,[38] and others.[39-41]

Conclusions from these national studies and other individual program studies[42-44] confirm that palliative care programs generally have low budgets and receive a significant percentage of their revenue from donations from individuals, grants from foundations, and Medicare and Medicaid.

The National Hospice Study

The most complete and detailed data about the costs of palliative care come from the National Hospice Study (NHS). The purpose of the study was to develop a knowledge base from which informed decisions regarding public policy and legislation could be made. The three-year NHS, begun in 1980 by researchers at Brown University, used 11 hospital-based hospice programs and 14 home care programs as demonstration sites, and 14 other hospices and 12 conventional care programs as nondemonstration sites or controls. The demonstration sites were given virtually a blank check for Medicare and Medicaid expenses engendered in providing nursing care, bereavement care, home and institutional respite care, and outpatient drugs. The 1983 Preliminary Final Report of the NHS documented a 44 percent difference in hospital-based hospice costs of $95 per day and home care hospice costs of $66 per day. However, the length of time that patients spent in a home care hospice (72.5 days) was longer than that spent in a hospital-based hospice (62.3 days). When the length of stay was considered, the total cost per hospice admission was a less marked 24 percent difference ($5,890 for hospital-based hospices and $4,758 for home care hospices), but still quite significant. Within these reported averages, the ranges were great. For example:

- 17.9 percent of home care patients and 9.4 percent of hospital-based patients had total costs (during the entire admission) of $500 or less.

- 22.8 percent of home care patients and 29.3 percent of hospital-based patients had total costs of $6,500 or more.

- The range of costs varied from a low of $30 per day in the lowest cost home care program to $153 per day in the highest-cost hospital-based program.

- Several home care programs had higher per day costs than hospital-based programs.

To explain these variations in cost, it is important to remember that palliative care programs vary in the type of services provided. Costs reflect the range of services provided, the actual utilization of those services, and the costs per unit of providing that service. Costs also vary according to the types of patients being served, the patient's diagnosis and prognosis, the stage at which the patient enters the program, availability of supportive help within the home, and other services in the community. According to NHS researchers,

> whether hospice saves money depends crucially on the type of hospice and the timing in which patients enter hospice. There is no simple, unambiguous answer as to the cost or savings of hospice care. While home care hospice always seems to lead to savings, hospital-based hospice care can lead to cost increases for patients with long hospice stays (longer than 2 months).[45]

What is clear is that hospice care is not necessarily cheaper than conventional care, nor does it always save money for patients, insurers, and society.

In 1978 Kenneth P. Cohen surveyed insurance companies to identify what, if any, hospice benefits they offered at that time. A 25 percent response rate was received to the 582 mailed questionnaires. Of the respondents only 17 percent provided any benefit at all. Coverage was typically limited to traditional nursing and medical care while omitting family counseling and bereavement services.[46]

In 1982 the Frank B. Hall Company found that, of 11 major insurance companies queried—Blue Cross and Blue Shield, Aetna Life Insurance Company, Connecticut General, Equitable Life Assurance Society, Hartford Life and Accident Company, Metropolitan Life Insurance Company, Mutual of Omaha Insurance Company, New England Life Insurance Company, New York Life Insurance Company, Prudential Insurance Company of America, and Travelers Insurance Company—most had hospice packages available or were developing them. By so doing the companies were hoping to be seen as adding new benefits and affirming their responsibility to provide appropriate care for dying patients and their families.[47]

The insurance industry is watching the palliative care movement carefully. Reimbursement often continues to be provided only for inpatient services or home health care services that would be covered even without their provision by a palliative care program. Where coverage is already being offered, no additional premium is being charged. In general, insurance companies support national accreditation of palliative care programs because it would help them know which programs to reimburse and which ones to avoid.

Medicare and Medicaid

In August 1982 a campaign was begun by palliative care administrators, lay persons, and legislators to include an optional hospice benefit for those eligible for Medicare as part of the Tax Equity and Fiscal Responsibility Act (TEFRA). The final regulations appeared in *The Federal Register* on December 16, 1983 and have been modified by the passage of the Catastrophic Health Care Bill of 1988. The law provides a hospice benefit as an option for Medicare patients who are diagnosed as terminally ill with 6 months or less to live. Patients may use this benefit only when receiving palliative care through a Medicare-certified program. To accept the hospice option means that the patient waives traditional Medicare benefits, but is given three opportunities (once during each of three certificate periods) to revoke the hospice option and resume traditional benefits. The three certificate periods include two of 90 days each and one of 30 days, for a total of 210 days. At the beginning of each benefit period, recertification of the diagnosis of terminal illness must be made. At the end of the 210 days if the patient is still alive but wishes to opt for continued hospice care and the hospice program certifies that the patient's prognosis is still less than six months, Medicare will continue to pay for the patient's hospice care.

For programs to be eligible to receive Medicare reimbursement, they must provide inpatient, outpatient, and home care services 24 hours per day, 7 day per week. In addition, four core services must be routinely and directly provided by hospice staff members: nursing services, physician services, medical social services, and counseling.

In addition, the regulations mandate that a program have a written plan for providing hospice care to each patient and that the plan must be established before care is provided. The plan must also be periodically reviewed by the patient's attending physician, the hospice medical director, and the interdisciplinary team. A minimum of 80 percent of a program's enrollment days must be home care; a maximum of 20 percent is reimbursed for inpatient days.[48]

The Medicare benefit also requires that volunteers participate in the provision of care and that a pastoral or other counselor be a member of the interdisciplinary team. Bereavement care is also mandated, but is not reimbursable. Reimbursement covers nursing care, physician services, physical therapy, occupational therapy, speech therapy, homemaker services, dietary counseling, and inpatient bereavement. Ninety-five percent of a patient's outpatient drugs and medical equipment is paid for out of the Medicare benefit; the patient pays the remaining 5 percent. Daily rates in 1988 for the Medicare benefit are shown in Table 3-1. Rates are set nationally, but are adjusted regionally.

Routine home care is defined by the Health Care Financing Administration to cover service provided at home, but not to include continuous care. Continuous home care predominantly covers professional nursing service in the home during

Table 3-1 Daily Medicare Reimbursement Rates, October 1988

Type of Care	Reimbursed Rates ($)
Routine home care	65.01
Continuous home care	379.39
General inpatient care	288.61
Inpatient respite care	66.83

Source: Medicare Flyer #88-14 Hospices, p.3. Provided by Blue Cross and Blue Shield, Chicago.

brief periods of crisis. General inpatient care covers the treatment of acute or chronic symptoms that cannot be managed in other settings. Inpatient respite care covers short-term inpatient care to provide respite for the family or caregiver.[49]

The views of hospice administrators concerning the Medicare hospice benefit are mixed. Although many hospice administrators are grateful for the federal funds, most think the reimbursement levels are too low to allow a program to provide the legislated services adequately. Several hail the action as an opportunity to bring true and reliable quality of care to hospice; others fear the benefits will legislate out the palliative care altruism and philosophy of care and replace it with a listing of services.

Participation in the Medicare hospice benefit has not been overwhelming. These reasons have been given for this poor participation:[50,51]

- Requiring that the four core services be delivered only by program employees (disallowing subcontracting) is a disincentive, especially for community-based and independently owned programs.

- The 80/20 split has deterred programs from seeking Medicare certification, especially hospital-based programs, skilled nursing facility programs, and free-standing hospices that control their own inpatient beds and that generally admit patients who live alone, have not had a primary caregiver, and who are likelier to be sicker. The inpatient rate is too low to cover the labor-intensive needs of hospitalized terminally ill patients who may need to be admitted for pain control or symptom management. The few patients who might require more than the allotted inpatient days could financially devastate a program, especially if prolonged hospitalization was required.

- Ethical concerns, such as who can have access to the program's services, are raised by participation in Medicare. Would certification result in the need to be more restrictive in delivering palliative care because of the financial limitations imposed by that certification? In addition, the physician is pressured to not admit patients whose prognosis may exceed six months. Yet, increased longevity is an inherent outcome of palliative care.

- The stipulation that a patient waive other Medicare benefits in lieu of the hospice option is problematic to patients, families, and health care team members alike and frequently interferes with helping the patient come to terms with death.

The Joint Commission on Accreditation of Hospitals Hospice Project

With funds from the W. K. Kellogg Foundation, a hospice standards project was undertaken by the Joint Commission in 1982.[52,53] The project's goals were three-fold.

1. assess the state-of-the-art of hospice care delivery
2. determine the feasibility of voluntary hospice accreditation
3. develop hospice standards

In August 1983, JCAH added hospices to other types of institutions already voluntarily accredited. In January 1984, surveys of hospices began. By December 1985, 60 hospices had been accredited by the Joint Commission.

These standards stress excellence of care irrespective of the program model chosen. As compared to what is allowed under the Medicare option, the Joint Commission's standards permit a wider definition of palliative care. Table 3-2 compares the Joint Commission standards and the standards required to obtain Medicare benefits on selected criteria.

It is important for palliative care program professionals, including the dietitian, to be cognizant of current palliative care financing issues because staff salaries are necessarily affected by the fiscal underpinnings of the program. Program administrators and staff, including the dietitian, should watch for changes in laws governing palliative care reimbursement. The Joint Commission standards for accreditation too will change as time passes.

Dietitians and other palliative care professionals must be flexible and ready for change, particularly in the areas of: (1) palliative care financing, such as prospective reimbursement, capitation payment, inclusion of nutritional services in third party and governmental regulations and policies, and (2) program incorporation, such as vertical integration and mergers in for-profit chains or as joint ventures, and in health maintenance organizations or preferred provider organizations.

Table 3-2 Comparison of Joint Commission Standards and Medicare Benefits on Selected Criteria

Criteria	Joint Commission Standards	Medicare Benefit
Emphasis	Continuity of care	Continuity of care and palliative support
Patient hospice days	No total days or election periods	Reimbursement criteria: two 90-day and one 30-day election periods, no total days
Ratio of home care to inpatient days	No ratio	80/20
Core services required	None	Four: nursing, physician, medical social services, counseling
Professional management provision	None	The hospice program is legally, clinically, and financially responsible for all other patient services rendered outside the hospice
Subcontracting of services	Allowed	Not allowed
Volunteer component	Recommended only; specific education and supervision of volunteers are required if volunteers are utilized; limits of practice are delineated	Required
Bereavement services	Not required but must have documented bereavement training program	Required
Quality assurance	Required quality assurance and utilization review	Required peer review and quality assurance activity
Survey procedures	Required visits with patient, in team conference, and in administrative meetings; tours of contracting facilities are required	Conducts patient interviews; attends team meetings; reviews medical records

NOTES

1. Sir George Young, "The Hospice Concept," in *Hospice: The Living Idea*, ed. Dame Cicely Saunders, Dorothy H. Summers, and Neville Teller (London: Edward Arnold Ltd., 1981), 1.

2. Peter A. Cassileth, "Common Medical Problems," in *Clinical Care of the Terminal Cancer Patient*, ed. Barrie R. Cassileth and Peter A. Cassileth (Philadelphia: Lea & Febiger, 1982), 15.

3. Ann G. Blues, "Hospice Philosophy of Appropriate Care," in *Hospice and Palliative Nursing Care*, ed. Ann G. Blues and Joyce V. Zerwekh (Orlando, Fla.: Grune & Stratton, 1984), 6–7.

4. Ibid., 7.

5. Herman Feifel, *New Meanings of Death: Death in Contemporary America* (New York: McGraw-Hill Book Co., 1977), 4–12.

6. Cicely M. Saunders, *The Management of Terminal Disease* (London: Edward Arnold Ltd., 1978), 1–2.

7. Robert W. Buckingham, *The Complete Hospice Guide* (New York: Harper and Row, 1983), 11–13.

8. Madalon O'Rawe Amenta, "The Hospice Movement," in *Nursing Care of the Terminally Ill*, ed. Madalon O'Rawe Amenta and Nancy L. Bohnet (Boston: Little, Brown & Co., 1986), 49–64.

9. Buckingham, *The Complete Hospice Guide*, 11–13.

10. Amenta, "The Hospice Movement," 49–64.

11. Buckingham, *The Complete Hospice Guide*, 11–13.

12. Amenta, "The Hospice Movement," 49–64.

13. Buckingham, *The Complete Hospice Guide*, 11–13

14. Saunders, *The Management of Terminal Disease*, 201.

15. Paul R. Torrens, ed., *Hospice Programs and Public Policy*, (Chicago: American Hospital Association Publishing, Inc., 1985), 7.

16. Elisabeth Kubler-Ross, *On Death and Dying* (New York: Macmillan Publishing Co., Inc., 1969), 1–289.

17. R. Schultz and D. Aderman, "Clinical Research and the Stages of Dying," *Omega* 5 (1974): 137.

18. Joan Carr, "The Dying Process: A Psychological Continuum," *American Journal of Hospice Care* 3, no. 4 (July/August 1986): 34–38.

19. Barbara A. McCann, "Keynote Address," Address presented at the Pennsylvania Hospice Network, Fifth Annual Meeting and Conference, Pittsburgh, Pa., 4 October 1985.

20. Madalon O'Rawe Amenta, "Hospice Care Prospectives," in *Nursing Care of the Terminally Ill*, ed. Madalon O'Rawe Amenta and Nancy L. Bohnet (Boston: Little, Brown & Co., 1986), 377–379.

21. Dottie C. Wilson and David J. English, "Issues in Hospice Administration," in *Hospice Programs and Public Policy*, ed. Paul R. Torrens (Chicago: American Hospital Publishing, Inc., 1985), 224–225.

22. Vincent Mor and Linda Laliberte, "Burnout among Hospice Staff," *Health and Social Work* 9 (1984): 274–283.

23. Wilson and English, "Issues in Hospice Administration," 224–225.

24. Claire Tehan, "Has Success Spoiled Hospice?," *Hastings Center Report* 15, no. 5 (October 1985): 10–13.

25. Alma Stanford and Joyce V. Zerwekh, "Integration of Hospice into the Acute Care System," in *Hospice and Palliative Nursing Care*, ed. Ann G. Blues and Joyce V. Zerwekh (Orlando, Fla.: Grune & Stratton, 1984), 294.

26. Ann G. Blues, "Establishing a Community Hospice," in *Hospice and Palliative Nursing Care*, ed. Ann G. Blues and Joyce V. Zerwekh (Orlando, Fla.: Grune & Stratton, 1984), 278.

27. Standards and Accreditation Committee, National Hospice Organization, *Standards of a Hospice Care Program* (McLean, Va.: National Hospice Organization, 1981), 8.

28. Hospice at Riverside, "Overall Program Description" (Columbus, Oh.: Riverside Methodist Hospitals, 1989), 1.

29. Dottie C. Wilson and David J. English, "Issues in Hospice Administration," in *Hospice Programs and Public Policy*, ed. Paul R. Torrens (Chicago: American Hospital Publishing, Inc., 1985), 237–238.

30. National Hospice Organization, *Standards of a Hospice Program of Care*, 6th rev. (McLean, Va.: National Hospice Organization, 1979), 10–12.

31. Cicely M. Saunders, "Hospice Care," *American Journal of Medicine* 65 (1978): 726–728.

32. National Hospice Organization, *Standards of a Hospice Program of Care* (Arlington, Va.: National Hospice Organization, 1982).

33. Jack McKay Zimmerman, *Hospice: Complete Care for the Terminally Ill* (Baltimore, Md.: Urban & Schwarzenberg, 1981), 5–6.

34. Standards and Accreditation Committee, National Hospice Organization, *Standards of a Hospice Care Program* (McLean, Va.: National Hospice Organization, 1979), 2.

35. Mary Cummings, "Current Status of Hospice Financing" in *Hospice Programs and Public Policy*, ed. Paul R. Torrens (Chicago: American Hospital Publishing, Inc., 1985), 140–141.

36. General Accounting Office, *Report to the Congress: Hospice Care — A Growing Concept in the United States (HRD-79-50)* (Washington D.C.: Government Printing Office, 1979).

37. P. Falknor and D. Kugler, *JCAH Hospice Project, Interim Report: Phase I*, (Chicago: Joint Commission on Accreditation of Healthcare Organizations, 1981), 1.

38. David S. Greer, Vincent Mor, S. Sherwood, John M. Morris, and Howard Birnbaum, "National Hospice Study Analysis Plan," *Journal of Chronic Disease* 36 (1983): 737–780.

39. National Hospice Organization, Health Services Foundation, and Hospital Research and Educational Trust, "Delivery and Payment of Hospice Services: Investigative Study. Final Report" (McLean, Va.: National Hospice Organization, 1979).

40. California Department of Health Services, "Palliative Care Service Pilot Project. Report to the 1980 California Legislature on the Hospice Project, Pursuant to Assembly Bill 1586, CH 1324" (Sacramento, Ca.: California Department of Health Services, 1980).

41. Robert W. Buckingham and Dale Lupu, "A Comparative Study of Hospice Services in the United States," *American Journal of Public Health* 72 (1982): 455–463.

42. Sylvia Ann Lack and Robert W. Buckingham, *First American Hospice: Three Years of Home Care* (New Haven, Conn.: Hospice, Inc., 1978), 12–13.

43. Carleton J. Sweetser, "Integrated Care: The Hospital-Based Hospice," *Quality Review Bulletin* 5, no. 5 (1979): 18–22.

44. Larry A. Van de Creek, "A Home Care Hospice Profile: Description, Evaluation, and Cost Analysis," *The Journal of Family Practice* 14 (1982): 53–58.

45. Howard G. Birnbaum and David Kidder, "What Does Hospice Cost?," *American Journal of Public Health* 74 (1984): 689–697.

46. Kenneth P. Cohen, *Hospice: Prescription for Terminal Care* (Rockville, Md., Aspen Publishers, Inc., 1979), 155.

47. P. Berger-Friedman and T. O'Hara, *Hospice Reimbursement Study* (Briarcliff Manor, N.Y.: Frank B. Hall Consulting Co., 1982), 40.

48. Department of Health and Human Services Health Care Financing Administration, *State Operations Manual Provider Certification Condition of Participation* (No. 418.68) (Washington, D.C.: U.S. Government Printing Office, 1982), 30.

49. Wilma Bulkin and Herbert Lukashok, "Rx for Dying: The Case for Hospice," *New England Journal of Medicine* 318, no. 6 (February 11, 1988): 376–378.

50. David S. Greer and Vincent Mor, "How Medicare is Altering the Hospice Movement," *Hastings Center Report* 15, no. 5 (October 1985): 5–9.

51. Ronald Bayer and Eric Feldman, "Hospice under the Medicare Wing," *Hastings Center Report* 12, no. 6 (December 1982): 5–6.

52. Barbara A. McCann, *The Hospice Project Report* (Chicago: Joint Commission on Accreditation of Healthcare Organizations, 1985), 1–83.

53. Barbara A. McCann and K. Hill, "The Hospice Project," in *Quality of Care for the Terminally Ill: An Examination of the Issues*, ed. Karen Gardner (Chicago: Joint Commission on Accreditation of Healthcare Organizations, 1985), 1–168.

Chapter 4

The Palliative Care Team

The process of dying is not only one of dying — it is also one of living. And whether patients have the opportunity to live and die in whatever way they find meaningful depends in large measure on who takes care of them. Palliative care programs recognize that, in order to help patients live to the fullest, even while dying, many more aspects of living and dying need to be addressed than can be done by any one person. Therefore, a key element of these programs is a care team, composed of many and varied members, the combined efforts of whom can help dying patients and their families live as fully as possible until the patient dies.

Patients and families are the center of the palliative care team. It is around them that the whole team revolves. In order to provide the best possible care to patients and their families, the team typically includes the following members:

- the patient's physician
- the program medical director
- the program administrative staff
- the program nurses
- the program clergy
- the program social workers
- the program psychiatrist or psychologist
- the program dietitian
- the program pharmacist
- the program therapists: enterostomal, physical, occupational, speech, art, and music
- the program dentist
- the nonprofessional volunteers

In this chapter the members of the palliative care team, their contributions, and the interrelationships among their roles are discussed. As a working group, conflicts between team members are bound to occur. Therefore, it is important to explore some of these common conflicts and suggest some potential solutions to them. Because it is the patient and family who comprise the unit of care for the palliative care team, it is important to first discuss them as that component through which all other members have reason for functioning.

THE FAMILY

The nature and definition of the family are fluid and ever changing. The family of today is different than the family of 20 years ago when palliative care programs began in the United States and, without a doubt, will be different than the families of 20 years in the future.

Defining the family is no easy task, because as Ginette Ferszt and Priscilla Houck note, "The family is more than just a collection of individuals; the whole is greater than the sum of its parts." [1] For our purposes, the word "family" is defined as a group of people who share some degree of a past, who currently are experiencing some degree of emotional bonding, and who are now or have in the past usually lived together. Examples of bonds that exist within the family structure include affection or love, caring, loyalty or commitment, responsibility or interdependence, and gratification. Traditional two parent–children families, single-parent families, unmarried couples with or without children, extended families, blended families, communal groups, homosexual partners, and religious orders are all families. As is often experienced in palliative care, the members may or may not be blood related, and the ties that unite may or may not be legal. To many of our dying patients, the family bond may extend past the definition used here to also include pets and co-workers with whom the patient feels a significant attachment.

No matter what the design, each family has its own unique history, traditions, values, communication patterns, and characteristic ways of handling the everyday experiences of life. Overlaid on the characteristics that define the family, each member brings a personal history and personal needs, expectations, skills, and values. Despite the changes in family functions over the years, the family is still the primary institution in which each member practices behavior; develops attitudes, beliefs, and values; and experiences growth through fulfillment, failures, health, and illness. Amidst change, the family continues to be the social institution concerned with the personal and private aspects of life. In so doing, it is a source of great strength and unity to its members, yet inherent in its very existence is risk.

The Family in Crisis

Because the family is the major source of emotional development in our lives, when it is struck with a crisis, such as the life-threatening illness of a member, it becomes vulnerable to disruption. Emotional needs of its members may be unmet. Changes in roles and relationships may be required but difficult to achieve. Finances may be ravaged. The palliative care team must recognize that families with a terminally ill member are at great risk for physical and mental health problems. The incidence of suicide, alcoholism, and divorce increases in families with a dying member, especially when grief and bereavement are handled inappropriately (see Chapter 2). It is the responsibility of each member of the palliative care team, individually and collectively, to assist the family in coping with the patient's illness so that the family as a unit can remain intact.

The Family as Caregiver

The word "caregiver" in palliative care terminology generally refers to the person or persons in the home who are primarily responsible for the care of the dying patient. In many families, the caregiver is the patient's wife, husband, mother, daughter, sister, or other family member. In other families, the caregiver may be a paid health care professional, volunteer, or friend. In this textbook the word "caregiver" is reserved for the family members who care for the patient, not the palliative care team members or other paid or volunteer personnel or friends unless they live in the patient's home.

In palliative care, conflicts often arise in determining who will be the caregiver. Traditionally, caregivers in palliative care have been spouses or blood relatives (usually parents, daughters, or sons). More recently, there has occurred a move from care being provided primarily by spouses or blood relatives toward care being provided by others.

It is likely that this trend will accelerate as palliative care programs expand to provide care for patients with such illnesses as acquired immune deficiency syndrome (AIDS). Often, with homosexual patients with AIDS, persons vying to be caregivers include both the traditional nuclear family (e.g., the mother and father) and the nontraditional new family (e.g., the homosexual partner with whom the patient has lived). Similarly, more than one family can become involved in the caring situation when a dying person has both grown children and a "new" spouse. In both of these examples, if the families have different values and beliefs about who should have decision-making power in caring for the dying person, conflicts can quickly arise.

Palliative care team members need to remember that the patient *and* family, which can include more people than just those designated as caregivers, is the unit of care, not just the patient alone. Therefore, the team needs to support each family member while at the same time accepting the patient's right to relate or not to relate to individual family members. Additionally, the team must accept the right of each family member to relate or not to relate to each other as desired. Although it is often difficult, team members must put aside personal views on how relationships between persons "ought" to be and instead must allow the patient and family to relate to each other as they choose.

Family Assessment

When a patient and family are admitted to a palliative care program, a program professional (usually a nurse) does the initial assessment of the patient and family. Data collected include a "who's who" in the family, each member's stage of development, and the multiple relationships among individual family members. However, gaining a complete understanding of the family's interrelationships will require more than an initial assessment interview. Other data gleaned during the initial visit should include the family's religious, cultural, socioeconomic, and ethnic characteristics; their community involvement and interactions; and information about the physical setting wherein the family reside.

After the initial assessment is performed, other team members become involved as necessary in establishing the goals for care and providing needed assistance. The goal of each team member must be to help the patient and family deal with the process of living and dying in ways that are most meaningful to them.

In most family situations, several team members are required to help the patient and family achieve a satisfactory death and remain intact as a family. The dietitian plays an integral role. The section, "Implications for the Dietitian" later in this chapter, begins to discuss the dietitian's role in assessing the patient and family, in providing professional services, and in functioning as an interdisciplinary team member. Chapters 7, 8, 9, 11, and 13 provide much more information in these areas.

Family Fears and Needs

More and more, patients are voicing their wish to die at home instead of in the hospital or in other health care institutions. Marion B. Dolan enumerates several advantages and disadvantages of home-care, noting that often the advantages to the patient can be disadvantages to the family.[2] Advantages to the patient include maintaining the continuity of long-time habits, creature comforts, family, and friends that have had meaning to the dying patient throughout life. Another advantage of home care to the patient is the lack of need to comply with outside-imposed routines, such as those that are necessary with hospitalization. Dying patients cared for at home can usually retain a higher degree of independence and control over their lives.

However, disadvantages of home care are also significant to the life of the family. In many families, the patient's presence dominates family life and disrupts normal routines. This disruption can place pressure on individual family members—on some more than others—which can cause them to grow weary. Such weariness is often perceived by the patient who in turn feels guilty for being a burden. A vicious cycle of uncomfortableness and guilt frequently arises. Additionally, family members who are not initially adept at home care will impart their uncertainties and fears to the patient, which adversely affects the patient's peace of mind. Finally, even though a tremendous amount of love may be present, there are some people who cannot tolerate the ambience of a sickroom or the ever-present threat of death.

The successful accomplishment of home care requires that the attitudes and abilities of family members caring for the patient mesh. By exploring these persons' attitudes and beliefs about home care, a host of fears will be brought to light. Identification of these fears and needs, development of a well-designed plan, provision of appropriate professional assistance, and commitment to trying home care are all required to provide home care effectively.

Patient and family members have many fears about performing the tasks of caring for a terminally ill family member.[3,4] The fear that the future will hold some unmanageable crisis for which they will be unable to obtain help is very real. Family members are often unable to distinguish a serious from a trivial problem and typically interpret small or large changes in the patient as "ominous." They fear not knowing what to do in emergencies and at the time of death. Life is frequently described as a roller coaster ride, with problems stabilizing only to result in the development of new problems. Family members worry about the effects of caring for the patient on other family members. Such heightened awareness is often exhausting. Feelings of isolation and being trapped are not uncommon. Yet, many terminally ill patients and families have gone through Elisabeth Kubler-Ross's stages of death and dying and now want help to cope and die peacefully without pain. Palliative care programs provide help in both types of situations. Reassurance is probably the most universal, often unstated, request that the terminally ill patient and family have.

The needs of a dying patient and of the family with a dying member have been extensively studied. The dying person's needs, regardless of age, do not differ much from those of the healthy person (Exhibit 4-1).[5–10] Most of all, persons want the physical comfort, security, love, and self-respect that come through performing the meaningful activities of life.

The needs of the family with a dying patient vary according to the family's degree of knowledge and experience with dying, their available support groups, and the interrelationships that exist among family members. These needs, as identified in Exhibit 4-2, have been summarized from several sources.[11–15]

When a family decides to be the caregiver for a dying patient in the home and invites the palliative care team to be part of this care, the family has the responsibility of deciding how active the team will be in the care of the patient. The team educates the family about the nature, symptoms, and predicted progression of the disease and teaches the family the skills that are needed for comfort-oriented care.

Exhibit 4-1 Needs of Terminally Ill Patients

1. To communicate openly and honestly with family members and health care team members, including the opportunity to ask questions, receive answers, and express feelings
2. To receive assurance that the truth about their condition, treatments, side effects, and prognosis is told and that they will not be abandoned
3. To live each remaining day of life to the fullest, with special emphasis on everyday pleasures
4. To make choices about big and little aspects of living, such as whether or not to undergo therapy and what to eat for breakfast
5. To prepare their loved ones for death
6. To conclude their life's business with dignity
7. To receive an abundance of affection
8. To be free of pain
9. To be relieved of the guilt they may feel by causing the family added burdens
10. To be surrounded by love as they are dying and to have someone loving with them at the time of death

After the palliative care team works with the family and reassures family members that they can anticipate and meet the patient's needs, the family's initial fears usually subside. The caregiving skills learned and practiced by the family leave them with the assurance that they did all that they could for their loved one before death.

Family Adaptation

Family assessment is a continuous responsibility of the palliative care team. The more that is known about the patient and family, the better their specific needs can be identified and addressed. Identifying the family's adaptive ability will help the team develop appropriate and realistic goals. Generally, the family's ability to adapt can be measured by assessing each member's communication patterns, roles, relationships, and degree of openness. Based on these factors, family adaptation continua have been developed. Ferszt and Houck[16] classify families as highly adaptive, midrange, and less adaptive. Virginia Satir[17] terms families as either open or closed. Salvador Minuchin[18] describes families as either enmeshed or disengaged.

Whatever terminology is chosen to describe the family's ability to adapt, the more adaptive the family, the greater their ease in dealing with death and the greater the likelihood for long-term appropriate adaptation following death. Highly adaptive families tend to accept the impact of terminal illness as temporary and do not become inflexible or overwhelmed with the stress of illness. Highly adaptive families communicate openly, clearly, and directly. They are able to express positive and negative feelings and acknowledge one another, allowing

Exhibit 4-2 Needs of Families with a Terminally Ill Patient

1. The need to know what is occurring physically and psychologically in the patient's body as the dying process continues
2. The need to know how to provide the best possible care for the patient and how to be involved actively in that care
3. The need to understand who from the palliative care team is responsible for which aspects of patient care and who will coordinate that care
4. The need to know that the patient is receiving competent care by the palliative care team and the family
5. The need to be acknowledged and supported by the team
6. The need to continue each family member's individual life at the same time that they care for the dying person
7. The need to maintain the family as an entity as they care for the dying person
8. The need to come to terms with the meaning of illness, death, and subsequent family reorganization
9. The need for information about resources that can help the family care for the patient at home

disagreements to exist between family members if necessary. Whereas the less adaptive family has little energy to acknowledge each member, the highly adaptive family can accurately perceive each other's needs and recognize contributions of each member. Warmth, caring, kindness, and hope can be felt in the highly adaptive family, although they are also able to express feelings of sadness and grief. Because highly adaptive families have an accurate sense of their needs, they can utilize their problem-solving skills to seek help, initiate actions, and use resources that will help them through periods of stress. The highly adaptive family is easier for the palliative care team to deal with than is the less adaptive family, but each has rewards.[19-22]

Appropriate nursing goals and actions for working with families with various adaptive styles have been described by Ferszt and Houck.[23] Their excellent table has been reproduced as Table 4-1 because dietitians need to be cognizant of appropriate nursing intervention when working with families with a terminally ill member.[24-26]

The fundamental goals identified in Table 4-1 will necessarily be the goals of every team member. For example, when working with the highly adaptive family, one goal that all team members share is to provide information, skills, and support in order to maintain and enhance the family's ability to cope. On the other hand, when working with the less adaptive family, a mutual goal of each team member is to maintain a consistent, realistic plan of care for the family and to support the family in order to minimize further disintegration.

The family's response throughout the dying process and at the time of death is based on several factors, including the significance of the members' interrelation

Table 4-1 Summary of Nursing Responses to Various Family Adaptation Styles

Family Interaction with Health Care Professionals	Nursing Responses
Highly adaptive family	
Communicate clearly, openly, freely express feelings	*Goal:* Provide information, skills, and support to maintain and enhance family coping
Flexible in role changes; able to prepare for change	Enable family to verbalize upset feelings; they benefit from support; recognize that even the most mature person regresses under stress
Able to tolerate anxiety	
Warm and affectionate	
Ease in problem solving and making decisions; work well together	Negotiate meeting times with the family to
Able to perceive needs accurately	Provide information
Able to verbalize needs	Discuss anticipated changes and what they can expect
Initiate contacts with health care team	
Able to establish support systems for themselves	Elicit from them what they identify as needs and/or problems
Welcome suggestions	Review options and choices to facilitate problem solving
Follow through on suggestions or recommendations	Provide health teaching to teach new skills to meet the physical needs of the patient
Use resources appropriately	
	Provide information regarding community resources (ACS, VNA)
Midrange family	
Mixed communication patterns; may blame one another or staff	*Goal:* Initially provide support to develop good working relationship, decrease anxiety, help family regain control
Often able to express feelings with support	Provide information, anticipatory guidance, teaching to assist coping
Overwhelmed emotionally; feel out of control; may either beset or avoid staff; may have a tendency to be passive or dependent initially	Model clear, open, and direct communication
Mixed feelings; negative may predominate	Establish consistent caregivers
Difficulty problem solving; may be resistant to change initially; difficulty absorbing information; may repeatedly ask same questions	Establish family meetings to initially discuss feelings; they usually benefit from verbalization, acknowledgment, and support
Difficulty perceiving their needs; may extend visits too long or want to help when they are unable to	Need much reassurance that they are doing a good job, that their feelings are OK
Difficulty focusing, identifying problems, or independently developing plans	Expect that their behavior may fluctuate and be erratic
	Recognize that initially they may need to be dependent until they regain control

continues

Table 4-1 continued

Family Interaction with Health Care Professionals	*Nursing Responses*
Midrange family	Patience and empathy usually result in family being able to work well together and follow through
	Establish clear goals, assign tasks, state expectations
	Establish structured and frequent brief family meetings to review information and progress
	Be comfortable setting limits; family needs external limits to regain control
	Provide structured opportunities for continued ventilation of feelings
	Structure ongoing meetings to assist with problem solving:
	Jointly identify problems and needs
	Discuss options and choices
	Develop plan
	Refer to community resources as needed
Less adaptive family	
Unclear, confused communication; may be argumentative or challenge staff	*Goal:* Initially focus on maintaining a consistent, realistic plan of care along with supporting the family to minimize further disintegration during this time of stress
Unable to express feelings; high level of anxiety; low tolerance for frustration	
Rigid roles; little or no support between parents	Model clear, open, and direct communication
Flat or negative affect; have great difficulty handling feelings produced by stress of illness	Establish who is information giver on hospice team and let family know
Poor problem-solving skills; often unable to accurately perceive needs or identify problems	Be prepared to handle your own anger and frustration because these families are difficult to deal with
May be hard to contact or involve them in plan	Be aware that anxiety is often transmitted to staff
Have great difficulty making decisions	Understand that for these families, this emotional tone is their normal experience; resist trying to make them express warmth, if it is not their style
May not be able to accept the reality of the situation or how the illness is and will be affecting them	
May pull away from staff as staff atttempts to confront them	Often these families will not benefit from interpretation or reflection of their feelings
Most vulnerable to family system disintegration and disequilibrium	Structure weekly team meetings to develop consistency and coordinate plan of care

continues

Table 4-1 continued

Family Interaction with Health Care Professionals	Nursing Responses
Less adaptive family	Define clearly what is expected of each member
	Ask them to identify their needs and priorities; they may be unrealistic; gently state your perceptions in a nonforceful manner
	Do not force reality since this will only lead to more anxiety and more rigidity
	Be able to tolerate family's tendency to deny while holding on to realistic plan
	Have appropriate expectations recognizing that they may not be able to follow through
	Consult mental health specialist (psychiatric clinical nurse specialist or psychiatric social worker) to assist in management of this type of family and to arrange for appropriate follow-up

Source: From "The Family" by Ginette G. Ferszt and Priscilla D. Houck in *Nursing Care of The Terminally Ill* by Madalon O'Rawe Amenta and Nancy L. Bohnet, Eds. Copyright © 1986 by Madalon O'Rawe Amenta and Nancy L. Bohnet. Reprinted by permission of Scott Foresman and Company.

ships and their emotional makeup, amount of unfinished business, ability to let go, self-confidence and self-esteem, age, sex, religion, occupation, educational level, and ethnic background. Families may have these varied reactions:

- welcomed relief: "It's a blessing for him to be at peace."
- numbness: "When will it really hit me that he's dying — my life is in limbo."
- fear: "When he dies, I'll die too — I don't think I can face life without him."
- anger: "How could he leave me with all these bills?"
- grief for a relationship that never was: "I'm sad and pained because I never had a good relationship with mother — now the chance is gone forever."
- emotional depletion: "Will it ever be over — I can't go on like this."
- withdrawal: "I can't even kiss her good night any more — do you think she notices?"

It is important for team members to look at how the family has dealt with crises before, who played what roles, and what resources were used. Then, the team, with the family's cooperation, aims to identify (1) roles and tasks that need to be performed and (2) roles that family members would like to perform. For example, the patient may need the services of a nurse from a community nursing association. Decisions about who will coordinate the plans with the nursing association then need to be made. Other needs and decisions, such as who will take charge of financial matters and who will be responsible for working with child care and patient care, may also need to be made.

IMPLICATIONS FOR THE DIETITIAN

When approaching each new family it is important for palliative care team members, including the dietitian, to put themselves in a positive frame of mind. Team members need to think of the family as primarily healthy (or as tending toward health) and as capable of learning and growing. This positive frame of reference should be maintained, despite what may have been previously discussed in team meetings or what another team member's experiences with the family might have been. As team members we should believe, when approaching a family, that the family members are trying to do the best they can. We must recognize that people react to circumstances differently and not necessarily the way we would. Overall, we must impart to the patient and family that we respect them, that we affirm their feelings (whatever they may be), and that our purpose in being with them is to support them and to enable them to cope effectively.[27]

The dietitian, as part of the palliative care team, has an especially important responsibility in assessing patients and their families. Many times, food, and whether or not it is eaten by the patient, becomes an issue around which family conflict occurs. Often patients think that they are eating enough, but one or more family members may disagree. Conflict can thus arise between the patient and family or among various family members who have different views on the importance and meaning of food. Frequently, one or more family members may want to force-feed a patient while another member considers force-feeding to be against the patient's wishes or best interests. The dietitian is a key member of the team who can not only identify this potential problem and the various issues involved but who can also suggest solutions.

Assessment of the patient and family by the dietitian is important in helping the team identify goals and objectives for the patient and family. Sometimes the patient does not need the services that a dietitian performs but the family does. The following four cases illustrate this point:

Case 1: A dying woman is cared for by her daughter. The daughter has a 3-month-old child and is breastfeeding. The dietitian recognizes that the emotional and physical stress the daughter is undergoing could result in decreased lactation. Therefore, the dietitian asks the palliative care team nurse during the interdisciplinary team meeting if the infant appears to be receiving adequate nourishment and growing properly. This question will also alert the nurse to ask if the infant is receiving necessary checkups and immunizations.

Case 2: A dying husband is cared for by his wife, who is an insulin-dependent diabetic. During the interdisciplinary team meeting the dietitian seeks information from the nurse about the wife's medical and dietary practices and volunteers to assess these issues and provide counseling if needed. Because the patient and wife have limited financial resources and are eligible to receive assistance from the local Meals on Wheels (home-delivered meals) program, the dietitian suggests that the social worker explore the possibility that this community service would be desired by the family. The dietitian further explains that the Meals on Wheels program could be especially helpful to this family because it provides well-planned diabetic meals that might help the wife take care of her own health needs.

Case 3: The nurse describes the family as highly intelligent, successful, and close. The youngest child, a girl, aged 13, is very thin and, like her two siblings, appears to be highly competitive and eager (almost too eager) to please. The dietitian asks the nurse to look for possible signs of anorexia nervosa in the 13-year-old girl. By making this suggestion, the consideration of nutritional and psychological counseling is thus raised, and the psychologist and dietitian can work closely together if needed.

Case 4: The female patient states that she is not hungry and does not want to eat. One of the patient's daughters, an anti-abortion activist who lives 1,500 miles from her mother, is coming for a visit. Mother and daughter have not seen each other or talked in 6 years because their views on the abortion issue are in conflict. The dietitian at the team meeting discusses the possibility that the daughter's "pro-life" views may extend into wanting to force-feed her mother and that conflict around this issue could occur. The nurse is thus alerted to the potential for conflict and has time to identify a plan of action should the situation arise.

Table 4-1 is especially important for dietitians to study. Understanding the ability of the family to adapt to the crisis of dying will aid you in working with the patient and family. Such knowledge will help you present information in the most usable form—sometimes in detail, sometimes with less detail—and sometimes, especially in the less adaptive family, doing a necessary task yourself, such as placing an order to the patient's pharmacy for a case of commercial nutritional supplement needed by the patient.

THE INTERDISCIPLINARY TEAM

Because the patient and family comprise a complex and interrelated system of physiological, psychological, social, and spiritual systems, no one person can address all of their needs. Therefore, palliative care programs often develop interdisciplinary care teams. Truly interdisciplinary teams of professionals are difficult to find. Such teams only exist when the precept is practiced that "it is the right and the responsibility of members to share in the patient's care." No team member should be denied a role on the team, and each role should be acknowledged by the other team members if interdisciplinary team practice is to succeed.

Just as the family is more than the sum of its members, the team is more than a collection of individuals. Each team member brings personal values and unique life experiences, in addition to a professional preparation and specific role expectations. An effective interdisciplinary team is made up of people who understand the importance of their unique knowledge and who are able both to accept the contributions of other members and to carry out decisions. It takes time, patience, and much hard work for a team to build itself into a functioning body that is more than an administratively determined plan recorded on paper.

Characteristics of an "Integrated" Palliative Care Team

Five elements should be evaluated when deciding if a team is effective or not in achieving integration. As identified by Ann G. Blues,[28] these five elements are (1) group purpose, (2) roles, (3) leadership, (4) communication, and (5) decision and actions.

Group Purpose

It is important for the palliative care team member always to be mindful that the reason for the team's existence is to care for dying patients and their families. In fulfilling this rationale, the team will have many goals to achieve, and individual team members should be included in deciding what these goals will be, who evaluates the progress toward the goals, and what each individual team member's role is in achieving the identified goals. Unfortunately, and too often, goals are established by the program's administrative staff and never shared with the entire team. The team's purpose and goals should be reviewed often, especially if the composition of the team changes frequently, as new members may come with other goals that need to be addressed. Goals of the team will necessarily change as the program changes and grows. The team that does not recognize the need to change as its composition and program change and grow will not develop a truly interdisciplinary nature.

Roles

Team members bring their beliefs of how they should act within that team, and they have a concept, albeit developed to a lesser extent, of how every other team member should act. These perceptions are based on many factors, including education, professional position, perceived importance of their own skills, past team experiences, and a variety of social concepts.[29] Irwin M. Rubin and Richard Beckhard note that there can be vast differences between the way individuals perceive their own roles and the way others see them.[30] These differences can lead to role ambiguity (individuals do not know what is expected), role conflict (expectations are not compatible), and role overload (multiple obligations cannot be met). For a team to be effective, it is imperative that team members know what their roles are on the team and what the roles of other team members are.

Leadership

The leader of the team has a vital obligation to (1) assist members in identifying their role, (2) develop the team concept, or (3) prevent uncooperative team members from sabotaging the concerted efforts of the rest of the team. Leaders should be highly committed to the group's purpose and goals and should have the necessary leadership skills and interpersonal sensitivity to get the job done under agreeable conditions. Leaders should want to lead, and they should be chosen for their ability to do so, not because of their professional stature. The leader can facilitate each team member's involvement on the team. With a supportive and sensitive team leader, the team can develop members who contribute appropriately and become an integral part of the team. Without a supportive and insightful leader, a truly interdisciplinary team will have difficulty coming into being.

Communication

Communication is the key to developing an effective interdisciplinary team. As Blues succinctly states, "All team members must be able to share their observations, frustrations, questions, and decisions and to receive feedback from those who, through different experience and education, can expand their levels of knowledge."[31] The leader has a great deal of influence in fostering this sharing because he or she can inform members what are the acceptable ways of communication, and how to get things done. Some groups allow disagreement and discuss problems openly; others do not tolerate even the mere thought of dissension. Team members, especially new team members, should be told how communication is best accomplished. Chapter 5 includes additional information on communication, staff stress, and burnout.

Decisions and Actions

Palliative care teams make decisions and take actions on those decisions. Team members are most likely to work for an idea or project that they have helped create. In the area of patient care, many team members have the ability and confidence to make decisions and carry them out without the need for team discussion. When complex problems arise, however, that need to be discussed by a larger body of professionals, team discussions can be very beneficial. Interdisciplinary team meetings are an important source of information for all team members and a mechanism to develop team cooperation.

Team cooperation requires that the members have common sense, sensitivity, and a healthy self-image. Whether or not dietitians feel involved, needed, and valued in a palliative care program depends to a large measure on how involved they want to be, how much they extend themselves, and how valued they are by the rest of the team. Becoming an integral member of the palliative care team requires that dietitians be available to patients and team, practice excellence in dietetics, sell themselves to the team, and "toot their own horns." Specific actions that the dietitian can take to become involved, needed, and valued include

- asking to have a written statement of the purpose, goals, and objectives of the program and discussing with the team's leader how the dietitian can assist in accomplishing them
- sharing with the team leader the dietitian's perceived role in patient care and team involvement
- discussing with the team leader the dietitian's perceived roles of the other members of the team, clarifying their roles, and exploring how the dietitian can best work with team members to achieve the goals of the program
- asking the team leader how communication is best achieved within the group; identifying what types of information the dietitian should share with the group during team meetings, what are the appropriate questions to ask, what should not be asked, and the openness of the team to discussion of possible areas of disagreement
- attending meetings, such as staff meetings, inservices, and continuing education events
- volunteering to be on program committees in order to share expertise and foster team cooperation

STAFF MEMBERS OF THE PALLIATIVE CARE TEAM

Staff members of the palliative care team vary according to the type and location of the palliative care program. For example, most palliative care teams that have developed as full-fledged programs and are accredited by the Joint Commission have a diversified and well-integrated team. Palliative care teams located in local health departments may also be multidisciplinary, but tend to have such a large patient load that integration of the team is often negligible. Programs in small nursing homes and day care centers often have no interdisciplinary team and instead rely on volunteers or consultants for expertise that is often not integrated into the program. As improvement occurs in program organization, financial status, and quality and quantity of volunteer or paid professionals, interdisciplinary and integrated care can be expected also to improve.

Acute care settings, such as hospitals and large nursing homes, are increasingly developing palliative care programs and teams that, depending on finances and administrative support, can become well-integrated interdisciplinary efforts. Dietitians should especially be involved in this type of program. The members of such a palliative care team, in addition to the patient and family around which the care team revolve, typically include the following:

- the patient's physician and the program's physician
- the administrative staff, such as a program director, nursing director, patient care coordinator, and bereavement coordinator
- the program's nurses
- the program's social workers
- the program's clergy and the patient's personal spiritual leader, such as a chaplain, rabbi, priest, or pastor
- the program's professional staff members or volunteers, including the dietitian, enterostomal therapist, physical therapist, occupational therapist, speech therapist, pharmacist, psychologist, psychiatrist, dentist, music therapist, and barber or beautician
- the program's lay volunteers

Primary Physician and Program Physician

Most often, the patient's primary physician continues to follow the patient throughout the patient's terminal illness, although the physician may elect to transfer responsibility to the palliative care program's physician.

The program's physician serves as the program's medical director and should have expertise in symptom management and palliative care. He or she writes standards of medical care and may also be the program's administrator and chief spokesperson. As medical director, the physician usually represents the program to the medical community and educates physicians and others about issues surrounding death and dying, medications and other therapies used to control pain and symptoms, and the role of the interdisciplinary team in assisting the patient and family to achieve a dignified and comfortable death.[32]

Administrator

The administrator manages and coordinates all aspects of patient and family care. The administrator can be the team's medical director, but is often a highly skilled nurse, a member of the clergy, or a business leader depending on the type and location of the program. It is the administrator's job to be the liaison between the team and the advisory board or board of directors of the program. The administrator must direct all aspects of the program and its resources in conformity with the philosophy, goals, and policies established by the governing board. The administrator is usually the team member who represents the program to the community and other health care agencies and may or may not lead the interdisciplinary team. Without this person who determines, secures, and manages the financial resources of the program, a program would soon crumble.

Director of Nursing or Patient Care Coordinator

The director of nursing coordinates the program's nursing staff which may consist of inpatient nurses, home care nurses, nursing aides, and homemaker aides depending on the type and location of the program. The director of nursing makes patient assignments and supervises the work of the nurses. In some cases, he or she may perform the initial intake assessment of patients and families. In large programs, there may be another professional, a patient care coordinator, who coordinates the appropriate care and services available with those needed by the patient and family. One or the other professional is responsible for implementing the policies of the program. Both usually work directly under the administrator, or one may be the administrator, or both may be co-directors.[33] Usually one of the professionals leads the discussion at team meetings.

Team Nurses

Generally, team nurses are the most visible team members. They are the professionals who visit the patients and families in their homes, hospitals, or other settings; assess their needs; deliver the needed care; evaluate the care; and document the plan and its achievement throughout the patient's illness. Team nurses teach, counsel, support, and coordinate the services planned for the patient and family. Because nurses are often the only team members to provide patient and family care on a continuing basis, they must keep track of the care that other team members provide and must identify the roles of each provider relative to the care needed by the patient. The nurses are often the team members with the most knowledge of the family and thus continue to be involved in the bereavement phase of care that usually extends at least 1 year after the patient's death.[34]

Social Worker

Community resources for patients choosing home care can be invaluable aids in achieving a dignified death. The social worker and the nurse are the key professional team members who furnish information about programs and services available in the community, such as supplemental feeding programs, homemaker services, and medical equipment available for free or at a nominal charge. They also determine the patient's eligibility for these and other assistance programs. Both work with other team members as necessary and may develop a support system of volunteers from a religious group or social organization to which the patient or family belongs that can augment the team's services.

The social worker can also help the patient and family deal with the emotional, social, and financial impact of illness and death. Social workers are skilled at obtaining maximal benefit from the health care system, including Medicare and Medicaid, insurance, and retirement benefits. Working through the legal process of establishing and executing wills and other legal documents is within the realm of the social worker. The social worker is trained in providing mental health consultation not only to the patient and family but also to the program's staff. Along with the nurse, clergy, and psychologist, the social worker is well qualified to assist the family during bereavement.[35]

Clergy

Clergy persons assess and help meet the spiritual needs of the patient and family. In so doing, they are of great assistance not only to the patient and family but also to the team. If the patient or family has a satisfying tie with a place of worship or a particular minister, priest, or rabbi, then the role of the program's clergy is to support that relationship. The program's clergy will also honor the decision of any patient and family not to receive spiritual assistance. If the patient or family expresses a need for spiritual counseling, however, the program's clergy fills this need. This professional represents the program to the religious community. Expertise in bereavement matters often places clergy in a leadership role in bereavement care. Likewise, because of their experience in exploring ethical issues, clergy persons often coordinate the ethics committee of the program and help the team explore ethical dilemmas during interdisciplinary team meetings.

Professional Volunteers

Palliative care programs have traditionally depended on the services of volunteers to develop and maintain the program. Volunteers, professional and lay, are an invaluable component of palliative care, serving as resources to the staff, patients, and families. In many programs, professional volunteers serve as dietitians, pharmacists, psychiatrists, psychologists, family counselors, dentists, and enterostomal, physical, occupational, art, music, and speech therapists.

Pharmacist

A pharmacist or pharmacologist is an extremely valuable resource for physicians, nurses, other team members, and the patient because of his or her professional knowledge of medications for pain and symptom management. This professional is often asked for technical advice regarding appropriate drug therapy for patients not only during team meetings but also during the middle of the night when no medication being tried is appearing to benefit the patient. The pharmacist may also dispense drugs as needed.

Psychiatrist or Psychologist

The team psychiatrist's services include diagnosis and treatment of organic and functional psychiatric disorders. The psychologist plays a crucial role in counseling the patient, family, and interdisciplinary team. As consultants, psychologists and psychiatrists are very helpful in the resolution of extreme emotional problems that may be due to anxiety, guilt, fear, or grief. Their skills are often directed toward reassurance and support of the normalcy of the patient's and family's responses to grief and stress. They frequently serve also as family counselors. Because of their expertise in bereavement and ethical decision making, psychiatrists and psychologists are frequently called on to serve on bereavement and ethics committees. The psychologist and psychiatrist educate colleagues and team members about psychological issues in death, dying, and bereavement.

Dentist

The dentist can be an invaluable member of the palliative care team. Patients frequently require dental work that can make their lives more comfortable and their dying easier. Dental work often includes tooth extraction or filling, treatment of gum and mouth problems including periodontal disease and stomatitis, denture replacement or repair, and dental relining. Many dental treatments can take place in the patient's home.[36]

Therapists: Enterostomal, Physical, Occupational, Art, Music, and Speech

The goal of each of these therapists in working with terminally ill patients and their families is to maximize the patient's potential to live as fully as possible. The enterostomal therapist is an especially important member of the team when the patient has a colostomy, gastric tube, fungating wound, or pressure sore. Suggestions from this professional are invaluable in treating open wounds, in preventing leaks around stomas, and in preventing or treating complications resulting from colostomies, fistulas, and pressure sores.

Unless the patient's life is expected to be long, therapists rarely attempt rehabilitation. Instead, they suggest ways to help the patient maintain current abilities and functions. Each therapist assesses the patient's potential, works with the patient and family to enable the patient to function with the greatest possible independence, helps the patient understand personal limitations, and advises the team and family regarding the patient's expectations and goals. By their unique contributions, each professional therapist can help the patient and family achieve release from tension, add some recreation to life, and experience some degree of accomplishment and pride in independence.

Lay Volunteers

Lay volunteers often provide personal care for the patient. They may relieve the family at the patient's bedside by giving the patient back rubs or ice chips, reading to the patient, or writing letters for the patient. They may also assist the family by cooking, cleaning, shopping, or running errands. Sometimes they stay with the patient while the family leaves the house for a few hours. At other times the volunteer may just sit and talk with patients and families.[37] Many volunteers are helpful in offering spiritual support and in helping with occupational, art, and music therapy.[38] Other volunteers prefer to work in the office of the program; still others have wonderful skills in representing the program to the community and in fund raising.

Teams profit from having a corps of volunteers who have a wide range of backgrounds, ages, language, professions, hobbies, and ethnic origins. Volunteers are the frequent recipients of a patient's deepest thoughts because they are seen by the patient more as family members than as health professionals. Because of their extremely valuable insights in identifying needs of the patient and family, volunteers should be included in team meetings. Communication and coordination between volunteers and program staff are most important, and without both, patient care suffers. Many large programs have a director of volunteers who selects, trains, and supervises volunteers. The presence or lack of volunteers in a program can mean the difference between success and failure.

TEAM BUILDING

In order to build an effective team, members of the various disciplines must work together and value each other's contributions. Members must never put selfish pride above the patient's goals, nor think they can be all things to all people. Building a truly interdisciplinary team requires work. According to Balfour Mount and J. Voyer, "Teams don't just happen. They slowly and painfully evolve. The process is never complete."[39] Teams that do not have scars have not truly worked as a team.

In order to evaluate how well team members work together, members need to ask themselves the following questions identified by Blues. Do they[40]

- help identify and prioritize tasks
- keep the group's purpose in mind when suggesting new ideas
- help implement personal suggestions and assume a leadership role if necessary
- compromise when necessary and remain flexible to suggestions
- obtain and share information freely
- evaluate personal responsibility and actions
- understand and respect genuinely the contributions of other team members
- accept the proven efficacy of another person's plan over a personal plan?

An honest "yes" answer to each of these questions suggests that that team member is involved and constructive. Substantial and positive actions can occur when members make an effort to facilitate team achievement.

INTERDISCIPLINARY TEAM MEETINGS

The palliative care team should strive for mutual understanding of the patient's condition, goals of care, and plans for management. The interdisciplinary team meetings, usually held weekly, are ideal times for developing this understanding. At team meetings, the patient's and family's acceptance of palliative care and their views of the program are also discussed.

Angry patients often try to pit family members and team members against each other. In fact, angry patients may try to make a particular team member the "scapegoat" for deep-seated family problems. Such behavior does not always have to be resolved, but it does need to be discussed by team members, lest they become victimized by it. Team meetings are appropriate times for gaining an understanding of these situations.

Patients and family members may test the team for consistency. The expression of a difference in philosophy and treatment by team members may distress the patient and family. Often, patients and families care obsessively about medications, therapies, and physical care details and repeat these details to each team member in turn. Team members should not show disagreement with team-determined goals and therapy. Avoidance of team splitting or suspicion and conflict among team members is of paramount importance. Team meetings are ideal times to discuss these potential problems.

As a team member who visits patients' homes less frequently than other team members, such as the nurse and social worker, you may feel uncomfortable at interdisciplinary team meetings when you have differing perceptions about the patient, family, home atmosphere, and the way in which the patient and family are coping. Yet, striking differences in perceptions even occur among those team members who often visit any one patient's home. In part, these differences occur because patients and family members have different levels of frankness or degrees of discretion with various health professionals and at various times. Unfortunately, this "situational" frankness may make members of the team who enjoy less openness and time with the patient feel that they may have misunderstood or not developed an honest relationship with the patient and family. It should be remembered, however, that variability in candor is inevitable because patients do not need to deal with truth constantly. Patients and families appreciate team members with whom they can minimize their sadness; visits may indeed be very gratifying to the patient and family, yet seem very shallow to the dietitian. At team meetings it is not necessary to resolve discrepancies in a patient's behavior. What is important, however, is the expression of these perceived differences so that the team members realize that the patient has many different sides and these sides are shared differently with different persons at different times. It is up to team members to tolerate the variability of the patient's frankness. Failure to express opinions regarding patient perception and the development of intimidation or resentment between team members are definite threats to team stability and must be avoided at all costs.

NOTES

1. Ginette G. Ferszt and Priscilla D. Houck, "The Family," in *Nursing Care of the Terminally Ill*, ed. Madalon O'Rawe Amenta and Nancy L. Bohnet (Boston: Little, Brown & Co., 1986), 175.

2. Marion B. Dolan, "If Your Patient Wants to Die at Home," *Nursing '83* (April 1983): 50–55.

3. J. Andrew Billings, ed., *Outpatient Management of Advanced Cancer: Symptom Control, Support, and Hospice-in-the-Home* (Philadelphia: J. B. Lippincott Co., 1985), 173–194.

4. V. Schubert, "Anticipatory Guidance for Family Caregivers to Manage the Last Few Days at Home" (Paper presented at Hospice of Seattle Advanced Symposium on Care of the Terminally Ill, Seattle, Wa., 26 February 1982).

5. Ann G. Blues, "Grief and Bereavement," in *Hospice and Palliative Nursing Care*, ed. Ann G. Blues and Joyce V. Zerwekh (Orlando, Fla.: Grune & Stratton, 1984), 198–227.

6. Susan Hackler Fetsch and Margaret Shandor Miles, "Children and Death," in *Nursing Care of the Terminally Ill*, ed. Madalon O'Rawe Amenta and Nancy L. Bohnet (Boston: Little, Brown & Co., 1986), 199–226.

7. Debra P. Hymovich, "Child and Family Teaching: Special Needs and Approaches," *The Hospice Journal* 2, no. 1 (Spring 1986): 108–109, 112.

8. G.R. Gates, "Terminal Care in Country Practice," *Australian Family Physician* 11 (1982): 338–342.

9. E.M. Pattison, "The Living-Dying Process," in *Psychosocial Care of the Dying Patient*, ed. Charles A. Garfield (New York: McGraw-Hill Book Co., 1978), 133–168.

10. M. Adams and R. Moynihan, "Issues of Children with Seriously Ill and Dying Parents" (Paper presented at the American Cancer Society Workshop, Portland, Ore., July 1982).

11. Dolan, "If Your Patient Wants to Die at Home," 50–55.

12. Ibid., 50–55.

13. Lynne Talley Walters, "The Family as the Unit of Care," in *Hospice and Palliative Nursing Care*, ed. Ann G. Blues and Joyce V. Zerwekh (Orlando, Fla.: Grune & Stratton, 1984), 246.

14. Ginette G. Ferszt and Priscilla D. Houck, "The Family," in *Nursing Care of the Terminally Ill*, ed. Madalon O'Rawe Amenta and Nancy L. Bohnet (Boston: Little, Brown & Co., 1986), 184–187.

15. Phyllis Anderson, "Common Psychosocial Problems of Home Hospice Patients," *American Journal of Hospice Care* 1, no. 4 (Fall 1984): 4, 45.

16. Ferszt and Houck, "The Family," 179–184.

17. Virginia Satir, *Peoplemaking* (Palo Alto, Ca.: Science and Behavior Books, 1972), 112–122.

18. Salvador Minuchin, *Families and Family Therapy* (Cambridge, Mass.: Harvard University Press, 1974), 54–56, 130, 144.

19. Murray Bowen, "Family Reaction to Death," in *Family Therapy: Theory and Practice*, ed. Philip J. Guerin (New York: Gardner Press, 1976), 335–348.

20. Ruth F. Craven and Benita H. Sharp, "The Effects of Illness on Family Functions," *Nursing Forum* 11, no. 2 (1972): 186–193.

21. Irene Goldenberg and Herbert Goldenberg, *Family Therapy: An Overview* (Monterey, Ca.: Brooks/Cole, 1980), 201.

22. Lisa Begg Marino and J. Kooser, "The Psychosocial Care of Cancer Clients and Their Families, Periods of High Risk" in *Cancer Nursing*, ed. Lisa Begg Marino (St. Louis: C.V. Mosby Co., 1981), 55.

23. Ferszt and Houck, "The Family," 196–198.

24. M. B. Leavitt, *Families at Risk: Primary Prevention in Nursing Practice* (Boston: Little, Brown & Co., 1982), 133.

25. Judith Fine, "Family Treatment in a Medical Hospital Setting," in *Family Treatment in Social Work Practice*, ed. Curtis Janzen and Oliver Harris (Itasca, Ill.: F. E. Peacock, 1980), 200–258.

26. Rae Sedgwick, "The Family as a System: A Network of Relationships," *Journal of Psychiatric Nursing and Mental Health Services* 12, no. 2 (March/April 1974): 17–20.

27. Walters, "The Family as the Unit of Care," 244–249.

28. Ann G. Blues, "The Hospice Team," in *Hospice and Palliative Nursing Care*, ed. Ann G. Blues and Joyce V. Zerwekh (Orlando, Fla.: Grune & Stratton, 1984), 67–80.

29. Ibid., 70.

30. Irwin M. Rubin and Richard Beckhard, "Factors Influencing the Effectiveness of Health Teams," *Milbank Memorial Fund Quarterly* 50, Part I (1972): 317–335.

31. Blues, "The Hospice Team," 71.

32. Wilma Bulkin and Herbert Lukashok, "Rx for Dying: The Case for Hospice," *New England Journal of Medicine* 318, no. 6 (11 February 1988): 376–378.

33. Louise M. Manetta, "The Primary Care Clinical Nurse Specialist: Director of a Hospice Program," *American Journal of Hospice Care* 4, no. 4 (July/August 1985): 15–17.

34. Helen Budd, "The Art of Being a Hospice Nurse," *American Journal of Hospice Care* 2, no. 3 (May/June 1985): 11–13.

35. Larry D. Pollock and Martha Isacson Pollock, "St. Joseph's Hospice and the Role of the Social Worker," *American Journal of Hospice Care* 1, no. 3 (Summer 1984): 32–34.

36. Bennett D. Tucker, Jr., "The Hospice Patient—Dental Aspects: Indications, Contraindications, and Limitations," *American Journal of Hospice Care* 1, no. 3 (Summer 1984): 21–24.

37. Theresa M. Stephany, "Identifying the Roles of Hospice Volunteers (Letter)," *American Journal of Hospice Care* 1, no. 3 (Summer 1984): 6–7.

38. Kirsten Eckberg, "Touching a Patient through Music," *American Journal of Hospice Care* 3, no.4 (July/August 1986): 23–25.

39. Balfour Mount and J. Voyer, "Staff Stress in Palliative/Hospice Care" in *The RVH Manual on Palliative/Hospice Care*, ed. Ina Ajemian and Balfour Mount (New York: The Free Press, 1980), 466.

40. Blues, "The Hospice Team," 79.

Chapter 5

Needs of Palliative Care Team Members

UNDERSTANDING PERSONAL FEELINGS REGARDING DEATH AND DYING

The dying patients who place their lives in our care ask two things—that we understand and that we respond. Understanding is the harder to do. If in order to understand we need to experience what the patient and family are going through, many of us would fail because we have little or no frame of reference about death. Because most dietitians do not routinely deal with death, many of us can remember the name of our first patient who died. And many more of us can identify the first time we were confronted with thoughts about our own death or the possible death of a loved one.

During our professional education and career, dietitians are taught that "compassionate detachment" is a necessary trait to develop in order to provide effective professional care. In caring for terminally ill patients and their families, this is difficult to do because we are dealing with the deepest and most emotional of issues—those of life and death. In working with the terminally ill patient and family, dietitians must feel, yet not become overwhelmed, and we must care without losing ourself in the process.

In order to help others live as fully as possible while dealing with death and dying, we must be comfortable with our own mortality so we do not have to deal with it each time we are confronted by the mortality of our patients. To be sure, if we have not explored the fact of our own death, we can have little to say to someone who is forced to explore his or her own end.

Traditionally, dietitians do not study death and dying to any great extent in undergraduate educational programs.[1,2] The stages of the dying process and the ethnic practices of coping with death and dying are the focus of most teaching. In most dietetic curricula, little time is spent on personal beliefs and experiences, and, students are rarely asked to explore and understand their personal lifelong fears

Exhibit 5-1 Questionnaire on Dying

Try to choose one best response to each question. Some questions clearly present an opportunity for discussion or for multiple choices as to answer, but select the concept that most closely agrees with your belief.

1. I remember that when I was a child my family talked about death
   a. openly, including me
   b. openly, in front of but not including me
   c. as if it were taboo
   d. only when I wasn't present
   e. rarely or never

2. My first encounter with dying was with
   a. grandparent/great-grandparent
   b. parent
   c. brother or sister
   d. pet
   e. friend
   f. other family member
   g. hero
   h. someone close to a friend or to a family member but not to me

3. When I was a child, my concept of what happens after death was that one
   a. went to heaven or hell
   b. went to sleep
   c. stopped breathing and moving
   d. joined nature
   e. disappeared mysteriously
   f. no concept

4. Today, I believe that after death one
   a. has a spiritual after-life
   b. sleeps eternally
   c. is nonexistent
   d. cannot know what will happen
   e. joins with the universe, nature, life's energy
   f. no concept

5. I think about my own death
   a. almost every day
   b. frequently
   c. once in while
   d. almost never or never

6. My main reason for not wanting to die is that I'd
   a. be unsure of the kind of after-life I would have
   b. be unable to provide for my family
   c. not be able to complete my plans
   d. die with pain
   e. not have control over what would happen to people I care about

7. Some people believe that we can will ourselves to start dying. I believe this
   a. substantially
   b. partially
   c. not at all

8. Thinking about dying makes me
   a. angry
   b. afraid
   c. uncomfortable
   d. depressed
   e. happy to be alive
   f. other

9. If my physician knew that I had a terminal disease, I would want him or her to tell me.
   a. True
   b. False

Exhibit 5-1 *Continued*

10. If my physician did not tell me of my terminal diagnosis, I would want a nurse to tell me.
    a. True   b. False

11. If I knew I was terminally ill, I would want to talk about it to
    a. no one   d. clergy
    b. my mate   e. physician
    c. close family   f. nurse
                                     g. a close friend

12. If someone I really cared for was terminally ill and wanted to talk about it, I would feel
    a. awkward   c. honored
    b. willing and comfortable   d. very sad

13. The thing I dread most about the dying process is
    a. pain   d. dependency
    b. mental deterioration   e. fears about after-life
    c. being someone I wouldn't like f. sadness of loved ones

14. I find the sight of a dead body
    a. revolting   c. disconcerting
    b. frightening   d. satisfying
                                     e. natural

15. When there is a funeral for someone I care about I
    a. usually do not go   c. am pleased to go
    b. go but dislike it   d. go if it is convenient

16. When people begin talking about death in a casual situation I
    a. feel anxious   c. think it is too personal
    b. feel embarrassed   d. am interested in their ideas
                                     e. am bored

17. The illness that I would least like to have is
    a. heart disease   e. arthritis
    b. cancer   f. multiple sclerosis
    c. diabetes   g. stroke
    d. kidney disease   h. other

Source: Reprinted from *Hospice & Palliative Nursing Care* by A.G. Blues and J.V. Zerwekh (Eds.), pp. 331–333, with permission of W.B. Saunders Company, © 1984.

about death. In order to work effectively with terminally ill patients, it is important for us to explore our inner selves for our views of life and death.

Ann G. Blues, in her classic book on palliative care nursing, includes a questionnaire eliciting thoughts about death. Because of its universal application to health professionals, it is recommended that dietitians and other palliative care team members complete the questionnaire (Exhibit 5-1).[3]

Dietitians wanting to work with terminally ill patients should discuss these questions with others. Palliative care staff members, spouse, friends, or colleagues with whom one feels a supportive bond are appropriate choices for sharing beliefs and experiences. In contrast to the brevity of the questionnaire, which takes about 20 minutes to complete, the understanding of its answers takes much longer.

There is no general prescription for experiences that must be undergone in order to be competent in working with terminally ill patients and their families. While exploring your experiences and views on death and dying, it is important to understand that no two people's experiences or views on the subject are, or need to be, identical. This is appropriate because no two patients or families will be identical either. All of us will feel more comfortable and work more effectively with some families than others.

In working with terminally ill patients, it is helpful to understand that people die much in the same manner that they have lived. They may be kind and considerate, stoic and brave, philosophical and accepting, or they may demonstrate other less endearing qualities. Some dying patients will be extremely difficult to care for by anyone. Therefore, dietitians and other health care professionals should not feel that they have to be equally effective or have the same degree of commitment toward each terminally ill patient and family with whom they work. To do so would be to deny very real feelings. Feelings must be recognized as your human response to another's very human behavior.

In order to develop a base for understanding your experiences and beliefs, exploring attitudes and experiences in addition to those in Exhibit 5-1 is helpful. The following 12 activities can be used as a springboard for discussion in staff meetings and when considering whether or not you want to work with terminally ill patients and families.

1. Identify the values and beliefs that guide your life.
2. Identify what you like and dislike about yourself.
3. List your roles in life, such as wife, mother, husband, father, dietitian, church worker, and auxiliary leader, and identify honestly how people with whom you regularly come into contact feel about you, your personality, abilities, and attitudes.
4. Identify your goals in life.
5. Reflect back on your life to its peaks and valleys, when major life experiences occurred, and what you learned from them. Identify your proudest moments and your failures. Try to free yourself from immobilizing past resentments and preoccupations with failures of self or others by identifying them and looking at them honestly .
6. Identify your fantasies and fears. Are there any deep-seated fears that may impinge on your feelings or fears of death?
7. Identify your "energy sources" and "energy sappers."

8. Identify how you feel and what you tend to say to someone who has just lost a loved one.
9. Speculate about your own death. Can you identify what might be the cause of your death? How would you like to die? How would you least like to die? What will your funeral be like? Who might attend? How will those who are closest to you grieve?
10. Identify your thoughts if you were told you had less than a year to live. What would you do in your remaining days? Write (but do not send) a letter to someone you love telling him or her about your impending death.
11. Write your eulogy or the few words of tribute that you would like to see on your tombstone.
12. By answering the above, can you identify why you might want to care for terminally ill persons and their families? Do the objectives of palliative care agree with your overall views of life and death?

The Adaptation Process in Dealing with Death and Dying

In 1977, Bernice Harper described a predictable five-step normal process that health professionals undergo as they adapt to working with the dying.[4] These stages of professional anxiety are diagrammed in Figure 5-1 and described more fully in Table 5-1.

Intellectualization Stage

During the first 3 months of working with dying patients and their families, professionals focus primarily on trying to gain a cognitive understanding of the multiple aspects of their job and the responsibilities of others. Feelings during this period are usually characterized as unorganized, anxious, and uncomfortable. Withdrawal is a common coping device. This stage is called "intellectualization" because intellectualization is the predominant process that the professional undergoes during this time.

Emotional Survival Stage

Between 3 and 6 months of working with terminally ill patients, professionals experience their first real involvement with patients and families and their suffering. Feelings of helplessness and anger commonly surface during this time. The professional may experience guilt about personally enjoying good health while knowing that the patient is going to die and the family will grieve. During this time, many health professionals return to the intellectualization stage as a means of coping. Harper terms the second stage of adaptation "emotional survival."

Figure 5-1 Stages of Professional Anxiety

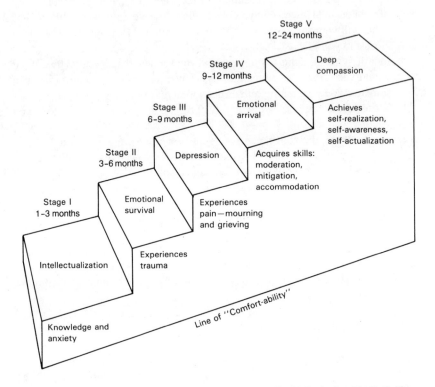

Source: Reprinted from *Death: The Coping Mechanism of the Health Professional* by B. C. Harper, Southeastern University Press, © 1977.

Depression Stage

The depression stage usually occurs between 6 and 9 months as professionals greatly identify and empathize with the patient's tragedy. The professional experiences pain, mourning, and grief and begins to come to terms with the universality of death. This is a critically important stage after which the professional either will continue to care for the terminally ill and "grow" or will call it quits and "go."

Emotional Arrival Stage

The fourth phase, emotional arrival, occurs somewhere between 9 and 12 months after professionals begin to work with terminally ill patients. During this

Table 5-1   Stage Characteristics and Differences of the Schematic Growth and Development Scale

Stage I	Stage II	Stage III	Stage IV	Stage V
Professional knowledge	Increasing professional knowledge	Deepening of professional knowledge	Acceptance of professional knowledge	Refining of professional knowledge
Intellectualization	Less intellectualization	Decreasing intellectualization	Normal intellectualization	Refining intellectual base
Anxiety	Emotional survival	Depression	Emotional arrival	Deep compassion
Some uncomfortableness	Increasing uncomfortableness	Decreasing uncomfortableness	Increasing comfortableness	Increased comfortableness
Agreeableness	Guilt	Pain	Moderation	Self-realization
Withdrawal	Frustration	Mourning	Mitigation	Self-awareness
Superficial acceptance	Sadness	Grieving	Accommodation	Self-actualization
Providing tangible services	Initial emotional involvement	More emotional involvement	Ego mastery	Professional satisfaction
Utilization of emotional energy on understanding the setting	Increasing emotional involvement	Overidentification with the patient	Coping with loss of relationship	Acceptance of death and loss
Familiarizing self with policies and procedures	Initital understanding of the magnitude of the area of practice	Exploration of own feelings about death	Freedom from concern about own death	Rewarding professional growth and development
Working with families, rather than patients	Overidentification with the patient's situation	Facing own death	Developing strong ties with dying patients and families	Development of ability to give of one's self
		Coming to grips with feelings about death	Development of ability to work with, on behalf of, and for the dying patient	Human and professional assessment
			Development of professional competence	Constructive and appropriate activities
			Productivity and accomplishments	Development of feelings of dignity and self-respect
			Healthy interaction	Ability to give dignity and self-respect to dying patient
				Feeling of comfortableness in relation to self, patient, family, and the job

Source: Reprinted from *Death: The Coping Mechanism of the Health Professional* by B. C. Harper, Southeastern University Press, © 1977.

time, health professionals put off the tendency to overidentify with patients and rid themselves of depression and guilt. Although there is no freedom from pain, the professional is able to grieve and recover each time a patient dies.

Deep Compassion Stage

Following the fourth phase—about 1–2 two years after beginning to work exclusively with dying patients—the professional develops deep compassion, self-awareness, and solid professional expertise at a faster and faster rate. The professional now has a realistic acceptance of illness and death and has entered the "deep compassion" stage identified by Harper.

The dietitian who neither works full time with terminally ill patients and families nor follows most patients as long or as indepth as full-time palliative care professionals is likely to go through Harper's adaptation stages at a slower rate, albeit in the order identified. Many professionals progress quickly through some stages and linger at others. Intellectualization and overidentification with patients are common traits that all health professionals tend to display at times.

YOU AND PALLIATIVE CARE PROGRAMS: IS IT A MATCH?

Team Selection

It has been demonstrated time and time again that a palliative care program is only as good as its paid staff and volunteer team members. Are there characteristics that all staff and team members should possess? Regardless of their area of expertise, staff and team members should demonstrate (1) competence, (2) sensitivity, (3) flexibility, and (4) maturity.[5]

Competence

Competence cannot be underestimated. Without it, the needs of patients and families cannot be determined, goals cannot be identified, and care should not be given. Assessment skills must be highly developed in all team members. Without an accurate assessment and without knowledge of appropriate intervention, proper care cannot be rendered. As team members become more experienced in palliative care, skills in assessment, planning, implementation, and evaluation become honed.

Sensitivity

Sensitivity and compassion are the pillars upon which palliative care is based. Because palliative care is a high-touch and high-caring program, its team must comprise high-touch and high-caring people. Team members should have a personal desire to serve. They must also want to grow. In addition, team members must recognize that they have a responsibility to care not only for their patients and families but also for themselves and for other members of the team.

Sensitivity flows out of those persons who know who they are, like what they see, and want others to know about them. Sensitivity can be learned. As we care for terminally ill patients and their families, our skills in caring improve if we remain open to learning. This growth instills self-confidence. And as our abilities improve and our self-confidence develops, we receive positive feedback from patients and others that encourages the development of even greater sensitivity. Patients, families, and other palliative care team members can increase our sensitivity by reinforcing our importance as a professional.

Sensitivity training, popular in the 1960s, may be a focus of palliative care team inservice gatherings in which the entire team participates. A weekend retreat, frequently needed to foster creativity and growth, would be an ideal setting for a modified, nonthreatening, and uplifting sensitivity training workshop. In such a workshop team members develop an awareness of the need for sensitivity and learn techniques for fostering sensitivity in self and others.

Flexibility

Palliative care is different from traditional medical care because of its emphasis on flexibility which is frequently not tolerated in medical care. By welcoming change and being adaptable, palliative care team members demonstrate flexibility. For most of us, it takes flexibility to integrate palliative care principles into our formerly held attitudes about health care delivery systems. Usually secure in our professional practice, we must recognize when in palliative care it is appropriate to deviate from the norm of traditional medical practice. Team members who thrive on creativity will find palliative care to be an ideal area for practice.

Maturity

Maturity may but does not need to be an age- or experience-related phenomenon. Instead, it is more a function of how much self-confidence one has, how much one values growth, and how supportive one can be of others. Our philosophy about life, death, and after-life is a reflection of our maturity. Holding meaningful philosophy about these issues is important. Such a philosophy gives us strength when we are called on to maintain a balance through what can be difficult situations in palliative care work, such as the death of a favorite patient or the death of many patients in a short period of time.

Developing and maintaining priorities are a demonstration of maturity. As a palliative care team member you will be asked to serve the program, patient, family, and team in many ways. Setting priorities and keeping these utmost in mind when responsibilities seem insurmountable will help you choose what to do when. Maturity not only helps one maintain a sense of priorities during times of stress but it is also helpful during times of failure. Maturity is demonstrated when one takes responsibility for personal actions, admits mistakes when they occur, and grows from these mistakes. Likewise, whenever we demonstrate self-forgiveness and forgiveness of others, we demonstrate maturity. Maturity is an act of becoming.

Other Characteristics

There are many other characteristics that are desirable in palliative care team members. Some programs value the independent worker; other programs do not. Some programs prefer a homogeneous group of members; others prefer a heterogeneous group. However, in order to build a team that truly provides interdisciplinary care, all team members must be respectful of each other and willing to be leaders at times and followers at other times.

One characteristic not mentioned above that dietitians might consider important in working with terminally ill patients is educational background. Your area of prior experience—whether clinical, community, management, education, or consultation and private practice—is probably not of major importance in your ability to function in palliative care. If the basic skills as a generalist dietitian are mastered and the characteristics of competence, sensitivity, flexibility, and maturity are possessed, the dietitian can be effective and valued as a member of a palliative care team or when working with terminally ill patients without a team. The knowledge base and clinical practice skills necessary in providing competent nutrition care to terminally ill patients and their families are identified later in this chapter and in upcoming chapters.

Team Education

All team members need staff education through an initial orientation program and through ongoing continuing education events. Orientation programs for new staff need to reflect the member's previous professional experiences in and outside of palliative care work. The orientation program should aim to supplement the individual's knowledge and clinical experience.

Most new team members will require education in the fundamentals of palliative care. Orientation should include discussion and reference materials on the topics of death and dying, bereavement, palliative care concepts, pharmacology, pain and symptom control, and program policies and procedures.

"Palliative care is not a 'once-trained always-trained' proposition."[6] Instead, there is always need for continuing education. Regularly scheduled inservices should combine theory and practice. Case studies are an extremely valuable teaching tool, especially if personnel from other programs are brought in from time to time to discuss their experiences. Sending staff members to other programs and to national meetings is valuable, as is the stimulation that comes when staff members serve as resources at conferences and meetings.

Staff Evaluation

Staff and program evaluation are important in helping team members and the program achieve their fullest potential. Dietitians working as paid staff or volunteers in a palliative care program should expect to receive performance evaluations and provide program evaluations. Joint Commission standards require that individual performance evaluations be part of the total program evaluation process. Therefore, as a member of the palliative care team, dietitians should have individual, regularly scheduled conferences with a designated program administrator. These conferences should include time for both performance and program evaluation. Evaluations should be a time for honest feedback, as well as a creative and sharing time wherein goals and expectations for the future are set.

Each team member brings unique gifts to the experience of caring for dying patients. The evaluation process presents the opportunity to acknowledge these attributes and to inform the team member how these relate to the palliative care program in general. And as with narcotic doses, for the patient with chronic pain (see Chapter 10), praise needs to be administered in regularly scheduled doses rather than on an "as needed" basis or saved for a yearly overdose.

All palliative care team members need to be involved actively in program development and policy-making efforts. Team members who are involved in the development of guidelines and policies are likely to be committed to the program and its framework. Active participation in performance and program evaluation has another very important effect—it helps prevent staff stress, distress, and burnout.

STAFF STRESS, DISTRESS, AND BURNOUT

Stress is a normal and important part of life. In just the right dosage, stress can produce growth and progress; on the other hand, too much or too little can be paralyzing.[7]

Working with terminally ill patients brings many stressful situations. When stress becomes harmful, the result is burnout.[8] Burnout is characterized by emotional exhaustion and depletion and behavioral changes including irritableness, withdrawal, crying, sleeplessness, and indulgence in alcohol, drugs, or foods. Anger and disinterest in work, colleagues, and patients are frequently noted.[9]

Causes of Burnout

Causes of burnout are numerous and have been discussed at length by several authors.[10-19] Factors commonly causing stress, distress, and burnout in palliative care work are listed in Exhibit 5-2.

Because the very nature of palliative care requires a high degree of personal involvement, the hospice dietitian cannot resort to comfortable defense mechanisms, such as depersonalization, detachment, and stereotyped responses, when trying to cope with stress even when it would be easy to do so. In addition, the lack of strict role definitions for team members and an emphasis on flexible and innovative responses to situations are stress-provoking aspects of palliative care.[20] Economic insecurity caused by low salaries and unstable fiscal bases of several programs, crisis and changes in home and social life, and threats to personal relationships posed by overinvolvement at work can be additional stresses.

Exhibit 5-2 Stresses of Palliative Care Work

Patient

1. Frequent confrontation with death and loss
2. Feelings of sadness and loss
3. Uncertainty, fear of the unknown regarding terminal illness
4. Demanding, broad-spectrum needs of patients and families and inability to meet psychosocial and physical needs of patient

Personal

5. Evolving identity and philosophy
6. Challenges to values
7. Need to express intense feelings
8. Painful feelings regarding one's own death or death of a family member
9. Personal perceptions of inadequacy
10. Idealistic, perfectionistic personality traits
11. Too high expectations
12. Inadequate preparation

Program

13. Lack of support from the institution, health care administrators, or interdisciplinary team
14. Undesirable physical characteristics of the program or institution, inadequate resources
15. Gap between reality and ideal, inability to change a situation when it is possible or accept a situation when it is not possible to change
16. Interpersonal team and staff conflict
17. Ambiguous job description
18. Work overload
19. Limited power

As can be expected, one of the most difficult problems in working with the terminally ill patient is the constant need to establish and then relinquish relationships with people. It is difficult to experience grief and pain in others because it touches grief and pain in ourselves. The hard fact facing palliative care professionals each day is the probability that no patient on the team's caseload is likely to get better. And whether we feel it in large or small measure, death does convey an element of defeat, which can be a source of frustration.

Dietitians normally hold idealized expectations of achievement, even when they work with terminally ill patients. Because dietitians who work with a well-integrated interdisciplinary team have the opportunity to see patients in their homes and follow-ups either by telephone call or home visit are frequent, they are frequently reminded of personal success or failure at helping a patient and family. Because they are constantly faced with people who have very different personalities and philosophies of life, dietitians must continually develop and modify plans to meet patient's and family's needs. Palliative care team dietitians are continually challenged to question their own identity, values, and philosophy of life. Discussion of these feelings and beliefs with others is important for growth. Not to be able to share one's experiences can lead to burnout and rigid behavior that interfere with the dietitian's ability to perform responsibly.[21]

Characteristics of Burnout

Palliative care team dietitians often feel an energy deficit in palliative care work, despite the continual generally positive feedback received from patients, family, and the interdisciplinary team. Exhibit 5-3 is a stress and burnout self-examination tool that may be helpful in self-assessment. The characteristics of burnout have been identified from several sources.[22-28] Using the tool periodically and modifying it to include your own personal indicators of stress are important.

In seeking to become more aware of your feelings, it is helpful to learn to recognize your own bodily warning signs as tensions mount. In addition, it is helpful to become aware of your bodily sensations when you are rested and enjoying life. This knowledge can help you return to the desired feelings and identify how far afield stress can affect you.

Distress is inevitable in adapting to work with dying patients and their families. Fostering professional and individual well-being and prevention of burnout are, however, possible.

Prevention of Burnout

The best offense in preventing burnout is adequate professional training and continuing education and meaningful self-expression. Taking care of ourselves is

Exhibit 5-3 Stress and Burnout Self-Examination

Commitment Characteristics

1. Spend more time routinely with patients than planned; come to work early and leave late or vice versa; spend less time with patients

2. Do things myself, rather than ask for help when demands build up

3. Care for other needy people outside of work

Overextended Characteristics

4. Feel pressured and overwhelmed with work and patient needs; excessive death-watch behavior

5. Feel I'm not doing a good job; negative self-image and excess guilt

6. Feel isolated or withdrawn; distance self from job and co-workers; increased absenteeism

7. Feel irritable, resentful, sarcastic

8. Feel my needs are not being met; uncontrollable crying

9. Feel depressed and powerless

10. Intellectualize or overidentify with patients

Social Characteristics

11. Discuss work routinely with family and friends

12. Marital and family conflict

13. Find that work is my major source of personal satisfaction and self-esteem

14. Socialize little outside of work

15. Indulge in alcohol, drugs, food, or tobacco

Physical Characteristics

16. Fatigue

17. Sleep problems

18. Gastrointestinal disturbances

19. Weight loss or gain

20. Back and/or neck pain

21. Headaches

22. Heart palpitations

23. Tightened jaw

24. Recurrent virus infections

our professional responsibility. Exhibit 5-4 identifies the general knowledge, skills, and attitudes of dietitians that are helpful in decreasing the risk of developing burnout when the stresses of palliative care work mount.

Exhibit 5-4 Knowledge, Skills, and Attitudes of Dietitians That Can Decrease the Risk of Developing Burnout

- Be sure your professional skills match the job requirements and that you have received adequate on-the-job palliative care training
- Be sure your professional skills include good clinical dietetic and people skills
- Possess a thorough knowledge of the following:
  1. anatomy, physiology, and pathophysiology
  2. assessing patient's nutritional status, needs, and nutritional concerns
  3. ability to teach nutritional intervention techniques at the foods level to patients and families
  4. ethical and legal considerations surrounding feeding issues
  5. uses, side effects, and nutrient interactions of medications and modalities used in cancer treatments and palliative care
  6. basic psychology and family interaction
  7. community nutrition resources, such as Meals on Wheels and other feeding programs, food stamps, and local representatives of companies producing nutritional supplements from whom free samples may be provided
- Possess personal and social skills, including the following:
  1. sense of purpose in life
  2. high self-esteem
  3. sensitivity in human relations and a sense of humor
  4. assertiveness and ability to discuss concerns objectively as they arise
  5. creativity and imagination
  6. self-motivation and independence as a thinker
  7. healthy self-care habits and personal support systems outside of work

The continuing education needs of the dietitian (Exhibit 5-5) are important to consider when inservice workshops are offered to palliative care team staff. Do not be afraid to suggest these topics and others as your continuing education needs arise. No doubt other team members have the same needs.

Exhibit 5-5 Continuing Education Needs of the Dietitian

1. Concepts in death and dying
2. Legal and ethical issues relating to death and dying
3. Funeral practices and responses to death and dying of various cultural and ethnic groups
4. How to maximize interdisciplinary teamwork
5. Bereavement education
6. Exercises that stimulate awareness of feelings
7. Psychiatric and mental health issues surrounding death and dying

SUMMARY

Working with dying patients and families demands insight and the willingness to explore oneself. The result of such endeavors is growth in self-awareness and understanding of life. As professionals work with terminally ill patients and their families, it becomes vital that they (1) explore their personal history and reactions regarding death itself and (2) identify unresolved conflicts and destructive coping mechanisms that may have been used to keep such conflicts out of conscious awareness.

We provide higher levels of care when we have low levels of death anxiety.[29] Therefore, we must find and use ways to be fulfilled and to nourish our own spirit, heart, and body. Techniques include being still, listening to our inner voice, and finding our center. Quiet mornings in our gardens, late evening gazes at the stars as they appear on a dimming sky, relaxing walks on an ocean's beach, or uninterrupted listening to Mozart's *Eine Kleine Nachtmusik* (A Little Night Music) in the quietness of our living rooms can provide us with time to rid our minds of the day's clutter and focus on the meaning and purpose of our lives. Solitude is a necessary part of life wherein we can listen to our heart's secrets and redirect our activities toward achieving those aspirations we hold most dear.

Being with good people, taking time for small joys, and tapping into our "energy sources" are also helpful techniques in reducing anxiety. Seeking affirmation from others through sharing ourselves is important. To expect our family and friends to absorb the heaviest portion of our need to debrief and discharge emotion, however, places such relationships in jeopardy. Sometimes, physical activity can rid us of pent-up feelings; at other times a counselor is needed to lend a listening ear. Rest, good food, activity, and loving are needed to bring out the best in us and to enable us to be willing to serve and be served.

A word of caution may be in order. After undergoing rigorous self-examination, it is easy to overidentify with patients and their problems and to want to share your new-found life understandings and experiences at the drop of a hat. Try to avoid placing patients and other team members at a level of self-understanding that you have set or achieved for yourself.

In addition, it is important not to fall into the trap of perceiving patients and families as helpless and in need of care. The dietitian who attempts to take over the burdens of the patient and family will become burdened and overstressed. Instead, our responsibility is to help patients and families set goals for care that are realistic and achievable. We must make a contract with the patient and family in areas of mutual agreement. The final responsibility for choosing to help themselves or not is thereby left to the patient and family.

Setting clear boundaries between your professional and personal lives is important. It is also important to limit our responsibilities to what is reasonable, remembering that it is impossible to do everything *now* and *alone*. We must be wary of making promises we cannot keep. It is important to recognize our own limits and to identify them clearly. Team members have a responsibility to help one another prevent and deal with distress. We are our brother's keeper.

Caring for the dying can be a learned skill. Most dietitians can learn to work full-time with dying patients and their families, but some will learn the necessary skills easier than others. Stress management requires a good deal of self-awareness and personal responsibility. The dietitian who takes the time to understand personal feelings and behavior and who takes the responsibility for learning how to cope effectively will be rewarded with satisfaction and fulfillment in caring for the dying patient and family.

NOTES

1.   Roberta Smith Hurley, M. Rosita Schiller, Elizabeth A. Kmiecimski, and Carol E. Dixon, "Preprofessional Education on Death, Dying, and Nutrition in Terminal Illness," *Journal of the American Dietetic Association* 88, no. 6 (June 1988): 713–715.

2.   Mary Jane Oakland, "The Effectiveness of a Short Curriculum Unit in Death Education for Dietetic Students," *Journal of the American Dietetic Association* 88, no. 1 (January 1988): 26–28.

3.   Ann G. Blues, "Understanding One's Own Feelings About Death," in *Hospice and Palliative Nursing Care*, ed. Ann G. Blues and Joyce V. Zerwekh (Orlando, Fla.: Grune & Stratton, 1984), 331–333.

4.   Bernice Harper, *Death: The Coping Mechanism of the Health Professional* (Greenville, S.C.: Southeastern University Press, 1977), 1–123.

5.   Kathleen Roche, "Staff Selection, Education and Evaluation" in *Hospice: Complete Care for the Terminally Ill*, ed. Jack McKay Zimmerman (Baltimore, Md.: Urban & Schwarzenberg, 1981), 113–114.

6.   Ibid., 116.

7.   Hans Selye, *The Stress of Life* (New York: McGraw-Hill Book Co., 1956), 64–65.

8.   Christina Maslach, *Burnout: The Cost of Caring* (Englewood Cliffs, N.J.: Prentice-Hall, Inc., 1982), 2–14.

9.   Ayala M. Pines, E. Aronson, and D. Kafry, *Burnout: From Tedium to Personal Growth* (New York: Free Press, 1981), 17–21.

10.   Joyce V. Zerwekh, "Professional Stress and Distress," in *Hospice and Palliative Nursing Care*, ed. Ann G. Blues and Joyce V. Zerwekh (Orlando, Fla.: Grune & Stratton, 1984), 348–361.

11.   Kathleen Roche, "Staff Selection, Education and Evaluation," 117–122.

12.   Nancy L. Bohnet, "Staff Stress," in *Nursing Care of the Terminally Ill*, ed. Madalon O'Rawe Amenta and Nancy L. Bohnet (Boston, Mass.: Little, Brown & Co., 1986), 291–304.

13.   P.A. Gray-Toft and J.G. Anderson, "Sources of Stress in Nursing Terminal Patients in a Hospice" (Paper prepared for the National Health Symposium on the Role of the Community Hospital in Dealing with Life-Threatening Disease and Bereavement, Bethlehem, Pa., 10-12 January 1980).

14.   Dorothy H. Moser and Diana A. Krikorian, "Satisfaction and Stress Incidents Reported by Hospice Nurses: A Pilot Study," *Nursing Leadership* 5, no. 4 (1982): 9–17.

15.   Mary L.S. Vachon, W.A.L. Lyall, and S.J.J. Freeman, "Measurement and Management of Stress in Health Professionals Working with Advanced Cancer Patients," *Death Education* 1 (1978): 365–375.

16. R. Yancik, "Coping with Hospice Work Stress," *Journal of Psychosocial Oncology* 2, no. 2 (1984): 19–35.

17. R. Yancik, "Source of Stress for Hospice Staff," *Journal of Psychosocial Oncology* 2, no. 1 (1984): 21–31.

18. Virginia Major Thomas, "Hospice Nursing—Reaping the Rewards, Dealing with the Stress," *Geriatric Nursing* 4, no. 1 (January/February 1983): 22–27.

19. Diana A. Krikorian and Dorothy H. Moser, "Satisfactions and Stresses Experienced by Professional Nurses in Hospice Programs," *American Journal of Hospice Care* 2, no. 1 (January/February 1985): 25–33.

20. Ann M. McElroy, "Burnout: A Review of the Literature with Application to Cancer Nursing," *Cancer Nursing* 5 (1982): 211–217.

21. Mary L.S. Vachon, "Staff Stress in Care of the Terminally Ill," *Quality Review Bulletin* 5, no. 5 (1979): 13–17.

22. Cary Cherniss, *Professional Burnout in Human Service Organizations* (New York: Praeger, 1980), 6–7.

23. Maire Friel and Claire B. Tehan, "Counteracting Burnout for the Hospice Caregiver," *Cancer Nursing* 3, no. 4 (August 1980): 285–293.

24. Ramon Lavandero, "Burnout Phenomenon: A Descriptive Study Among Nurses," *Journal of Nursing Administration* 11 (1981): 17–23.

25. Maslach, *Burnout*, 56–85.

26. Edwina A. McConnell, ed., *Burnout in the Nursing Profession: Coping Strategies, Causes, and Costs* (St. Louis: C. V. Mosby Co., 1982), 70–74.

27. Ayala Pines and Christina Maslach, "Characteristics of Staff Burnout in Mental Settings," *Hospital and Community Psychiatry* 29 (1978): 233–237.

28. Avery D. Weisman, "Understanding the Cancer Patient: The Syndrome of Caregiver's Plight," *Psychiatry* 44 (1981): 161–168.

29. Thomas, "Hospice Nursing," 22–27.

SUGGESTED READINGS

Korda, Lois. "Compassion, Conviction, Commitment: Creed for Quality Hospice Care, Core of Hospice Burnout." *American Journal of Hospice Care* 4, no. 5 (September/October 1987): 39–44.

McElroy, Ann M. "Burnout—A Review of the Literature with Application to Cancer Nursing." *Cancer Nursing* 5 (1982): 211–217.

Paradis, Lenora Finn, ed. "Stress and Burnout Among Providers Caring for the Terminally Ill and Their Families." *The Hospice Journal* 3, no. 2/3 (Summer/Fall 1987): 1–276.

Selye, Hans. *Stress without Distress*. New York: Signet, 1974.

Smith, Manuel J. *When I Say No, I Feel Guilty*. New York: Bantam Books, 1975.

The Overall Goal in the Provision of Nutritional Care

As members of the profession of dietetics, dietitians are committed to providing optimal nutritional care to patients. To identify a terminally ill patient's problems and the appropriate treatment goals, dietitians work with the patient, the patient's family, and, when it exists, the palliative care team. The advances in nutritional assessment and support techniques during the last few years have given dietitians the opportunity to identify and to reverse malnutrition frequently. Although identifying malnutrition is prudent in palliative care, reversing malnutrition may not be possible or appropriate in terminally ill patients.

In arriving at specific nutritional goals, the palliative care dietitian must never lose sight of the larger clinical picture and major goal of treatment for the terminally ill patient. We must remember that the goals of care are palliative, not curative; therefore, all treatment goals, including specific nutritional goals, should parallel this overall medical goal.[1] "Dietary care can be effective . . . only when dietitians reorient their practice skills in a manner consistent with the palliative care . . . philosophy, which views patient choice as important in the decision-making process."[2]

Palliative nutritional care does not imply indifferent or inferior care. Instead, it reflects the nature of palliative care that was summarized in 1982 by Dame Cicely Saunders, the mother of modern-day palliative care:

> To accept a situation where treatment is directed to the relief of symptoms and the alleviation of general distress will no longer mean an implicit "there is nothing more that we can do" but an explicit "everything possible is being done."[3]

Nor does palliative nutritional care automatically preclude the use of such aggressive nutritional support techniques as tube or intravenous feedings. If their use is considered, however, it must be shown how they aid in achieving palliation, comfort, and enjoyment in living.

97

Part II is the heart of this book. In Chapter 6 the role of the dietitian in palliative care is defined. Although the dietitian may have food service responsibilities, as well as patient care responsibilities, the food service responsibilities are not discussed because they do not differ significantly from such responsibilities in other health care settings.

The components of nutritional care for terminally ill patients are discussed in Chapters 7 (assessment), 11 (planning), 13 (implementation), and 14 (evaluation and documentation). Each of these chapters describes a practical approach to achieving the responsibilities of the palliative care dietitian. It is recognized that dietitians caring for terminally ill patients are sometimes a member of an interdisciplinary palliative care team and at other times are functioning in a setting without well-integrated efforts. Therefore, the amount and availability of data and the expertise of other professionals in developing a plan of care that meets the patient and family's many needs will vary with settings and personnel involved.

Chapter 8, which describes the meaning of foods and dying to peoples of different ethnic backgrounds, will aid you in assessing and developing individualized plans of care. In Chapter 9 appropriate nutritional intervention is described for the multiple potential problems facing the terminally ill patient and the patient's family. Because nutritional problems are multicausal, stemming from and affecting nursing and medical conditions, the medical and nursing strategies as adjunctive therapy for nutritional problems are also delineated. Pain is the primary concern of terminally ill patients, and its importance and treatment are discussed in a separate chapter (Chapter 10). Legal questions are more and more entering into decisions regarding palliative care and quality of life. The ethical considerations and the latest legal cases concerning feeding issues during terminal illness are described in Chapter 12. In total, Part II provides the dietitian and others with the knowledge base in nutrition to care humanely and effectively for terminally ill patients.

NOTES

1. Cathy Arnold, "Nutrition Intervention in the Terminally Ill Cancer Patient," *Journal of the American Dietetic Association* 86 (1986): 522–523.

2. Dian O. Weddle, T. Elaine Prewitt, and Audrey K. Gordon, "Perspectives on Nutrition Care for the Geriatric Hospice Patient," *Topics in Clinical Nutrition* 3, no. 4 (October 1988): 25.

3. Cicely M. Saunders, "Principles of Symptom Control in Terminal Care," *Medical Clinics of North America* 66 (1982): 1171.

Chapter 6

The Role of the Dietitian in Palliative Care

Over the past two decades, dietitians and other members of the health care team have increasingly recognized the need for nutritional expertise in meeting the needs of terminally ill patients. As more dietitians have become involved in providing palliative care, the role of the dietitian has been elucidated more clearly and what the dietitian needs to know in order to serve the patient and family best has become more defined.

Dietitians involved in palliative care in the early-and-mid 1900s had little to offer patients and their families, except to promote quality of life through enjoyment in eating whenever possible. With the advent of nutritional support in the form of parenteral nutrition in the mid 1960s, however, decisions regarding aggressive nutritional support and the role of the dietitian changed dramatically. No longer did palliative care mean "nothing more could be done." Thus, the role of the dietitian in dealing with terminally ill patients grew to include ethical decisions regarding whether and what to "feed" terminally ill patients.

As all health care practitioners experience, it is often the patient, initially more so than the professional, who teaches practitioners about their roles. Indeed, it has been so with the role of the dietitian in caring for terminally ill patients.

Three important documents have also aided in the task of defining the dietitian's role.

1. *Hospice Standards Manual*, Chapter 5: Inpatient Services, by the Joint Commission on Accreditation of Hospitals

2. "Code of Ethics for the Profession of Dietetics" adopted by the House of Delegates of The American Dietetic Association in 1987

3. *Standards of Practice* issued by The American Dietetic Association in 1986

A brief description of the influence of these three documents in defining the role and responsibilities of the palliative care dietitian follows.

STANDARDS FOR INPATIENT DIETETIC SERVICES OF THE JOINT COMMISSION ON ACCREDITATION OF HEALTHCARE ORGANIZATIONS

In 1983 the Joint Commission on Accreditation of Hospitals (now the Joint Commission on the Accreditation of Healthcare Organizations [Joint Commission]) issued its first *Hospice Standards Manual*,[1] which was revised in 1986. Although this manual (Standard IX) primarily identifies the services that the dietetic services department must provide in order for a hospice program to be accredited by the Joint Commission, it also provides a basis for identifying the responsibilities of the dietitian in caring for terminally ill patients.

The 1983 Joint Commission standards state that: the nutritional aspects of hospice patient care are supervised by a dietitian who is registered by the Commission on Dietetic Registration of The American Dietetic Association or who has the documented equivalent in education, training, and/or experience, as well as evidence of continuing education.[2]

The standards also define the responsibilities of the dietitian, including (1) the assessment, planning, implementation, and evaluation stages of providing nutritional care; (2) the need to develop policies and procedures for nutritional care; and (3) the participation in interdisciplinary team conferences as appropriate. It further delineates specific policies and procedures that must be written in order to provide dietetic services. The palliative care dietitian should be familiar with the most current Joint Commission standards for hospice programs.

CODE OF ETHICS FOR THE PROFESSION OF DIETETICS

The Code of Ethics of The American Dietetic Association (ADA), which in 1989 replaces the old Standards of Professional Responsibility that have been in effect since January 1984, must be thoughtfully considered when defining the role of the dietitian.[3] The revision is more inclusive of the practitioner's responsibility to withdraw voluntarily from practice under specified conditions; it also specifies circumstances under which the practitioner is subject to disciplinary action. Because of its importance, the Code of Ethics is reproduced in Exhibit 6-1.

Exhibit 6-1 Code of Ethics for the Profession of Dietetics

A new phase of support for ethical practice by members of The American Dietetic Association and credentialed dietetic practitioners will be ushered in January 1, 1989. At that time, ADA's Code of Ethics for the Profession of Dietetics will become applicable to non-member RDs and DTRs as well as to members. The revised code has drawn from the current Standards of Professional Responsibility and principles reflective of other credentialing agencies, professional associations, and state dietetic licensing boards.

The purpose of the new code is to provide guidance to dietetic practitioners in their professional practice and conduct. It will also assist in protecting the nutritional health, safety and welfare of the public by enforcing ethical behavior among ADA members and non-member RDs and DTRs.

ADA's House of Delegates adopted the revised code on October 18, 1987. During 1988, the Ethics Committee and the Commission on Dietetic Registration developed and approved the procedures for the review process. The procedures were accepted by the Board of Directors on June 8.

Preamble

The American Dietetic Association and its credentialing agency, the Commission on Dietetic Registration, believe it is in the best interests of the profession and the public it serves that a Code of Ethics provide guidance to dietetic practitioners in their professional practice and conduct. Dietetic practitioners have voluntarily developed a Code of Ethics to reflect the ethical principles guiding the dietetic profession and to outline commitments and obligations of the dietetic practitioner to self, client, society, and the profession.

The purpose of the Commission on Dietetic Registration is to assist in protecting the nutritional health, safety, and welfare of the public by establishing and enforcing qualifications for dietetic registration and for issuing voluntary credentials to individuals who have attained those qualifications. The Commission has adopted this Code to apply to individuals who hold these credentials.

The Ethics Code applies in its entirety to members of The American Dietetic Association who are Registered Dietitians (RDs) or Dietetic Technicians Registered (DTRs). Except for sections solely dealing with the credential, the Code applies to all American Dietetic Association members who are not RDs or DTRs. Except for aspects solely dealing with membership, the Code applies to all RDs and DTRs who are not ADA members. All of the aforementioned are referred to in the Code as "dietetic practitioners."

Principles

1. The dietetic practitioner provides professional services with objectivity and with respect for the unique needs and values of individuals.
2. The dietetic practitioner avoids discrimination against other individuals on the basis of race, creed, religion, sex, age, and national origin.
3. The dietetic practitioner fulfills professional commitments in good faith.
4. The dietetic practitioner conducts himself/herself with honesty, integrity, and fairness.
5. The dietetic practitioner remains free of conflict of interest while fulfilling the objectives and maintaining the integrity of the dietetic profession.
6. The dietetic practitioner maintains confidentiality of information.
7. The dietetic practitioner practices dietetics based on scientific principles and current information.

Exhibit 6-1 *continued*

8. The dietetic practitioner assumes responsibility and accountability for personal competence in practice.
9. The dietetic practitioner recognizes and exercises professional judgment within the limits of his/her qualifications and seeks counsel or makes referrals as appropriate.
10. The dietetic practitioner provides sufficient information to enable clients to make their own informed decisions.
11. The dietetic practitioner who wishes to inform the public and colleagues of his/her services does so by using factual information. The dietetic practitioner does not advertise in a false or misleading manner.
12. The dietetic practitioner promotes or endorses products in a manner that is neither false nor misleading.
13. The dietetic practitioner permits use of his/her name for the purpose of certifying that dietetic services have been rendered only if he/she has provided or supervised the provision of those services.
14. The dietetic practitioner accurately presents professional qualifications and credentials.
    a. The dietetic practitioner uses "RD" or "registered dietitian" and "DTR" or "dietetic technician registered" only when registration is current and authorized by the Commission on Dietetic Registration.
    b. The dietetic practitioner provides accurate information and complies with all requirements of the Commission on Dietetic Registration program in which he/she is seeking initial or continued credentials from the Commission on Dietetic Registration.
    c. The dietetic practitioner is subject to disciplinary action for aiding another person in violating any Commission on Dietetic Registration requirements or aiding another person in representing himself/herself as an RD or DTR when he/she is not.
15. The dietetic practitioner presents substantiated information and interprets controversial information without personal bias, recognizing that legitimate differences of opinion exist.
16. The dietetic practitioner makes all reasonable effort to avoid bias in any kind of professional evaluation. The dietetic practitioner provides objective evaluation of candidates for professional association memberships, awards, scholarships, or job advancements.
17. The dietetic practitioner voluntarily withdraws from professional practice under the following circumstances:
    a. The dietetic practitioner has engaged in any substance abuse that could affect his/her practice;
    b. The dietetic practitioner has been adjudged by a court to be mentally incompetent;
    c. The dietetic practitioner has an emotional or mental disability that affects his/her practice in a manner that could harm the client.
18. The dietetic practitioner complies with all applicable laws and regulations concerning the profession. The dietetic practitioner is subject to disciplinary action under the following circumstances:
    a. The dietetic practitioner has been convicted of a crime under the laws of the United States which is a felony or a misdemeanor, an essential element of which is dishonesty and which is related to the practice of the profession.
    b. The dietetic practitioner has been disciplined by a state and at least one of the grounds for the discipline is the same or substantially equivalent to these principles.

Exhibit 6-1 *continued*

> c. The dietetic practitioner has committed an act of misfeasance or malfeasance which is directly related to the practice of the profession as determined by a court of competent jurisdiction, a licensing board, or an agency of a governmental body.
> 19. The dietetic practitioner accepts the obligation to protect society and the profession by upholding the Code of Ethics for the Profession of Dietetics and by reporting alleged violations of the Code through the defined review process of The American Dietetic Association and its credentialing agency, the Commission on Dietetic Registration.
>
> *Source*: Reprinted from *Journal of The American Dietetic Association*, 88, No. 12, pp. 1592–1593, with permission of The American Dietetic Association, © December 1988.

STANDARDS OF PRACTICE OF THE AMERICAN DIETETIC ASSOCIATION

In July, 1986, The ADA Council on Practice, Quality Assurance Committee, published *Standards of Practice: A Practitioner's Guide to Implementation.*[4] These standards of practice were developed for the purpose of helping the dietitian plan, implement, evaluate, and adapt performance systematically, regardless of area of practice.[5] Exhibit 6-2 identifies the standards of practice and the preliminary criteria as published by the ADA. The author's application of these standards and criteria in establishing a personal quality assurance program for working with terminally ill patients is also delineated in Exhibit 6-2.

Exhibit 6-2 Standards of Practice for a Dietitian with Responsibilities in Palliative Care

> **Standard 1.0**
> *The dietetic practitioner establishes performance criteria, compares actual performance with expected performance, documents results, and takes appropriate action.*
>
> **Preliminary Criteria**
> 1.1 Establish performance criteria to measure quality practice.
> 1.2 Compare actual to expected performance.
> 1.3 Document action taken when discrepancies exist between actual and expected performance.
> 1.4 Document the result(s) of action taken.
>
> **Performance Criteria for Responsibilities in Palliative Care**
> 1.1 Develop an annual personal plan for practice that recognizes the evolving nature of the palliative care dietitian's roles and responsibilities, is based on the ADA Standards of Practice and the Code of Ethics, and includes criteria to assess personal accomplishments.

Exhibit 6-2 *continued*

1.2 Identify the need for improvement in practice based on comparison of personal performance (via collected data from patient and colleague evaluations) to established criteria identified in the personal plan for practice.

1.3 Revise personal plan for practice based on an identified need for improvement, and share with palliative care/dietetics administrators.

1.4 Use initial and revised personal plan for practice, including self-, peer, and patient evaluations in yearly performance evaluations with palliative care/dietetics administrators.

Standard 2.0
The dietetic practitioner develops, implements, and evaluates an individual plan for practice based on assessment of consumer needs, current knowledge, and clinical experience.

Preliminary Criteria

2.1 Complete a needs assessment.

2.2 Develop goals and performance criteria.

2.3 Document implementation steps.

2.4 Evaluate process and outcomes continuously.

Performance Criteria for Responsibilities in Palliative Care

2.1.1 Identify the consumers of palliative nutritional care, including terminally ill patients and their families, interdisciplinary team members, other dietitians and health professionals, and the public.

2.1.2 Identify the consumer needs for palliative nutritional care by surveying consumers on the need for services rendered and services that consumers feel should be offered.

2.1.3 Continue to read and study literature, including textbooks and journals on palliative care, death and dying, psychology and sociology, pain and symptom control, and interdisciplinary team building and networking.

2.2.1 Develop long- and short-term goals and objectives for the position of palliative care dietitian.

2.2.2 Develop an annual plan and measurable performance criteria to accomplish goals and objectives.

2.2.3 Develop a tool to screen palliative care patients and families who need the services of the dietitian.

2.2.4 Develop and implement educational programs on nutrition for interdisciplinary team members so that other team members can meet the nutritional needs of those patients and families who do not require the services of the dietitian.

2.2.5 Develop a nontraditional inpatient food service department that can meet varying patient and family needs.

2.3 Develop a medical record charting system and food service charting system to reflect the nutritional needs of patients and families and the services rendered to patients, families, team members, other professionals, and the public.

2.4 Review productivity and compliance with screening, charting, and food service standards with program administrators on a monthly basis.

Exhibit 6-2 *continued*

Standard 3.0
The dietetic practitioner, utilizing unique knowledge of nutrition, collaborates with other professionals, personnel, and/or consumers, in integrating, interpreting, and communicating nutritional care principles.

Preliminary Criteria

3.1 Demonstrate integration of nutritional care with other professionals, personnel, and consumers.

3.2 Document interpretation of nutritional information to other professionals, personnel, and consumers.

3.3 Document results of communication regarding nutritional care principles with other professionals, personnel, and consumers.

Performance Criteria for Responsibilities in Palliative Care

3.1.1 Provide nutrition mini-lectures at interdisciplinary team meetings/patient care conferences.

3.1.2 Participate as a panel member in educational programs on palliative care that are provided to other health professionals and the public.

3.1.3 Participate in interdisciplinary team meetings/patient care conferences, program staff meetings, inservices, and team development seminars.

3.1.4 Participate actively on the program's Ethics Committee.

3.2.1 Serve as liaison between the hospital inpatient dietetics program, the free-standing building program, the home care program, and the day care program for staff update and administrative coordination.

3.2.2 Write policies and procedures regarding nutritional care procedures and food service operations for the palliative care program.

3.2.3 Review documentation of nutritional care rendered by program staff to evaluate the effectiveness of nutrition mini-lectures and staff inservices provided by the dietitian.

3.3 Document results of communication regarding nutritional care principles with other professionals, personnel, and consumers.

Standard 4.0
The dietetic practitioner engages in lifelong self-development to improve knowledge and skills.

Preliminary Criteria

4.1 Conduct self-assessment to identify professional strengths and weaknesses.

4.2 Identify professional development goals.

4.3 Write a plan for self-development.

4.4 Record self-development achievements.

4.5 Adhere to high standards of ethics.

Exhibit 6-2 *continued*

Performance Criteria for Responsibilities in Palliative Care

4.1   Conduct personal self-assessment, listing areas of strengths and weaknesses in:
- interdisciplinary team participation
- comfortability level with terminally ill patients
- flexibility in professional role
- listening and communication skills
- personal management skills
- clinical nutrition knowledge
- food service management skills and knowledge
- medical, pharmacology, and palliative care philosophy knowledge

4.2   My long-term goal is to establish registered dietitians as integral members of palliative care interdisciplinary teams. My short-term goals are (1) to share my experiences as a palliative care team dietitian with my colleagues through publishing a book on nutrition and terminal illness, and (2) to market the role of the dietitian to health care administrators and government policy makers.

4.3   Based on my professional development goal and self-assessment, the following action plan is projected:
1. Attend seminars on marketing and leadership development. Time frame: annually
2. Attend National Hospice Organization conferences on legislation and policy development. Time frame: annually
3. Review the *Federal Register* for pertinent legislative activities. Time frame: monthly

4.4   Identify progress toward achievement of the action plan shown in 4.3 above and revise the plan as necessary.

4.5   Adhere to the Code of Ethics for the Profession of Dietetics. Seek to establish ethical standards for palliative care by serving on the program's Ethics Committee.

Standard 5.0
The dietetic practitioner generates, interprets, and uses research to enhance dietetic practice.

Preliminary Criteria

5.1   Use research findings in practice.
5.2   Conduct research (see operational definition).
5.3   Ensure that valid data are collected.

Performance Criteria for Responsibilities in Palliative Care

5.1.1   Review critically literature and conference information on nutritional care of terminally ill patients and the impact of legislation on palliative care programs.
5.1.2   Use critically reviewed information to forecast future ventures and design innovative nutrition and food service programs.
5.2.1   Use experiences with patients to identify innovative practices in nutritional care of terminally ill patients and their families. Implement carefully researched practices only after their efficacy has been proven.

Exhibit 6-2 *continued*

5.2.2 Generate cost effective data on reimbursement of nutritional services in palliative care programs.

5.2.3 Collaborate with other interdisciplinary team members in planning and implementing program research.

5.3 Develop valid research protocols and publish findings in peer-reviewed journals.

Standard 6.0

The dietetic practitioner identifies, monitors, analyzes, and justifies the use of resources.

Preliminary Criteria

6.1 Document use of resources.

6.2 Analyze use of resources in practice.

6.3 Document that use of resources is consistent with the plan for practice.

Performance Criteria for Responsibilities in Palliative Care

6.1 Keep a log of activities and time required to perform the duties of the palliative care dietitian in the following categories: counseling, patient and program documentation, administrative work, research, and public service.

6.2 Perform a self-productivity audit to assess personal use of resources.

6.3.1 Document use of resources through activity logs, productivity tables, and client evaluation summaries.

6.3.2 Compare the plan for practice and performance with the established standards.

DEFINING A POSITION DESCRIPTION FOR A DIETITIAN WITH PRIMARY RESPONSIBILITY IN PALLIATIVE CARE

When identifying the role that a professional will play in a palliative care program and when writing the professional's position description, these issues should be addressed.[6]

- scope and nature of the services to be provided by the discipline, noting the interrelationships among disciplines comprising the palliative care program
- potential recipients of services provided, such as the patient, family, interdisciplinary team members, program administrative personnel, and the public
- program components, such as inpatient, home care, day care, and bereavement
- who provides what services and under whose supervision, again noting overlapping of services within and outside each discipline

- qualifications and educational requirements of staff
- responsibilities of each discipline to the program, such as in the following areas
  1. educating program staff, including volunteers
  2. public education
  3. participation in ethical decision-making activities
  4. interdisciplinary team activities
  5. overall program planning, evaluation, quality assurance
- responsibilities to patients, including the screening and assessment of patient and family needs and planning, implementing, evaluating, and documenting the plan of care

Based on these components, a position description for a dietitian with primary responsibility in palliative care can be written, as shown in Exhibit 6-3.

ROLE PERCEPTION

Before delineating the role and responsibilities of the palliative care dietitian in more depth, it is important to examine a concept that affects the role and responsibilities of all professionals—that of role perception. Role perception is how we feel about ourselves and our profession and how others perceive us.

The perception we have of our role as a health professional is colored by several factors. John Horwitz identifies the following four factors:[7]

1. our own personal and professional identity
2. our view of our professional role in a particular setting
3. our understanding of the competencies of our colleagues
4. our image of how we feel our colleagues perceive us

Each of these four factors is important, regardless of whether we work full-time with terminally ill patients or whether we see terminally ill patients on a less frequent consulting basis. However, role perception usually seems to have greater importance when the dietitian is a member of a health care team such as a palliative care team, working primarily with terminally ill patients and their families, than when he or she is working independently.

It is common to find differences in perception among team members regarding others' roles. In addition, individuals may not understand or have an appropriate perception of their own role. Role conflict can develop between or among team members, and between the individual team members and program administrators when role misunderstanding exists.

Exhibit 6-3 Position Description for a Palliative Care Dietitian

Summary of Position

   The palliative care dietitian will be responsible for providing nutritional services to terminally ill patients and their families, to the interdisciplinary palliative care team and administration, and to the public as necessary to carry out the overall goals and objectives of the palliative care program, including the free-standing inpatient program, the home care program, and the day care program. The dietitian shall be registered by the Commission on Dietetic Registration of The American Dietetic Association. The dietitian will be committed to the philosophy, goals, and objectives of the program and will be directly responsible to the Director of Patient Services of the program.

Nature and Scope of Responsibilities

The dietitian will perform the following responsibilities:

- Assume responsibility for providing or supervising the provision of all aspects of nutritional care to terminally ill patients and families, including food service in the inpatient and day care settings and nutritional counseling in home care settings.
  1. Evaluate on a yearly basis the performance of food service employees assigned to the palliative care unit.
  2. Plan and assume responsibility for the menu and food service system in the inpatient and day care settings consistent with palliative care unit philosophy and objectives.
  3. Prepare, defend, and ensure compliance with a yearly budget for palliative nutrition and food service programs consistent with the institution's mandate for a balanced budget.
- Develop nutritional care policies and procedures for inpatient, home care, and day care services consistent with palliative care unit objectives and philosophy.
- Screen all patients and families for the presence of or the potential for nutritional problems and further assess those who are or who are likely to be in need of nutritional services.
- Develop an appropriate nutritional care plan for patients and families consistent with the care plans of other members of the interdisciplinary team.
- Implement an individualized nutritional care plan through patient and family counseling, diet instruction, and provision of food as appropriate.
- Evaluate the nutritional care rendered and document the plan, implementation procedures, and evaluation of personal performance and client behavior in the patient's medical record.
- Contribute nutritional expertise to interdisciplinary team meetings, staff meetings, bereavement sessions, and inservice programs, and serve on the program's Ethics Committee and other committees as appropriate.
- Consult with interdisciplinary team members about specific patient nutritional problems. Provide inservice education to the interdisciplinary team as requested. Provide leadership in identifying overlapping responsibilities of program employees concerning provision of nutritional care to clients.
- Establish and use personal performance standards in self-evaluation and in evaluation with the program's Director of Patient Services. Evaluate the goals, objectives, and accomplishments of the program on a yearly basis. Conduct patient care audit and quality assurance activities as requested.
- Create and collaborate in research projects, publish findings, and share research expertise with other professionals.

Causes of role misunderstanding and role conflict vary, but they usually develop because of role ambiguity, role overlap or blurring, and role overload. Adding new people to the team brings additional perceptions regarding roles, and blurring of roles frequently occurs as a team grows.

A detailed description of each professional's role should be written and shared with each member of the palliative care team in order to avoid role ambiguity and overlap. Consider the example of "assessment," a process that must be performed on each terminally ill patient and family, to demonstrate the need for role under-standing and appreciation. Every team member "assesses" the patient and family. Each professional assesses some of the same patient and family characteristics, but each has a particular area of professional expertise around which most of his or her assessment efforts center. Because areas of assessment overlap to some extent and assessment abilities vary, assessments of professionals for any given area may differ. Certainly, no one assessment at any one time will be 100% complete. The importance of sharing and accepting each professional's insights cannot be over-emphasized.

Another reason for role conflict is role overload. Role overload can occur when a team member either has too large a role or has too many roles to perform. Role overload frequently leads to professional burnout (see Chapter 5); a frequent indicator is when the team member misses many interdisciplinary team meetings. Only when roles comfortably fit the professional and are understood and valued by others on the team can professionals function effectively as an interdisciplinary team.

RESPONSIBILITIES OF THE DIETITIAN AS A TEAM MEMBER

The dietitian as a member of the palliative care team is usually expected to function more as a team player than as an individual professional. This means that dietitians should establish themselves as supportive colleagues instead of as consultants to whom patients are passed for treatment. As a team player, the dietitian is expected to engage in the following group-supporting activities:

- participate regularly in team meetings
- keep accurate and up-to-date patient records
- develop respect and a general liking for other team members
- develop interpersonal networks and trust without being greedy for personal power
- understand and support the team's structure and the stage of growth of the team and the program
- avoid the "groupthink" situation

Participate in Team Meetings

The dietitian should regularly participate in team meetings; each team member should be "seen *and* heard," not "seen and not heard." Of all the important actions a dietitian should take, being seen and being heard are two of the most important. Timely oral communications are essential if we want to be an integral and respected member of the team. Know what to say, and say it well. Be judicious in the amount of time spent talking during team meetings and other meetings, but do not sit quietly and hope others will request your opinion. Silence will be perceived as having nothing to say. Speak, and be well-spoken.

Keep Appropriate Patient Records

Accurate and timely communications are essential for coordination and continuity of patient care. Written documentation is also essential for quality control purposes and to meet standards established by the Joint Commission. Therefore, keep accurate and up-to-date patient records and write appropriately in the patient's medical record.

Most palliative care programs do not specify a format that must be used when writing in the patient's medical record. Use whatever format you prefer or that is used by other members of the team. The SOAP format is appropriate and frequently used. Documentation may be brief or elaborate, whichever is needed to inform accurately and completely the other team members of your findings and accomplishments with regard to the patient and family situation.

Respect Team Members

The dietitian is well advised to develop an "affection" for other team members. Such affection should be built on respect and a general liking for others. This does not mean that you must frequently interact socially with the other team members, but getting to know them as people, knowing something about their families, and sharing yourself with them are important in fostering camaraderie and developing value and respect in the work environment. One way to gain the respect and appreciation of other team members is to commend team members for exemplary care of patients, especially if you witnessed it in a patient's home. Be honest and do not exaggerate. Properly timed, a word of praise can mean a great deal to team members and can endear you to them.

Simple acts of kindness given to the team will not be forgotten. On occasion, especially for a team member's birthday or on a bleak day in winter, take a nutritious (and sometimes not so nutritious) goodie to team meetings. Kindness, on a more serious note, will be appreciated by others if you attend calling hours, funerals, wakes, or memorial services of patients with whom you worked. Not only will this act support the family and palliative care team, but it will help you bring closure to your involvement with the patient.

Develop Networks and Trust

It is important that dietitians not force themselves onto a palliative care team, but instead be asked to join. Forcing acceptance is not likely to result in eager recognition by other team members, especially if program administrators felt coerced into accepting a professional as a team member. To be asked to join because the profession and the professional are viewed favorably is essential in order to be granted the rights and privileges due a member. A benefit to being a valued team member is the ability to be effective in causing change.

It is likely that the dietitian joining a palliative care team will experience a power dilemma. The tenets of Western society and our profession encourage us to develop our individual sense of power. Countering this personal power, however, is the power frequently wielded by the hierarchial authorities at employing institutions. These and other authorities often discourage us from developing a power base in our work environment. As a result, we withdraw from self-assertion and do not develop a clear professional identity. As the dietetics profession continues to affect health care in the United States, as it has begun to do during the 1980s, the dietitian can expect to enjoy an increased power base.

Within a palliative care team, however, the dietitian should not be immediately hungry for power. Power comes as trust is developed. "Building trust is difficult in a marriage of equals, let alone in an interdisciplinary team wherein people have not been taught how to interact across traditional professional disciplines."[9]

Although nutrition is a frequent problem for terminally ill patients and their families, a discussion around nutrition rarely becomes the focus of attention within the group. As a result, the dietitian must demonstrate skills and fulfill assigned roles well before co-team members will "trust" him or her. When the professional has earned the trust of team members by consistently demonstrating good clinical skills and consistently dealing fairly with others, the professional will be granted power within the group. It takes time and patience, a high degree of flexibility, and a good dose of professional expertise to achieve power within a team. If the care a professional demonstrates for patients and their families is applauded by those served, the professional's image within the interdisciplinary team will be heightened. The patient and family are the strongest voices in singing the praise of a compassionate and valued palliative care team member.

Support the Team's Structure

In order to understand the position of a dietitian in the palliative care program, it is important first to understand the following four team characteristics: (1) how leadership of the team is determined, (2) the goals of the program, (3) the team's structure, and (4) the stage of growth of the team and the palliative care program within the health care system in which it operates.

Usually, but not always, the leadership of team meetings is based on functionality, which means leadership is allocated based on a task basis. Because the nurse or nursing administrator usually coordinates patient and family care and has the best balance of technical and psychosocial skills, one or the other of these professionals often leads the patient care discussions at interdisciplinary team meetings. However, other team members may take the leadership role for specific tasks and may lead the discussion about a particular patient. The team member who develops the most meaningful communication or trust with the patient and family is the one who usually leads the discussion about the patient at team meetings.

The dietitian should understand the overall goals and objectives of the palliative care program and be able to contribute to their accomplishment. An astute dietitian will recognize when changes in program goals or objectives are appropriate and as a team member should support those changes.

In order to effect needed change in the program, you must understand the group structure. And in order to understand the group structure, it is helpful to participate in task-oriented group interaction in which you work to help the team accomplish a given goal or objective. As a member of a task-oriented group, you will be in a good position to seek and give information and opinions; clarify, elaborate, and summarize what is happening or is being said; and join in consensus. Through such participation in the process-oriented group interaction, you can help the team work together, develop and maintain a harmonious working relationship, and, at the same time, develop your own sphere of influence.

As a team member, you should help maintain harmony. Help police or gate-keep the group's relationships when necessary. Help set standards of care. Compromise if necessary. Never be manipulative or complaining; manipulation and complaining only raise the team's frustration level, create resentment, and adversely affect the quality of care to be rendered to patients and their families.

It is important that the dietitian exhibit behavior in both the "task-oriented" and the "process-oriented" realm of group interaction. The productivity of the palliative care team is determined by the demands of the team's workload, the resources available to the team, and the dynamics of the group.[10] Effective teamwork results in a quality of care that exceeds the level of care that a team member working alone can give.

Avoid "Groupthink"

Avoid the groupthink situation in which the team becomes so cohesive that cohesion itself becomes a goal and members develop behaviors that protect it.[11] This situation can occur in teams who have been together for years, who have gone through tough developmental situations together, or who have struggled together for survival. As is anticipated, the problem with groupthink is that its rigidity damages the group's decision-making ability and its potential for change by clouding or rejecting alternatives.

If you find yourself involved in a groupthink situation, it is important to remember that group change will be difficult and often impossible. If you try to cause change, recognize that your efforts will be met with great resistance. Do not attempt to bring about change until you have become an accepted and valued part of the group. To try to effect change before you have "paid your dues" will alienate you from the "controlling majority" and your efforts likely will be stonewalled.

In closing, it is important to remember that conflicts on teams are inevitable. Conflicts may serve a dysfunctional or a creative purpose. Conflicts that involve interpersonal friction are often due to role blurring, ambiguous role delineation, unclear role expectations, inflexible norms, jealousy, and distress or burnout. If conflicts are not interpersonal (which may mean that they stem from work overload or inadequate or poor working conditions), action can be taken to depersonalize the problem. Then, attempts can be made to change the conditions causing the friction so that the tasks of caring for the patient and the patient's family can be facilitated.

NOTES

1. Joint Commission on Accreditation of Healthcare Organizaitons, *Hospice Standards Manual* (Chicago: Joint Commission on Accreditation of Healthcare Organizations, 1983), 1–60.

2. Ibid., 28.

3. "Code of Ethics for the Profession of Dietetics," *Journal of The American Dietetic Association* 88, no. 12 (December 1988): 1592–1593.

4. The American Dietetic Association Council on Practice, Quality Assurance Committee, *Standards of Practice: A Practitioner's Guide to Implementation* (Chicago: The American Dietetic Association, 1986).

5. Ibid., 3.

6. Madalon O'Rawe Amenta, "Spiritual Concerns," in *Nursing Care of the Terminally Ill*, ed. Madalon O'Rawe Amenta and Nancy L. Bohnet (Boston: Little, Brown & Co., 1986), 148.

7. John J. Horwitz, "Dimensions of Rehabilitations Teamwork," *Rehabilitation Record* 10 (1969): 36.

8. Mary L. S. Vachon, "Team Stress in Palliative/Hospice Care," *The Hospice Journal* 3, no. 3 (Summer/Fall 1987): 86–87.

9. Ibid., 88.

10. Ivan Dale Steiner, *Group Process and Productivity* (New York: Academic Press, 1972), 1–13.

11. Irving Lester Janis, *Victims of Groupthink* (Boston: Houghton Mifflin, 1972), 1–13.

Chapter 7

Screening and Assessment

The first component in providing nutritional care to terminally ill patients and their families is assessment. A nutritional care plan can only be as good as the completeness and accuracy of the assessment of the patient's condition and the family's situation.

In this chapter, screening and assessment instruments are provided and discussed. Depending on the setting in which the dietitian functions, one or more of the instruments can be helpful in data collection and assessment.

SCREENING

Regardless of the setting, the dietitian or designated other, such as a nurse or diet aide/technician, will need to screen terminally ill patients for their need to receive nutritional services. Screening patients is easily done during the initial assessment of the patient for admission to a palliative care program.

Exhibit 7-1 is a screening instrument that includes nutrition-related questions that the intake professional and assessment nurse should ask the patient and family during the intake session and subsequent sessions. Answers to these questions will give clues about the nutritional status and eating behavior of the patient and the patient's family. This information will also help shape the nutritional and nursing care plan. A positive answer to any one or more of the questions should alert the intake and assessment professionals to the probability that the dietitian could be of help to the patient and family.

Offering the services of the dietitian is highly appreciated by the patient and the patient's family. If the patient, family, or nurse perceive the need for the dietitian to visit the patient and family, the nurse will generally request a visit at interdisciplinary team meetings. Thus, the nutritional screen performed by the intake professional or palliative care nurse has two primary purposes: (1) it identifies

Exhibit 7-1 Nutrition Screening Questions Appropriate to Ask during Initial Intake and Subsequent Assessment Sessions

---

1. Are the following symptoms uncontrolled by medications and a bother to the patient or family?
   - nausea   Yes ☐   No ☐
   - vomiting   Yes ☐   No ☐
   - diarrhea   Yes ☐   No ☐
   - constipation   Yes ☐   No ☐
   - mouth sores/difficulty swallowing or chewing/dry mouth
                                         Yes ☐   No ☐
   - anorexia   Yes ☐   No ☐

2. Does the patient have a gastrointestinal or intravenous feeding tube in place?
                                         Yes ☐   No ☐

3. Does the patient or family express significant remorse regarding weight change or food intake?
                                         Yes ☐   No ☐
   Comments:

4. Does the family exhibit any of the following behaviors:
   - inappropriate use of food as a crutch for emotional problems
                                         Yes ☐   No ☐
   Comments:

   - belief that disease is caused by what the patient did or did not eat
                                         Yes ☐   No ☐
   Comments:

5. Would the patient or family members like to discuss any nutrition- or food-related concerns with the dietitian?
                                         Yes ☐   No ☐
   Comments:

---

those patients and families who could benefit from the services of the dietitian, and (2) it lays the groundwork with the patient and family that a dietitian is available for counseling as part of the palliative care program.

If nutritional screening data are not compiled at the initial assessment session, the dietitian can screen patients during interdisciplinary team meetings. At these regularly scheduled meetings, each terminally ill patient and family are discussed and the team arrives at a sense of direction for the individual patient and family situation. Such a sense of direction is essential to the maintenance of consistency of patient and family goals among team members.

Exhibit 7-2 is an example of a form that can be used by the dietitian as a patient summary and nutritional screen. This form can be completed easily and quickly during interdisciplinary team meetings, using information discussed there or extracted directly from the patient's medical records (which are frequently made available), to ascertain whether the patient or family needs a more indepth nutritional assessment. The patient's medical record can also assist the dietitian in identifying whether the dietitian could be of benefit to the patient and the patient's family.

ASSESSMENT

If the results of the nutritional screen indicate a need for nutritional intervention and if the patient and the patient's family desire the dietitian's assistance, the dietitian should visit them to conduct a more indepth nutritional assessment. Sometimes a telephone conversation can take the place of a personal visit.

Before visiting or phoning the patient and the patient's family, you should be armed with more information than that on the nutritional screening form. From the interdisciplinary team meetings, the patient's medical record, or the palliative care nurse, obtain the following additional information:

- the patient's ethnic status and socioeconomic background
- the patient's activities of daily living
- the level of pain that the patient experiences
- the patient's prognosis
- the stage of death and dying of the patient and individual family members
- the palliative care goals and patient care plan
- the patient's address and telephone number, as well as directions to the patient's house

Being aware of the stage of acceptance of death and dying that the patient and the patient's family are in helps you anticipate and answer their questions. Patients and families in the denial stage, may say such things as

- a family member: "If he gets too bad, we will need to hospitalize him, won't we?"
- a family member: "If he can't eat, we will find other ways to feed him, won't we?"

If the patient or family members are in the anger stage, they may make such comments as

Exhibit 7-2 Patient Summary and Nutritional Screening Form

Patient Profile

Name:_____ Referring M.D.:_____

Caregiver:_____ Hospice Nurse:_____

Age:_____ Date of Intake:_____

Diagnosis:_____ Date of Death:_____

Additional Medical Information: (medical history and condition on admission)

Medications: (admission and updates; D/C meds by marking through medication name with colored marker)

Date: Medication:

_____

_____

_____

Weekly Team Update: (prognosis, medical-nursing conditions, family concerns, etc.)

Date: Update:

_____

_____

_____

_____

Nutritional Assessment

Nutritional Status (admission):   excellent ☐

adequate for ADL ☐

poor ☐

PO Intake (admission):   good ☐   fair ☐   poor ☐

Nutritional Problems:

Date Identified	Date Resolved	Problem

Patient/Family Views on po intake, tube feeding, parenteral feeding:

Nutritional Action Needed: ☐ none by R.D.; nurse can handle

☐ R.D. to phone patient/family

☐ R.D. to visit patient/family

- the patient: "She's to blame; the beef she fed me all these years has caused my colon cancer."
- the patient: "All those additives I ate for years caused my stomach cancer; the federal government is not strict enough on industry, which is trying to poison us all these days."

Patients or family members in the bargaining stage may make such statements as

- the patient: "If I give up alcohol now, will it help me live longer?"
- the patient: "If I lose weight, will my tumor also shrink?"

Exhibit 7-3 is a sample nutritional assessment form that the author has used successfully to obtain information from the patient and family, to plan an appropriate nutritional care plan, and to serve as an official form in the patient's medical record. The nutritional assessment tool is divided into six sections: (1) patient symptoms, (2) simple dietary history, (3) patient losses, (4) family concerns, (5) family nutritional health, and (6) summary and action plan.

Some of the appropriate nutritional parameters for a nutritional assessment tool for terminally ill patients differ from those appropriate for a nutritional assessment of patients who are not terminally ill. History taking and physical examinations are performed to elicit the specific information and diagnostic measurements that are actually useful in understanding the course of the patient's illness and in determining appropriate palliative treatments. Accordingly, some assessment parameters, especially biochemical laboratory tests for visceral protein status assessment, anthropometric measures, and immune function tests, may not be performed during a palliative care assessment session. What an "eyeball" test does not tell probably does not need to be known. In contrast, dietary assessment and the assessment of possible nutrient and drug interactions are often important. The rationale for performance of a particular nutritional assessment test should be whether the result will make a difference in palliative treatment.

When doing a dietary assessment as part of the overall nutritional assessment, it is important that you only ask questions with a purpose. For example, why ask how much fruit the patient eats? Is it to estimate if the patient is receiving enough vitamin C? If you found the fruit intake was poor but the patient did not exhibit signs of scurvy and he or she disliked fruits or said they hurt the mouth to chew them, would you do anything about it? If, on the other hand, you know that a constipated patient likes and can tolerate fruit and you suspect that added fiber from fruit might help overcome the constipation, you should ask the question. Keep in mind, however, that laxatives are used by 90 percent of palliative care patients, and they are usually more efficacious in relieving constipation than is an increase in foods high in fiber. Also, remember that a question about how much

Exhibit 7-3 Nutritional Assessment Form

Patient Symptoms

1. Presence of the following symptoms
   - nausea?   Yes ☐   No ☐
   - vomiting? Yes ☐   No ☐
     - Is nausea and/or vomiting associated with?
       (circle all that apply)
       1. meals?
       2. taste of foods (sweet, spicy, tart, salty, bland, protein-containing)?
       3. sight, smell of particular foods?
       4. temperature of foods (hot, cold)?
       5. mealtimes?
       6. depression, anxiety?
       7. any conditioned response, e.g., medication box, perfume, thoughts of
          doctor's office, abdominal pain, etc.?
     - Do any foods lessen nausea or vomiting?

	Yes ☐		No ☐	
   - mouth sores? | Yes ☐ | | No ☐ |
   - dry mouth? | Yes ☐ | | No ☐ |
   - drooling? | Yes ☐ | | No ☐ |
   - ill-fitting dentures? | Yes ☐ | | No ☐ |
   - inability to chew properly? | Yes ☐ | | No ☐ |
   - inability to swallow easily? | Yes ☐ | | No ☐ |
   - diarrhea? | Yes ☐ | | No ☐ |
   - constipation? | Yes ☐ | | No ☐ |
   - fluid accumulation? | Yes ☐ | | No ☐ |
   - dehydration? | Yes ☐ | | No ☐ |

2. Presence of the following conditions
   - colostomy?   Yes ☐   No ☐
   - urinary catheter?   Yes ☐   No ☐
     - If present, do you modify what you eat or drink because you do not want your
       caregiver to have to mess with the bag or tube?
                                    Yes ☐   No ☐
   - functioning GI feeding or drainage tube?
                                    Yes ☐   No ☐
   - functioning IV feeding or hydration line?
                                    Yes ☐   No ☐

Exhibit 7-3 *continued*

Simple Dietary History

1. Is eating a pleasurable experience for you?
   Yes ☐   No ☐
2. What are your favorite foods?

3. Are there any foods that you do not like or avoid? If so, what?

4. Are you allergic or intolerant to any foods? If so, what?

5. What are "sick foods" to you?

6. Do you have any cultural or religious food preferences?

7. Have you developed any food changes since being ill?

8. If appropriate, obtain a dietary history including:
   - when, what, how much, where, and with whom the patient eats during the day

9. Do you take any vitamin/mineral supplements?
   Yes ☐   No ☐
   If so, what?

10. If appropriate, try to determine the following:
    - average daily intake of
      1. kilocalories
      2. fluid (particularly the amount just before bedtime)
      3. fiber
      4. alcohol
      5. methyl xanthines

    - cause of anorexia, such as
      1. pain or other symptoms
      2. depression, anxiety
      3. early satiety, fatigue, weakness

Patient Losses
1. Appetite
   - Do you have your usual appetite?
     Yes ☐   No ☐
     If yes, go on to #2 on weight change.
   - Is your appetite usually, but not always pretty good?
     Yes ☐   No ☐
   - Do you have to force yourself to eat?
     Yes ☐   No ☐

Exhibit 7-3 *continued*

- Do you usually feel like you cannot stand the thought of food?

    Yes ☐   No ☐

2. Weight Change
   - Has your weight basically been stable?

       Yes ☐   No ☐
   - Has your weight gotten a "little" or a "lot" worse? (circle which)
   - If your weight has gotten worse, are you a "little" or a "lot" concerned about it? (circle which)
   - Does your weight change make you more dependent on others?

       Yes ☐   No ☐

     If so, how?
     If so, does it bother you?   Yes ☐   No ☐
   - If we can, do you want us to try to do something about your weight?

       Yes ☐   No ☐

3. Inability to eat or feed self
   - If you become unable or find it undesirable to eat or drink, would you want to be "tube" fed or "intravenously" fed to be kept alive?

       Yes ☐   No ☐

     If yes, circle which.
   - Do you find it difficult to let others feed you?

       Yes ☐   No ☐
   - Do you find it difficult to let others shop, cook, or clean up for you?

       Yes ☐   No ☐
   - Do you want "more," "less," or the "same" socialization at mealtimes? (circle which)
   - To the respiratory troubled patient if appropriate: Do you sometimes feel you'll drown or choke to death if you drink or eat?

       Yes ☐   No ☐

Family Concerns
1. Anticipate and answer questions the caregiver(s) may have, such as (put checkmark [√] beside those answered)
   - If he doesn't eat or drink and becomes dehydrated, will he suffer? [ ]
   - If he doesn't eat, won't he feel hunger pains? [ ]
   - If he doesn't eat, will he die sooner? [ ]
   - If he quits eating and drinking, doesn't it mean he hasn't long to live? [ ]
   - Did I contribute to his illness by what I fed or didn't feed him? [ ]
   - What about nutritional therapies, such as vitamin C, laetrile, the macrobiotic diet, enzymes? [ ]

Exhibit 7-3 *continued*

2. Ask the caregiver(s) questions, such as
   - How well do you think the patient is eating?
     good ☐   fair ☐   poor ☐
   - Are the amount and variety the patient eats acceptable to you?
                      yes ☐   no ☐
   - Is there anything you would like to tell the patient or express to me about the patient's eating that concerns or hurts you?
                      yes ☐   no ☐
     If so, what?
   - Are there community services I can facilitate access for you, such as Meals on Wheels, food stamps, or commercial nutritional supplements?
                      Yes ☐   No ☐
     If so, what?

Family Nutritional Health
1. Ask the caregiver(s) questions about their own health such as
   - Do you enjoy eating?   Yes ☐   No ☐
   - Are you eating regularly?   Yes ☐   No ☐
     A variety of foods?   Yes ☐   No ☐
   - Are you eating your favorite foods often?
                      Yes ☐   No ☐
     If not, why?
   - Since the patient's illness, have you gained or lost weight unintentionally?
                      Yes ☐   No ☐
     If so, why?
   - Do you find that food or beverage helps you cope?
                      Yes ☐   No ☐

Summary and Nutritional Care Plan

any type of food, such as fruit, is eaten carries the implied suggestion that patients need to eat more of that type of food. Unless the patient actually does need to change eating patterns to achieve other palliative goals, it is best to avoid both subtle and overt statements designed to effect behavioral change. Instead, encourage patients to continue eating if they enjoy it and also advocate other ways to bring enjoyment.

Appropriate dietary assessment questions generally include the following:

- Do you enjoy eating?
- If so, what are your favorite foods?
- Are there any foods you can think of that you would like to eat and that your family or others could get for you?
- Do you want to change how much you eat? If so, how can we help you do so?
- Is there any assistance such as Meals on Wheels, food stamps, or food supplements that we can try to obtain for you?

Indeed, asking about weight, a common and appropriate question asked in nutritional assessments of acute care patients, may not be appropriate with the terminally ill patient. It is only appropriate when the patient expresses sadness about weight loss (or weight gain that occurs with some medications) and the change in the patients' views of their bodies.

One purpose of your visit with the patient and the patient's family is to elicit their views on aggressive nutritional support. Before being accepted into most palliative care programs, a patient and the patient's family will have signed an informed consent document indicating they do not want extraordinary treatments to be instituted to keep the patient alive. Usually, the intake professional, assessment nurse, or palliative care nurse discusses aggressive nutritional support with the patient and the patient's family in regard to this informed consent document. In most palliative care programs, aggressive nutritional support, especially total parenteral nutrition, is considered extraordinary treatment. Tube feedings are often but not always considered extraordinary as well.

When conducting the nutritional assessment, the palliative care dietitian should ascertain whether the patient and/or the patient's family are comfortable with their acceptance of the policy of no aggressive nutritional support. If you find that a patient and/or individual family member(s) want to discuss aggressive nutritional support, be open and straightforward in responding to their wish. As part of the discussion, explore the patient or family's reasons for desiring such treatment and support the patient and the patient's family in their choice after identifying what aggressive nutritional support can and cannot do for the patient. It is essential that you immediately share the information discussed with the patient's palliative care nurse and then discuss the conversation further with other team members at the first subsequent interdisciplinary team meeting. For a much deeper discussion of aggressive nutritional support and its place in palliative care, the reader is referred to Chapter 9 on symptom control and Chapter 12 on ethics.

During the nutritional assessment, the patient and the patient's family will often, in an offhanded manner, mention serious concerns that are easily missed by an inattentive clinician. For example, the patient and the patient's family may sometimes pose questions that indicate hidden fears, such as

- "Do you think my bowels some day will just 'spill out' into my colostomy?"
- "If I don't drink or eat anything, will dehydration be painful?"
- "I like to drink liquids, but will I choke and be unable to breathe or drown if I drink too much?"
- "If he doesn't eat at all, won't he get hunger pangs?"
- "If I had eaten 'right' would I have avoided cancer?"
- "If he quits drinking and eating, doesn't it mean he hasn't long to live?"

Dietitians need to probe what the patient or the patient's family mean when they ask such questions by posing these questions in turn to the patient or family.

- "What do you make of your condition now?"
- "How do you think [the condition] should be treated?"
- "What do you think caused [the illness]?"
- "How long has the problem been going on?"
- "What do you foresee happening in the next few days? Weeks?"
- "Are you worried about (e.g., looking thin in the casket)?"

When posing these questions, tact and sensitivity are critical; if the patients or families feel threatened or confronted, they will react with anger and denial and will not answer further questions.

During these visits, the patient or the patient's family will often tell you information that does not directly pertain to nutrition. Because this information will be valuable to the entire palliative care team, listen and take notes. Reporting significant findings at interdisciplinary team meetings is imperative.

Chapter 8

Food, Dying, and Ethnic Background

Despite the well-known adage that it is hazardous to apply cultural stereotypes to individual patients, peoples of various ethnic backgrounds *do* have different views and *do* respond differently to food, symptoms, pain, health, health care delivery systems, and dying. The views and responses of others are often greatly different from our own. To be helpful to patients and their families, dietitians must not only recognize that cultural and individual differences exist but must also be supportive of these differences.

Entire books have been written on the cultural views of various ethnic groups on food, health, and dying. The suggested readings at the end of this chapter provide the reader with information about the practices of several large ethnic groups living in the United States. The Indochinese culture, a relative newcomer to the melting pot that characterizes American culture, provides a good example of the ethnic characteristics that a dietitian must consider when working with people from different cultures. Therefore, a discussion of the food patterns and the health and dying practices of Indochinese is included in this chapter, along with a description of the broad range of views regarding death and dying of several cultural groups that have lived in the United States for a long time.

MEANING OF FOOD

Food carries biological, emotional, and sociological meanings.[1] Biologically, food provides nutrients essential for life. Without nutrients and a constant source of energy, the body dies. Emotionally, food means different things to us at different ages. The infant attaches love and bodily security to food. The toddler may see food as a reward or punishment. From early life experiences, we can remember "comfort" foods such as ice cream, hot cereal, broth, toast, popsicles, or tea, that were given to us by a loving parent when we were ill. Children and adolescents may use food as a crutch for emotional problems, to attract attention, or to control their parents. Adults often maintain many of these same associations with foods. Like children, the adult attaches security to familiar foods. Perhaps this is best illustrated by the fact that immigrants to new countries usually give up their native speech and dress before they give up their native foods.[2] Too, immigrant children often give up ethnic food practices before their parents.

Foods have different meanings to us whether we are ill or well.[3] To a dying patient, food may have a positive or a negative meaning. On the positive side, food is equated with *hope* ("if I can eat, I can live"), *comfort* ("Mother always gave me chicken soup when I was ill"), and *joy* ("now that my pain is gone, my appetite has improved").

On the negative side, food can cause *guilt* ("I know I should eat, but I just can't"), *fear* ("I can't breathe and swallow at the same time; solid foods cause me to choke"), and *pain* ("even if the sores in my mouth would allow me to eat, my stomach would rebel"). Patients can also use food as a tool to hasten death by refusing to eat or drink, or by the same technique, patients can use food to manipulate family members when they know that others are greatly concerned about their intake.

Similarly, to individual family members of a dying patient, food may have different meanings. Food can support *hope* ("as long as he eats he can live") or represent *despair* ("what can I do when he refuses to eat; I think he has just given up") and *guilt* ("I fed him too much red meat"). Family members can also use food in a passive-aggressive manner in an attempt to control the patient or accomplish another, often hidden agenda ("If I don't eat and let my health go, I'll show him how much care he requires of me.").

The consumption of food is an intellectual as well as an emotional process. People frequently choose foods on an intellectual basis because of the desired taste, the known nutrient content, or some perceived health benefit. Self-expression can be exercised through the choice or rejection of certain foods.

Certain foods also have social meanings. To a grieving person, a gift of food is a message of sympathy,[4] which is why foods are usually brought to the home of a dying or deceased patient and why funeral dinners are common worldwide. Tabooed foods, special foods, and feast days are an integral part of many religions. Sociologically, several foods are identified solely with certain ethnic, cultural, and religious groups, and within these groups, certain foods may be proscribed to certain individuals depending on their status or class.

Many dietitians themselves have ambivalent feelings about the meanings of food. Because of their abhorrence of malnutrition, many novice dietitians working with terminally ill patients have the tendency to want to feed the patient as much as possible. The act of giving food represents the desire to give life to the patient. Answering this question honestly,—"Do I live to eat or eat to live?"—and exploring how the answer to this question influences feelings about feeding others are important for dietitians.

Terminally ill patients have taught us that, when eating is enjoyable for them, we should count it a blessing and encourage mealtimes to be shared with loved ones. Important goals of palliative care are to maximize enjoyment and minimize pain. When eating and mealtimes can accomplish either of these goals, they should be used to advantage. If eating is not an enjoyable experience, however, its practice should not be overemphasized. It is at this time that the dietitian can be a strong patient advocate and family ally by reassuring both that loving care can be demonstrated in ways other than through feeding.

FOOD PRACTICES OF RELIGIOUS AND ETHNIC GROUPS

The various cultures and religions of the world have had a profound influence on dietary practices. In the classic textbook, *Food and Man* by Miriam E. Lowenberg and colleagues, the food practices of five major religions of the world—Christianity, Judaism, Islam, Hinduism, and Buddhism—are discussed.[5] Of these religions, the dietary practices of Christians, including Roman Catholics, Eastern Orthodox, and such protestant denominations as the Seventh Day Adventists and the Church of Jesus Christ of the Latter-Day Saints, and Jews are best understood by people living in the United States.

Most American Jews today do not observe strict dietary laws, and Orthodox, Conservative and Reform Jews hold divergent views on food practices. It is important to remember that an individual can be Jewish (or of other religious persuasion) and not concur with all the tenets of his religion's doctrine. It is the patient's values and opinions that should be honored. In reality, religious dogma becomes of primary importance when it is embodied in the mission statement of the institution that is caring for the patient. Certainly, the possibility of a conflict exists between an individual patient's values and wishes and the facility's philosophical imperatives; such a conflict must be addressed by the patient, family, health care team, and institution. In the case of Jewish dietary laws, during illness (especially with terminal illness), many Jewish dietary laws and practices can be ignored in the interest of preserving life.

Culture, as well as religion, influences dietary practices. The food practices of various ethnic groups who have lived in the United States a long time, such as the Italians, Germans, French, and Japanese, have contributed to the melting pot that is today's American cuisine; these practices have been recently described in an appropriately titled annotated bibliography, *Melting Pot*, by Jacqueline M. Newman.[6]

Within the past two decades, the Indochinese have moved in greater numbers to the United States, and their traditional eating and health practices are just now becoming better understood. In addition, because greater numbers of Indochinese people are now seeking medical care, including palliative care, dietitians need basic information that will help in dealing appropriately with both their health care needs and food needs. The importance of considering dietary traditions when caring for terminally ill patients and their families is illustrated by the following description of Indochinese culture; their health care traditions are discussed in the next section.

Indochinese (Vietnamese, Laotian, and Cambodian)

Foods traditionally eaten by the Indochinese people in their native homelands include, most especially, rice, fish, fresh fruits, fresh vegetables, and tea. Traditionally, breakfast is composed of fewer foods than lunch and dinner. Lunch and dinner are heavier meals and usually comprise several foods that are served communal style. Condiments and seasonings include soy sauce, salt, fish sauce, and "nuoc nam," a Vietnamese soy sauce that has a strong fishy odor but a very mild taste.[7]

The food practices of Vietnamese who have come to the United States are similar to those of immigrants from the Hunan and Sichuan provinces of Southwest China, but spiced with French overtones. They eat traditional long grain rice and many salads and fruits. Vegetables may be served plain or with meat dishes. They prefer chicken to pork and enjoy eggs, fish, and seafood dishes, including heavily salted fish pastes and pates. The Vietnamese cook with little fat; lard is the preferred oil. Sweets, especially small cakes and candies, are often eaten.

A recent governmental report indicates that 30 percent of the Vietnamese immigrants living in the Washington, D.C. area since 1975 have modified their food behaviors since coming to the United States.[8] Rice remains a staple in the diet and is eaten at least once daily; rice noodles are also favorites. Rice, however, is often replaced or supplemented by bread or instant noodles at lunch and by cereals at breakfast. French breads and croissants remain popular breakfast foods; butter is the preferred spread.

Other changes include an increased consumption of pork, beef, and lamb because these foods are less costly in the United States than in Vietnam; a decreased consumption of fish and seafood parallels the increased meat consumption. Not surprisingly, the Vietnamese have expressed distaste for American hot dogs, stating a dislike for their texture and flavor. Stir-fried liver is a healthy food preference of Indochinese people living in the United States.[9] Black pepper, chili pepper, ginger, lemon, and lime remain popular condiments.

With the availability of a wide variety of foods in the United States, the Vietnamese are consuming fewer bananas, more fruit juices, and more soft drinks. Milk and milk products are not commonly consumed. Although the Vietnamese generally do not like milk or the flavor of cheese, they can be readily taught how to cook with cheese. In addition, they like ice cream and can learn to substitute cow milk for coconut milk using the ratio 2/3 coconut milk to 1/3 cow milk.[10]

The Indochinese in their native homelands, unless they were wealthy, had no available refrigeration. Meat was slaughtered and eaten fresh. Fish and chicken were usually alive when bought. Fruits and vegetables were purchased fresh and were usually picked that morning by the vendor. If refrigeration was available, refrigerated foods included water and other fluids, ice, and fruits. Therefore, when the Indochinese come to the United States they need to be educated on food handling procedures that help ensure the safety of their foods. They should be taught which foods should and should not be refrigerated. When visiting in the home of a Vietnamese family, do not be surprised to find eggs in the cupboards and cereal in the refrigerator. Refrigeration is a new concept to most Vietnamese.[11]

The Indochinese usually make rice in the morning and eat it throughout the day. It is generally kept on the stove without heat. Because they prepare many foods over an open flame, the concept of a stove is easily explained. However, the Indochinese are typically afraid of what they cannot see, such as the natural gas and electricity used for heat in many ovens. Explaining gas and electricity can be difficult, as is explaining how to bake cakes or casseroles. Kitchen fires and gas leaks are common occurrences in the homes of newly immigrated Indochinese to the United States. Skin burns are also common because it takes time and practice to learn how to regulate an electric burner; a hot burner does not always look dangerously red.

Indochinese families with school-aged children are usually more acculturated into the American life-style than families without children. Children generally become acculturated faster to the American diet than their parents, due probably in part to their involvement in school lunch programs. At first, Indochinese children may not eat much of their school lunches, but gradually they come to enjoy most American foods. If the Indochinese family has children in American schools, the family likely does its major food shopping in large, cheaper American grocery stores, but may still frequent the small, more expensive Asian markets for specialty foods. The dietitian may need to show them the difference between flour and sugar, or oil and syrup, because the packages and products often look very similar on store shelves.

The dietitian working with Indochinese family members will find them ready learners who are very gracious and accommodating. The Indochinese respect authority figures. They do not want to hurt or disappoint their teachers, so they will try very hard to do what is taught, although often they will be unable to incorporate suggestions into home practice.

Teachers should speak simply and slowly and should demonstrate what they want to teach. It is important to remember that, although many Indochinese may be illiterate in their own language, giving them written materials in their language tells them that they are respected and accepted. An acculturated Indochinese interpreter, who should always be a woman interpreter when working with a female client, is a ready source of help. It is important to remember that men traditionally are not allowed in an Indochinese kitchen, nor do they usually help with the physical care of a female. These are very important societal traits.

When trying to determine whether what you have tried to teach has been understood, do not ask a question, such as, "Do you understand?." Because it is culturally and socially important to Indochinese people to be viewed as agreeable, the answer to this question will invariably be "yes," and it will most likely be accompanied by an affirmative nod of the head. Instead, ask "What do you think about . . .?" or "How do you do . . .?." Answers to these questions are more likely to tell you whether the client has or has not understood the material presented.

MEANING OF HEALTH, HEALTH CARE DELIVERY SYSTEMS, AND PAIN

The meaning of health, health care delivery systems, and pain to persons of various ethnic backgrounds will have a major impact on the services that dietitians and other health care professionals should render and the manner in which these services will be received by patients and families.[12] Some of the characteristic styles of dealing with health care systems and with pain by a few major ethnic groups living in the United States are discussed next.

Indochinese Culture

Most Indochinese are Buddhist. They believe strongly in spiritual ties with the spiritual world, and if our advice to them conflicts with their spiritual beliefs, they will generally not compromise their religion. The Indochinese believe that sickness is caused by outside spirits or the unhappiness of their souls. When they are sick, the Indochinese visit chamins who are viewed as doctors and religious leaders, but who actually function as psychologists. The chamin may recommend that patients change their names in order to lose an evil spirit that is thought to be causing an illness. Strings and jewelry may be tied around the patient's neck, wrists, or ankles on the belief that doing so keeps good spirits within the body. The health care professional should not remove or suggest that the strings or jewelry be removed unless they clearly have a deleterious effect. Generally health care professionals should not interfere with or refute the chamin's advice.

"Koining" is an Indochinese medicinal practice in which herbal medicines that are ground into a balm are rubbed into the skin with the help of coins. The skin may appear bruised, and when koining is seen on a child's skin, it may erroneously be interpreted as child abuse. Koining does not hurt, but incorrect reporting of child abuse can be very painful to those wrongly accused offenders. Some falsely accused adults, even when they have done no wrong, have committed suicide because of loss of face and their cultural abhorrence of child abuse.

"Cupping" is another traditional remedy often recommended by the chamins. In this procedure, a short glass containing alcohol-soaked cotton is heated, placed on a painful part of the body, such as an arm or leg, and allowed to cool. As the cup cools, it creates a vacuum, causing the skin to redden under it. The Indochinese believe this procedure sucks out evil spirits and leaves a mark when the evil spirits depart the body.

Although it is not the dietitian's role to discuss medications with patients, you may at times be asked questions about medications. It is important to understand that the Indochinese often believe that, if one pill is good, five are better. Or these clients may look at a pill, decide it is too big for them, and cut it in half. Therefore, reinforce the concept that the patients' pills are made just for them and that they should not alter the medication given to them in any way.

Asian Culture

In this discussion Asians include the Chinese, Japanese, Koreans, and Filipinos. Because of the early and continuing Chinese migration throughout Asia, the Chinese influence pervades most Asian health traditions. Chinese medicine was vastly different from Western medicine until the reign of Chiang Kai-shek when many Western influences were adopted. Still, major differences persist. The major difference is one of emphasis; whereas Chinese medicine has traditionally emphasized prevention, the Western system has only recently added this emphasis to that of crisis intervention.[13]

Chinese medicine seeks to understand and keep human beings in a proper relationship with the universe and nature. It embodies philosophy, meditation, nutrition, martial arts, herbology, acumassage-acupressure-acupuncture, and spiritual healing. Nutrition is thought to be the most important force in maintaining this harmony. Foods are classified as yin (cold) and yang (hot), and a balance of both is thought to be required for health. An improper balance, such as too much of the wrong kind of food is thought to cause disease. Too much yang food is thought to cause a yang illness, and a yang illness may be counteracted by yin food.

Diseases are also classified as yin or yang. A yin condition is one in which the ill person feels drawn inward and suffers a cold feeling and loss of appetite. For such a condition certain foods are given that are thought to boost energy. A yang condition indicates an overabundance of energy and is characterized by fever, parched throat, crusty nose, and gritty eyes. A sore throat and fever (yang symptoms) may be treated with watercress or watermelon soup (yin foods).

The Chinese cook meat and vegetables together as this combination is believed to be a proper mixture of yang and yin. Moderation is an important principle of

Chinese cuisine. Dishes made with all protein, or all fruits and vegetables, or all extremely cold or extremely hot foods are frowned upon. In addition, certain foods are thought to be good for the eyes, for the muscles, for the blood, and for general health.

When proper nutrition fails to maintain one's health, the Asians use herbs as the next healing step. Herbs are thought to boost health and the body's natural energy level. Specific herbs are thought to be protective and/or healing for certain parts of the body. Herbs are generally brewed in about three cups of water, and then boiled down to one cup of tea, which is drunk.

Jewish Culture

Terminally ill Jewish patients hold well-defined views of health care and pain.[14–17] Jewish patients are commonly perceived as skeptical, pessimistic, and worried. They are sensitive to pain, express discomfort willingly, and feel entitled to complain. They expect sympathy from others, especially family and health care team members. Jews can usually explain their pain and their interpretations of pain in detail. Generally they seek knowledge regarding their illness, prognosis, life-expectancy, pain, medications, and treatments. Typically they are more concerned about getting rid of the underlying disease or cause of pain than about immediate symptom control. Most Jewish patients prefer home care to hospital care.

The Jewish view of terminal care is important for health care professionals to understand. Orthodox Jewish teaching emphasizes the sanctity of life, stating that every effort must be made to prolong life. The Orthodox Jew does not have the right to self-determination in questions pertaining to the body or to life and death; living wills are not considered valid. Because a terminally ill patient is viewed as a living person, no therapeutic procedure that could lengthen life can be omitted. However, despite the expectation that everything possible must be done to extend life, there are also teachings that allow for the withholding of treatment when medical care is of no avail, will not lengthen life, and the patient is within 72 hours of expiration. No act, however, may be performed that could in any way inadvertently hasten death.[18] As death approaches, it is forbidden to close the eyes of the patient until the soul has departed. Anyone who does so is committing an act tantamount to murder.[19] After death has occurred, the body should not be left unattended. Burial should be done as soon as possible in a wooden casket. No autopsy or body parts may be removed according to Orthodox Jewish beliefs.

Recent Jewish commentators have lent support to palliative care, stating that the relief of pain is a "mission of restoration" not an "intervention in the divine process." Julian Ungar-Sargon, physician and member of the advisory board of the National Institute for Jewish Hospice, believes that "hospice . . . is an appropriate and fitting ethical alternative for someone wishing to remain loyal to the theological obligations of reverence for life and preservation of life."[20] Some Jewish commentators even advocate that the patient has the right to decide to withdraw death-delaying procedures when they only prolong dying and not life.[21] And although there have been no test cases on passive euthanasia ("letting nature take its course") in Jewish courts, one can reasonably assume that it does occur; otherwise there would not be enough facilities to house all of the terminally ill Jewish patients who would be on life support systems.

Italian and Hispanic Cultures

The Italians and Hispanics tend to be dramatic in their views and actions and in their response to disease, pain, treatments, and members of the health care team.[22-24] They frequently cause anxiety in other family members, caregivers, and the health care team. Italian families who provide home care are usually highly stressed.

Italian and Hispanic patients and families are usually convinced that the patient "hurts all over." Patients have difficulty localizing the pain in any particular area. Problems appear magnified—which may or may not be the case. Unlike Jews who seek to treat their underlying problems, Italians and Hispanics generally do not try to discover the meaning of the symptom or review the course of the illness; rather, they want immediate physical relief. In general, Italians and Hispanics want sympathy, not worry. Like Jews they prefer home care to hospital care. If a setback occurs or the patient and family becomes depressed, they recover their spirits quickly, unlike the English person who tends to be unflappable in a crisis but who harbors feelings long after an event is over.

Latino/Chicano and Mexican American Cultures

The Latino/Chicano people are Americans whose origins were in Spain, Latin America, and Mexico. These people's health beliefs and values derive from the diverse Indian civilizations of Latin America and traditional fifteenth- and sixteenth-century European medicine and practices.[25]

Characteristically, Latino/Chicano people are strongly influenced by mystical, sacred, and ritualistic practices. How much they use medicinal herbs and plants, folk medicine and practices, and folk healers (curanderos), however, is determined by the person's or family's degree of acculturation and language, age, religion, and accessibility of such health care.

To the Latino/Chicano person, happiness and peace are associated with keeping God's commandments and leading a good life. Illness is often viewed as a punishment from God. When a person is ill, priests may be summoned for special blessings. Intercession through special patron saints is often requested on behalf of the ill person. During an illness, family members commonly gather and pray for the recovery of the ill person.

The Latino/Chicano person generally uses modern medicine along with folk medicine. In addition to pharmaceutical compounds, curanderos suggest treating illnesses through prayers, diet, rituals, chants, herbs, and spices. Many foods are thought to have magical properties, and certain foods are believed to possess curative properties. Herbs and spices are used to prevent complications of chronic illness and decrease susceptibility to disease.

It is important for health professionals dealing with dying people to respect their health beliefs and practices. Without being judgmental, the health professional can ask questions about the meaning of certain rituals and foods and then use this information to develop a meaningful and individualized plan of care that can be operationalized effectively. The Latino/Chicano patients who believe the health professional is honest and respectful of their culture will accept and appreciate help during the dying process.

In the southwestern United States, when a Mexican-American is dying, the entire extended family is usually in attendance, as well as friends. Generally, Spanish-speaking patients and families do not wish to discuss death, dying, and family problems outside the family. They rarely ventilate their feelings of loss, anger, or guilt, but tend to concentrate on the immediate needs of the patient. The macho image is strong, especially in the Mexican-American male.[26]

Irish Culture

The Irish tend to live in fear—fearing the truth about their disease. They are stoic and reluctant to express pain, symptoms, and worry. They tend to minimize symptoms, pain, and problems, and their families tend to reinforce this stoical nature. Because of these characteristics, Irish patients and their families frequently suffer needlessly when pain that could be treated is not expressed.[27–30]

American Indian Culture

The American Indians' traditions at the time of illness, death, and bereavement are uniquely tribal and personal, yet they are also highly social.[31] Stereotypes of Indians would have us believe that they are stoic and rarely show emotional extremes of any kind. In reality, Indians are much less stoic than generally assumed and when surrounded by a caring environment exhibit the most intense reactions, which range from sheer happiness to great remorse. The patient's extended family is usually a source of great support.

Many acculturated Indian patients and families desire traditional American burial and funeral processes with the addition of some tribal customs. Less acculturated Indians have prescribed rituals for burying their dead. Many tribal customs do not permit the body to be taken to a mortuary, but tribal leaders or family members perform the wrapping of the body themselves. The Pueblo prepare the favorite food of the deceased as an act of honor. Many times the belongings of the deceased are buried with the body so that the deceased will not need to return for them.

The singing of tribal songs and the burning of incense are religious ceremonies that aid in grieving. Such ceremonies show the beautiful symbolism of human beings in tune with nature and the "Great Spirit."

Health care providers should maintain a respectful attitude during the family's grief and strive to provide a quiet environment for the family. By showing respect, asking what the family wants done, and then abiding by their wishes, the health care professional can help the Indian family during this initial bereavement period.

White Anglo Saxon Protestants (WASPs) and "Older Americans"

There is great diversity among white, Anglo-Saxon, protestants (WASPs) and older Americans depending on where they live in the United States. The familiar Appalachian practice of "if it isn't broken, don't fix it" can be contrasted with the urban view of "let's prevent problems from occurring by preparing ahead of time." No one way of looking at health care should be judged superior over another.

Typically, most older Americans and WASPs tend to be future-oriented.[32-35] Pain is often less a problem in the present than the patient fears it will be in the future. Pain may be described in purely objective terms without emotion. Response by the health care team is demanded in terms of what can be done practically to rid the patient of pain. Maintaining a "stiff upper lip" and devaluing the expression of physical pain and psychological pain are common reactions. Most older WASPs feel that some pain is inevitable and should be tolerated, but that excess suffering should be unnecessary and treated. In contrast to older Americans, younger WASPs demand complete pain control, sympathy, and honest information regarding their disease, treatment, and prognosis.

WASPs tend to withdraw from family and social contacts when their bodies are not functioning well. Again, there are generational differences. Older WASPs tend not to seek support or sympathy as much as younger WASPs. The higher the educational and socioeconomic status of the patient, the more these trends seem to apply.

The health care professional can be of tremendous help to each member of the family at the time of the patient's death. It is most important at this time for health care professionals to follow the patient and family's religious or cultural preferences that should have already been elicited. Ensuring that each family member's needs are addressed, such as having a time and place for crying or silence, and touching the body or leaving the place of death if desired, is a task that any health care professional, including the dietitian, can perform.

SUMMARY

Ina Ajemian and Balfour Mount, two present-day leaders of the palliative care movement in India and Canada, respectively, have identified several cultural considerations that professionals should apply in palliative care.[36] Keep these in mind when caring for patients from ethnic backgrounds different from your own.

- Try to learn about the background of patients, their traditions, interests, and lives. Educate the palliative care team about caring for people of various ethnic backgrounds by organizing inservice education programs concerning cultural characteristics, customs, and needs during illness and grief.

- When communicating with people whose native language is different from your own, remember that most communication must be nonverbal. A warm smile and a quiet relaxed manner convey a sense of caring and security even when a language barrier is present. Support can be shown with an arm around a shoulder or a hand on an arm. However, watch for nonverbal cues indicating whether such overtures are appreciated or interpreted as an invasion of privacy.

- Keep in mind that music is a communicator that extends beyond a language barrier. It can evoke memories of the past—happy or painful. Music can be an effective catalyst of the expression of moods and emotions.[37]

- Remember that the elderly and the very ill tend to revert to the language and culture of childhood.

- Because ethnic traditions are expressed in dietary customs, encourage families to bring in favorite foods and specially prepared dishes. Facilities can usually be provided to prepare, store, and reheat foods as desired. Traditional seasonings can often be brought to the facility where the dietary department, patient, or family can use them to prepare foods. Special feeding utensils or favorite china and silverware can also be brought from home and used by the patient.

- Use ethnic community service centers that may be able to supply assistance with legal issues and social assistance; such centers may also be able to supply interpreters who can be of great service to health care professionals.

NOTES

1. Harriett Bruce Moore, "The Meaning of Food," *American Journal of Clinical Nutrition* 5, no. 1 (January/February 1957): 77–82.

2. George S. Queen, "Culture, Economics, and Food Habits," *Journal of the American Dietetic Association* 33, no. 10 (October 1957): 1044–1052.

3. E. Pumpian-Mindlin, "The Meaning of Food," *Journal of the American Dietetic Association* 30, no. 6 (June 1954): 576–580.

4. Mary Lou Chappelle, "The Language of Food," *American Journal of Nursing* 72, no. 7 (July 1972): 1294–1295.

5. Miriam E. Lowenberg et. al., *Food and Man* (New York: John Wiley & Sons, Inc., 1968), 125–158.

6. Jaqueline M. Newman, *Melting Pot: An Annotated Bibliography and Guide to Food and Nutrition Information for Ethnic Groups in America* (New York: Garland Publishing, 1986), 1–194.

7. "Vietnamese Americans," *Nutrition & the M.D.* 14, no. 5 (May 1988): 5.

8. Amy Tong, "Food Habits of Vietnamese Immigrants," *Family Economics Review* 2 (1986): 28–30.

9. Amy Tong, "Food Habits of Vietnamese Immigrants," *Journal of Nutrition Education* 19, no. 2 (April 1987): 59.

10. Cathy Cooper, "Indochinese Practices" (Presentation to the Ohio Nutrition Council, Columbus, Ohio, August 1986).

11. Karen A. Welzel, "Meeting the Challenge," *The Columbus Dispatch*, 22 October 1986.

12. Z.J. Lipowski, "Psychosocial Aspects of Disease," *Annals of Internal Medicine* 27 (1969): 1197–1206.

13. Effie Poy Yew Chow, "Cultural Health Traditions: Asian Perspectives," in *Providing Safe Nursing Care for Ethnic People of Color*, ed. Marie Foster Branch and Phyllis Perry Paxton (New York: Appleton & Lange, 1976), 99–114.

14. J. Andrew Billings, *Outpatient Management of Advanced Cancer: Symptom Control, Support, and Hospice-in-the-Home* (Philadelphia: J. B. Lippincott Co., 1985), 20–21.

15. Mark Zborowski, "Cultural Components in Responses to Pain," *Journal of Social Issues* 8 (1952): 16–30.

16. Irving Kenneth Zola, "Culture and Symptoms—An Analysis of Patients' Presenting Complaints," *American Social Reviews* 31 (1966): 615–630.

17. Irving Kenneth Zola, "Problems of Communication, Diagnosis and Patient Care," *Journal of Medical Education* 38 (1963): 829–838.

18. Catherine F. Musgrave, "The Ethical and Legal Implications of Hospice Care: An International Overview," *Cancer Nursing* 10, no. 4 (August 1987): 183–189.

19. J. David Bleich, *Judaism and Healing: Halakhie Perspectives* (New York: Ktav Publishing, 1981), 146–157.

20. Julian Ungar-Sargon, "Is Hospice Care in Conflict with Jewish Values?," *American Journal of Hospice Care* 4, no. 3 (May/June 1987): 43–45.

21. Maurice Lamm, "The Halachah of Caring" (Paper presented at the First National Conference of Jewish Hospice, Boston, Mass. 13 June 1984).

22. Zborowski, "Cultural Components," 16–30.

23. Zola, "Culture and Symptoms," 615–630.

24. Zola, "Problems of Communication, Diagnosis and Patient Care," 829.

25. Pauline Rodriguez Dorsey and Herlinda Quintero Jackson, "Cultural Health Traditions: The Latino/Chicano Perspective," in *Providing Safe Nursing Care for Ethnic People of Color*, ed. Marie Foster Branch and Phyllis Perry Paxton (New York: Appleton & Lange, 1976), 41–80.

26. Helen Budd, "The Art of Being a Hospice Nurse," *American Journal of Hospice Care* 2, no. 3 (May/June 1985): 11–13.

27. Billings, *Outpatient Management of Advanced Cancer*, 20–26.

28. Zborowski, "Cultural Components," 16–30.

29. Zola, "Culture and Symptoms," 615–630.

30. Zola, "Problems of Communication, Diagnosis and Patient Care," 829.

31. Jennie R. Joe, Cecelia Gallerito, and Josephine Pino, "Cultural Health Traditions: American Indian Perspectives," in *Providing Safe Nursing Care for Ethnic People of Color*, ed. Marie Foster Branch and Phyllis Perry Paxton (New York: Appleton & Lange, 1976), 81–98.

32. Billings, *Outpatient Management of Advanced Cancer*, 20–21.

33. Zborowski, "Cultural Components," 16–30.

34. Zola, "Culture and Symptoms," 615–630.

35. Zola, "Problems of Communications, Diagnosis and Patient Care," 829.

36. Ina Ajemian and Balfour M. Mount, "Hospice as a Style for Living. The Adult Patient: Cultural Considerations in Palliative Care," in *Hospice: The Living Idea*, ed. Dame Cicely Saunders, Dorothy H. Summers, and Neville Teller (London: Edward Arnold Ltd., 1981), 30.

37. S. Munro and Balfour Mount, "Music Therapy in Palliative Care," *Canadian Medical Association Journal* 119 (1978): 3.

SUGGESTED READINGS

American Dietetic Association. *Understanding Cultural Food Patterns in the USA*. Chicago: American Dietetic Association, 1975.

Aylard, F. "Food Habits in Western Tropical Africa." *Chemistry and Industry* 39 (1966): 1624–1627.

Babcock, Charlotte G. "Food and its Emotional Significance." *Journal of the American Dietetic Association* 24 (1948): 390–393.

Barker, Theodore Cardwell, McKenzie, J. C., and Yudkin, J. *Our Changing Fare: Two Hundred Years of British Food Habits*. London: MacGibbon & Keen, 1966.

Brewer, T. J. "Food Practices of Some Samoans in Los Angeles County." Los Angeles, Ca.: County of Los Angeles Department of Health Services, 1973.

Bruhn, Christine M., and Pangborn, Rose Marie. "Food Habits of Migrant Farm Workers in California: Comparisons Between Mexican-Americans and 'Anglos'." *Journal of the American Dietetic Association* 59 (1971): 347–355.

Casey, P., and Harrill. I. "Nutrient Intake of Vietnamese Women Relocated in Colorado." *Nutrition Report International* 16 (1977): 687–693.

Cassel, Bella. "Jewish Dietary Laws and Customs." *Public Health Nursing* 32 (1940): 682–687.

Chakravarty, Indira. *Saga of Indian Food: A Historical and Cultural Survey*. New Delhi: Sterling Publishers, 1972.

Corruccini, C.G., and Cruskie, P.E. *Nutrition During Pregnancy and Lactation*. Sacramento, Calif.: California Department of Health, 1975.

Darby, William J., et al. "A Study of the Dietary Background and Nutriture of the Navajo Indians." *Journal of Nutrition* 60, Supplement 2 (1956), 3–85.

Delgado, Graciela, Brumback, C.L., and Deaver, Mary Brice. "Eating Patterns Among Migrant Families." *Public Health Reports* 76 (1961): 349–355.

Duyff, Roberta L., Sanjur, Diva, and Nelson, Helen Y. "Food Behavior and Related Factors of Puerto Rican-American Teenagers." *Journal of Nutrition Education* 7 (1975): 99–103.

Foster, George McClelland, and Anderson, Barbara Gallatin. *Medical Anthropology*. New York: John Wiley & Sons, Inc., 1978.

Gladney, V.M. "Food Practices of Black Americans in Los Angeles County." Los Angeles, Ca.: County of Los Angeles Department of Health Services, 1966.

Gladney, V.M. "Food Practices of the Mexican-American in Los Angeles County." Los Angeles, Ca.: County of Los Angeles Department of Health Services, 1966.

Grivetti, L.E. "The Importance of Flavors in the Middle East." *Food Technology* 29 (1975): 38–40.

Hacker, Dorothy B., and Miller, Eleanor D. "Food Patterns of the Southwest." *American Journal of Clinical Nutrition* 7 (1959): 224–229.

Hickey, Gerald Cannon. *Village in Vietnam*. New Haven, Conn.: Yale University Press, 1964.

Judd, Judith E. "Century-Old Dietary Taboos in 20th Century Japan." *Journal of the American Dietetic Association* 33 (1957): 489–491.

Korff, S.I. "The Jewish Dietary Code." *Food Technology* 20 (1966): 76–78.

Kuhnlein, H.V., and Calloway, Doris H. "Contemporary Hopi Food Intake Patterns." *Ecology of Food and Nutrition* 6 (1977): 159–173.

Lewis, Jane S., and Glaspy, Maria Fe. "Food Habits and Nutrient Intakes of Filipino Women in Los Angeles." *Journal of the American Dietetic Association* 67 (1975): 122–125.

Munsell, Hazel E. "Food and Nutrition Problems in Puerto Rico." *Journal of The American Dietetic Association* 20 (1944): 305–307.

Roberts, Lydia J. "Nutrition in Puerto Rico." *Journal of the American Dietetic Association* 20 (1944): 298–304.

Sakr, Ahmad H. "Dietary Regulations and Food Habits of Muslims." *Journal of the American Dietetic Association* 58 (1971): 123–126.

Sakr, Ahmad H. "Fasting is Islam." *Journal of the American Dietetic Association* 67 (1975): 17–21.

"Scandinavian Food Habits." *Journal of the American Dietetic Association* 20 (1944): 234–236.

Scott, E.M. "Nutrition of Alaskan Eskimos." *Nutrition Reviews* 14 (1956): 1–3.

Stefansson, Vilhjalmur. "Food and Food Habits in Alaska and Northern Canada." In *Human Nutrition, Historic and Scientific*, edited by Iago Galdston. New York: New York Academy of Medicine, 1960, 23–60.

Valassi, Kyriake V. "Food Habits of Greek-Americans." *American Journal of Clinical Nutrition* 11 (1962): 240–248.

Whiting, Beatrice Blyth, ed. *Six Cultures*. New York: John Wiley & Sons, Inc., 1963.

Wittfogel, Karl A. "Food and Society in China and India." In *Human Nutrition, Historic and Scientific*, edited by Iago Galdston. New York: New York Academy of Medicine, 1960, 61–77.

Yohai, Fanny. "Dietary Patterns of Spanish-Speaking People Living in the Boston Area." *Journal of the American Dietetic Association* 71 (1977): 273–275.

Chapter 9

Nutritional Intervention and Symptom Control

GOALS IN SYMPTOM CONTROL

In few areas of life are our experiences so uniquely personal as in our experience of dying. The goals of dietitians and other health care professionals in working with terminally ill patients and their families are to maximize the pleasurable experiences of dying and minimize those experiences, such as pain and other symptoms, that separate patients and their families from the enjoyment of everyday living. Although dying often brings many less-than-desirable side effects, it would be wrong to view dying as a "disease" hungry for medical "remedies." Indeed, the patient may decide that saying farewell to family and friends is more important than having a wound dressed or an appetite improved.[1] By providing the patient and family with helpful suggestions for pain and symptom control, the dietitian gives them information that they can use in their best interests.

Symptom control demands a large part of the palliative care team's time and energy, and often requires relatively aggressive treatments. The most common symptoms occurring in dying patients were clarified in 1981 through a study in Ramsey County, Minnesota. The symptoms most frequently reported by patients were weakness (97 percent), loss of appetite (84 percent), pain (67 percent), difficulty in sleeping (59 percent), nausea and vomiting (58 percent), depression (56 percent), constipation (53 percent), dry mouth (48 percent), and difficulty in swallowing (48 percent).[2] Other studies provide similar findings.[3,4]

During the last few weeks of a terminally ill patient's life, changes affecting nutrition occur. The patient typically experiences anorexia with a subsequent decrease in food intake. Changes in the gastrointestinal tract, including reduced competence of the upper and lower esophageal sphincters, slowed gastric emptying, and reduced oral and hypopharyngeal sensation are common as body functions slow. With decreased food intake, the patient experiences weight loss, decreased energy levels, and fluid and electrolyte imbalances that are often exacerbated by anemia.[5]

The majority of dying patients that we currently care for are diagnosed with cancer. This may change as our population ages and chronic degenerative diseases, including renal disease, cardiovascular failure, pulmonary failure, and organic brain syndrome have more time to exert their ravishing effects. Because in palliative care we treat symptoms not diseases, it is appropriate to discuss symptoms, rather than diseases. Later in this chapter, several of the most common and significant nutrition-related problems are discussed. Chapter 11 describes treatment for anorexia and cachexia in detail. Reference is made to specific diseases but the diarrhea associated with postsurgical dumping and acquired immune deficiency syndrome (AIDS), and the nausea and vomiting associated with gastrointestinal obstruction and narcotic use, are included under the symptoms of diarrhea and nausea and vomiting, respectively. Not all of the identified treatments may be appropriate for all diseases or conditions. The reader is therefore encouraged to consult standard medical textbooks to obtain indepth information on specific diseases and conditions as necessary.

LABORATORY TESTS IN PALLIATIVE CARE: "TO DO, OR NOT TO DO"

Often dietitians caring for dying patients will wish for the results of several diagnostic studies to identify the cause of a symptom and to indicate whether a particular therapy would be appropriate. Diagnostic studies are not routinely done on terminally ill patients.[6] Peter A. Cassileth suggests the following four reasons to do diagnostic studies in the terminally ill patient:[7]

1. if the results will potentially alter the patient's management
2. if the test will help determine the etiology of symptoms before treatment is initiated and its invasiveness does not cause more discomfort than is warranted by the information to be gained
3. if the benefits of the results outweigh the physical, emotional, and financial costs of obtaining them
4. if the patient's life expectancy is longer than just a few days

COMMON NUTRITION-RELATED SYMPTOMS DURING TERMINAL ILLNESS

Anemia

Terminally ill patients often exhibit anemia frequently caused by diseases of chronic illness and bleeding. Bleeding sites in the terminally ill patient are generally the gastrointestinal tract (especially if intravenous solutions or tube feedings have been used in the past or are currently in place), brain, kidney, large vessel, and lung.

Symptomatic anemia in patients with the possibility of high quality of life can be treated with blood transfusions. If transfusions seem more like aggressive, curative treatment than palliative therapy, it should be remembered that transfusions can improve the quality of life when death is not imminent and improve the patient's physical and psychological well-being. Terminally ill patients living quality lives are also frequently transfused when bleeding cannot be controlled and when red blood cell production cannot be increased. Transfusion is also appropriate when a patient would benefit in order to attend a special event such as a grandchild's graduation or wedding. One to two units of packed red blood cells will often ensure adequate blood levels for up to a month. If response is not achieved with this amount, additional units are generally not appropriate.

Transfusions have several benefits. Added red blood cells will increase the oxygen-carrying capacity of blood and decrease fatigue. Use of packed red blood cells; correction of congestive heart failure; and supplemental oxygen delivery; especially when combined with small doses of morphine to relieve anxiety, are helpful in decreasing pulmonary problems associated with anemia.

Asymptomatic or mildly symptomatic anemia can be left untreated. In fact, hemoglobin levels as low as 6–7 g/dL in debilitated and bedridden patients are usually well tolerated. If these patients are transfused, physical discomfort, fluid retention, and congestion can occur with little or no overall improvement in well-being. Transfusions are rarely needed for hemoglobin levels of 8 g/dL or more unless the patient has severe lung dysfunction in addition to anemia.

The palliative care team will be faced with many difficult decisions in the care of terminally ill patients. One of the hardest decisions is whether to transfuse a patient who exhibits an acute bleeding episode. On one hand, death from exsanguination can be viewed as simple and painless as an unconscious patient drifts into shock. Transfusions in these patients are senseless if they momentarily delay a timely death. On the other hand, blood transfusions are certainly appropriate when exsanguination would mean the untimely death of a patient with an excellent quality of life or if spontaneous cessation of bleeding can be anticipated soon. The occurrence of a large amount of blood loss due to hemoptysis, hematemesis, hematochezia, or large vessel bleeding, is a gruesome sight for the conscious patient and family; use of red towels will reduce the sight of blood. Vigorous sedation is an additional palliative care consideration in the conscious patient.

Constipation

A major goal in symptom control for terminally ill patients is the prevention of constipation. Constipation is common in patients receiving narcotics for pain, in patients with poor fluid and food intake, and in patients who are depressed. An appropriate medical objective is to achieve a bowel movement at least every three days regardless of whether the patient is eating well or not. Often, patients have different goals. For example, patients may have had at least one regular bowel movement daily and are not satisfied unless this routine occurs.

Terminally ill patients receiving narcotics for pain control should be prophylactically treated for constipation. Treatment and preventive measures for constipation center on laxative administration. Laxatives should be taken daily unless loose stools develop. In addition, maintenance of adequate fluid intake is important, as is physical activity to the extent tolerated by the patient.

Constipation often deceives the terminally ill patient because it frequently presents itself as diarrhea or incontinence. Fecal impactions result when stools become progressively more and more dehydrated, hard, and large. The more liquid portions of the stool above the solid mass can ooze around the mass and cause fecal incontinence that is interpreted as diarrhea. Treatment includes breaking up and dislodging the mass, usually by digital manipulation, and following with enemas and appropriate laxatives.

Once constipation has been controlled, stimulant laxatives are usually able to keep the patient symptom-free. Stool softeners alone rarely are adequate to support regular defecation in the terminally ill patient, especially in those patients receiving narcotics and those whose gastrointestinal function is sluggish.

Medications for constipation have dietary implications. For example, whenever mineral oil is used as a laxative, the patient is at increased risk for aspiration. Whenever bulk-former medications, such as Metamucil, are administered, the patient is required to drink a significantly large amount of fluid for the treatment to be effective. Bulk-formers would therefore be an inappropriate treatment for the patient who is comatose, or otherwise unable to drink adequate fluids. Hydrophilic bulk-forming agents are also quite unpalatable, but can be masked in foods and fluids such as applesauce, mashed potatoes, gravy, orange juice, nectars, and other juices. Treatment with solutions such as Golytely (a balanced electrolyte solution with polyethylene glycol) also requires the patient to be able to ingest a large amount of liquid.

Diarrhea

Diarrhea is a major symptom in terminally ill patients occurring in as high as 90 percent of patients. Its control is necessary in order to achieve comfort for the patient and to lessen the tasks performed by caregivers. When not controlled, diarrhea can result in fluid and electrolyte losses and subsequent imbalances, severe perianal irritation due to fecal incontinence, and soiling that can cause pressure sores if not quickly and completely cleaned.

The most common causes of diarrhea in terminally ill patients without cancer or acquired immune deficiency syndrome (AIDS) are fecal impaction, sphincter failure, malnutrition, and drug toxicity, especially laxative, antacid, and antibiotic abuse.

Treatment of diarrhea involves alleviating impaction and modifying drug therapy. Diarrhea secondary to malnutrition is best treated by small frequent feedings of foods the patient likes, and concomitant treatment with anti-diarrheal medications. Aggressive treatment of malnutrition in an attempt to control diarrhea is not a realistic goal for terminally ill patients. Diarrhea and malabsorption in AIDS patients are primarily due to intestinal infection, malnutrition and hypoalbuminemia, bacterial overgrowth with long-term antibiotic use, and nonspecific enteropathy. Treatment involves appropriate antibiotics and a diet usually high in calories and protein, and low in fiber, lactose, and fat. Commercial medical nutritional products are often well tolerated and liked by the AIDS patient.

The most common reasons for diarrhea in cancer patients are obstruction secondary to tumor, and side-effects of radiation therapy, chemotherapy, and surgery. Diarrhea can occur in terminally ill cancer patients long after curative therapies have ceased.

Radiation therapy to the small intestine precipitates enteritis and decreases the absorptive surface area of the small intestine. If pancreatic secretions are decreased (common in pancreatic cancer, or with radiation therapy and surgery) a decreased bicarbonate production will prevent the optimal pH for small intestinal enzyme activity. In the absence of pancreatic lipase, the formation of micelles necessary for absorption of fats and fat-soluble vitamins will be decreased, and diarrhea and steatorrhea will result. Administration of oral pancreatic enzyme supplements can help correct this problem. Fat malabsorption due to obstruction of biliary flow, either extra-or intra-hepatic, is less easily managed. A diet high in medium-chain triglycerides and low in long-chain triglycerides helps, but does not cure, the problem.

Hypercalcemia

Hypercalcemia in terminally ill patients can be a true metabolic disorder or it can be a symptom of another disorder. A common manifestation of malignancy, it is often overlooked in patients receiving infrequent laboratory tests. Hypercalcemia has many causes in addition to the most common ones of multiple bony metastases, dehydration, and demineralization of bone secondary to limited weight bearing on bones and limited muscle action due to a bed-ridden state. Symptoms include anorexia, nausea, vomiting, constipation, lethargy and weakness, polyuria, pruritus, and coma.

When hypercalcemia occurs late in patients with terminal illness and is the result of overwhelming tumor, it is best to treat it by accepting that it is part of the result of many problems. On the other hand, when it occurs early and there is reason to believe that its treatment will be effective and will provide the patient with relief, it should be dealt with appropriately and aggressively.

Appropriate treatment for hypercalcemia is first and foremost hydration.[8,9] Home care should include pushing fluids as tolerated. Inpatient treatment might include an intravenous saline load with a loop diuretic such as furosemide. In debilitated patients or patients with renal or urinary dysfunction, intravenous diuretics may not be a wise choice of treatment. Intravenous volume loading is contraindicated in elderly terminally ill patients with anemia or borderline cardiopulmonary function because of the possibility of precipitating congestive heart failure.

Steroid administration (intravenous hydrocortisone or oral prednisone) may be added to inpatient or outpatient therapy. Corticosteroids are especially effective in decreasing blood calcium in patients with breast cancer and myeloma.

If hydration and steroids fail to control the hypercalcemia, intravenous mithramycin (Mithracin) might be considered for treatment. Mithramycin is a chemotherapy drug that inhibits osteoclast activation. Osteoclast activation can result from lymphoid neoplasms that release prostaglandins or an osteoclast activating factor that causes bone resorption and hypercalcemia. Mithramycin has limited side effects. Serum calcium levels fall within 1–2 days after its usage, and doses can be repeated 2–3 times per week if needed.[10]

Calcitonin (administered intramuscularly or subcutaneously) with or without steroids is another treatment for hypercalcemia. Lastly, oral phosphates (Fleet Phospho-Soda) may be given if the patient is not hyperphosphatemic. If resulting diarrhea is problematic, oral phosphates should be discontinued.

The dietitian can be of assistance to the patient with hypercalcemia by suggesting ways to keep hydrated. Encouraging carbonated beverages containing phosphoric acid is appropriate because they add needed fluid and phosphates. It is rarely helpful to restrict dairy products and other foods containing calcium in an attempt to reduce serum calcium.[11,12] If the dietitian ascertains that the patient is taking vitamin and mineral supplements that contain large amounts of vitamin D and calcium, it might be wise to suggest that these be eliminated. The patient should be encouraged to participate in some daily physical activity if possible, such as walking.

Jaundice and Hepatic Encephalopathy

Liver dysfunction in acutely ill patients is of urgent concern to the dietitian, but in terminally ill patients the resulting anorexia is usually best accepted as a common symptom that is rarely treatable. If laboratory tests were performed in terminally ill patients with liver dysfunction, impaired hepatic intermediary metabolism would reveal malutilization of protein, carbohydrate, fat, vitamins, and minerals. Liver failure results in decreased glycogenolysis and gluconeogenesis (therefore hypoglycemia) and decreased glycogen stores (therefore increased protein and fat catabolism for energy). Decreased aerobic glycolysis results in anaerobic metabolism of glucose with lactate accumulation and systemic acidosis causing nausea and anorexia.

Biliary obstruction and hepatic failure can be expected to occur in terminally ill patients with cancer of the liver, biliary tract, and pancreas, or with other malignancies that have metastasized to the liver. Drug toxicity also is a cause of hepatic failure in many terminally ill patients. Such patients often exhibit jaundice and hepatic encephalopathy.

Jaundice is alarming to the patient and family, and it often signals serious complications of advanced disease. It may or may not, however, signal rapid deterioration. Some patients live for weeks with severe jaundice, anorexia, pruritus, drowsiness, and weakness. If jaundice is caused by biliary obstruction, hepatic encephalophathy may also occur as a result of various abdominal cancers. Treatment is important only in those patients whose quality of life can be enhanced and is desired. Neomycin and Cephulac are appropriate treatment medications. Theoretically a protein restricted diet may be appropriate, but dietary restrictions are usually not desired by terminally ill patients and generally are not effective even when tried.

Death from liver failure is slow, gentle, and usually painless. The patient often slips first into a drowsy state, followed by stupor, and then coma. Symptoms include noncognitive and reflex movements such as groans and random motions. The family should be told that these movements are common and without meaning, but they should be encouraged to talk to the patient and assume that the patient hears and comprehends.

Nausea and Vomiting

Incidence and Pathophysiology

Nausea and vomiting are among the most frequently troubling symptoms experienced by terminally ill patients. Cancer patients especially experience nausea and vomiting due in large part to radiation therapy and some forms of chemotherapy. Most terminally ill patients on narcotics experience nausea and vomiting as side effects of narcotic administration.

The pathophysiology of vomiting is complex but is fairly well defined. Vomiting is controlled by an emesis center in the medulla of the brain (Figure 9-1). The emesis center receives stimulation from four major sources:

1. The chemoreceptor trigger zone (CTZ), also located in the medulla, is activated by chemical stimuli from the blood or cerebrospinal fluid. Chemical stimuli include several chemotherapy agents, narcotics, cardiac glycosides, anesthetic agents, tumor products, and metabolic problems, such as hypercalcemia, hyponatremia, uremia, hepatic failure, and adrenal insufficiency. The chemoreceptor trigger zone can be blocked by antiemetic drugs, such as Compazine, Thorazine, Phenergan, Haldol, and Reglan.
2. Peripheral input, primarily from the gastrointestinal tract and pharynx, can also cause vomiting by stimulating the emesis center. Distension or irritation of the gastrointestinal tract by radiation therapy; some chemotherapy drugs; dumping; constipation, ileus; gastric paresis; and abdominal, pharyngeal, biliary, and intestinal tumor obstruction are common causes of vomiting due to peripheral stimulation. Inhibiting peripheral input as a cause of nausea and vomiting is primarily achieved by treating the causes of peripheral stimulation. Antiemetics also help.
3. Cortical input, primarily due to cerebral edema; brain lesions; specific tastes, smells, and thoughts; and other psychogenic factors, can cause vomiting. Cortical input is decreased primarily through treating its causes. Antiemetic drugs which can inhibit cortical input include corticosteroids.
4. Vestibular inputs include motion sickness and ear disorders. Antiemetic drugs which act to inhibit vestibular causes of vomiting are Dramamine, Benadryl, Atarax, and Phenergan.

Assessment

Identifying the causes of the patient's nausea and vomiting, and managing them appropriately, are important goals in helping terminally ill patients achieve enjoyment in living. Questions you should elicit from the patient and family include:

- Is nausea and vomiting associated with meals?
- Does the taste, smell, or sight of any food or beverage cause nausea or vomiting? If so, what foods or beverages?
- Are there any foods or beverages that appear to lessen the incidence or severity of nausea and vomiting?
- Is nausea and vomiting caused by abdominal pain?
- Is nausea and vomiting associated with any medications?
- Is nausea and vomiting associated with emotional state?
- Is nausea and vomiting associated with positional change?

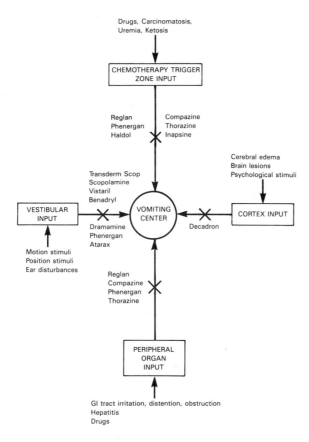

Figure 9-1 The Vomiting Center: Stimuli and Inhibitors. *Source*: Adapted from *Hospice: The Living Idea* by C. Saunders, D.H. Summers, and N. Teller, p. 97, with permission of Edward Arnold Publishers, Ltd., © 1981.

The dietitian should seek out the possibility that nausea and vomiting is a conditioned behavior to foods, beverages, drugs, odors, sights, experiences, or even thoughts that have caused nausea and vomiting in the past. If results from your history-taking imply that the patient has nausea and vomiting secondary to conditioned behavior, suggest that prophylactic antiemetics be given before the possible triggering episode occurs. Treatment should be swift and effective. Relaxation techniques may also be helpful. The patient who vomits frequently and in large amounts is a primary candidate for dehydration, electrolyte imbalance, malnutrition, pain, erratic absorption of oral medications, and risk of aspiration and death due to choking, pneumonia, or esophageal tear.

Drug Management

When the cause of the patient's nausea and vomiting can be diagnosed, treatment should be aimed at correcting the cause. Antiemetic drugs are generally chosen for their action on the CTZ or emesis center. When the cause for nausea and vomiting is not established, treatment is generally begun with the phenothiazine (Compazine, Phenergan, or Thorazine) class of antiemetics. If high doses of phenothiazines do not control the vomiting, or if Compazine causes sedation, a second phenothiazine may be added or a butyrophenone (Haldol or Inapsine) may be tried. If sedation is desired in an agitated, nauseated patient, Thorazine is a good choice. If these regimens do not result in symptom control, metoclopramide (Reglan) may be tried or added to the existing regimen, especially in patients with a gastric outlet obstruction.[13] Table 9-1 shows the most commonly used antiemetic drugs in palliative care programs, their site of action, and side effects.

Obstruction (Intestinal)

Intestinal obstruction in terminally ill patients is frequently caused by abdominal cancer, especially of the ovary or colon, or a less-than-adequate bowel regimen to prevent constipation when narcotics are given for pain management. Intestinal obstruction in terminally ill patients is not the acute emergency it was when "cure" was the goal. Instead, its onset can be insidious, intermittent, and not terribly debilitating. The patient may note abdominal discomfort, anorexia, and loud bowel sounds followed by abdominal distension and transient loose stools. The anorexia that accompanies such attacks frequently results in the avoidance of food. Such treatment is appropriate during an abdominal attack, although the drinking of fluids is usually welcomed and well tolerated. The bout usually subsides spontaneously over a day or two.

When treating intestinal obstruction, no one recipe can be followed for all patients. Criteria to assess include

1. cause of the obstruction
2. location of the obstruction
3. extent of the tumor
4. general condition of the patient
5. desires and goals of the patient and family

In patients who have incurable but limited tumors, and therefore several months life expectancy, the appearance of a total distal colonic obstruction may necessitate the performance of a colostomy to control the ensuing nausea, vomiting, hard stools, and lack of bowel movement. Vomiting frequently occurs if the obstruction is high in the intestinal tract. Sometimes, patients prefer to forego the placement of

Table 9-1 Most Commonly Used Antiemetic Drugs in Palliative Care Programs

Class of Drugs	Examples	Side Effects
Phenothiazines (inhibit CTZ and some peripheral action)	Compazine Thorazine Trilafon Torecan Phenergan	Sedation Hypotension Parkinson-like twitches Restlessness Some cardiac toxicity
Butyrophenones (inhibit CTZ)	Haldol Inapsine	Twitches Restlessness Sedation
Metoclopramide (inhibit CTZ and some peripheral action)	Reglan	Accelerates gastric emptying. Increases LES pressure. Worsens symptoms of intestinal obstruction.
Antihistamines (inhibit emesis center and vestibular disorders)	Marezine Dramamine Benadryl Vistaril Atarax Phenergan	Sedation Dry mouth
Anticholinergics (inhibit peripheral action)	Transderm Scop Scopolamine bromide	Decreases motion sickness Dry mouth
Tetrahydrocannabinol (THC) is not frequently used but is undergoing testing with varying results		

a colostomy, a restrictive diet, or a nasogastric tube, in favor of gentle, frequent vomiting that can be made tolerable by antiemetics, smooth muscle relaxants, and stool softeners. The choice should be the patient's.

For patients whose small bowel obstructions are only partial, but whose tumors are incurable and widely disseminated intra-peritoneally, the goal is usually palliation. Many patients live a prolonged time with intermittent partial obstruction. In this case, the choice may be to do nothing, or the choice may be the simple passage of a nasogastric tube that would be palliative and comfortable. If the choice is to do nothing, the crampy abdominal pain can be well controlled with smooth muscle relaxants. Nausea and vomiting may occur; therefore, the patient should also be given large doses of antiemetics and stool softeners. If pain occurs, adequate analgesics can alleviate it. Patients should be encouraged to eat and drink as desired, and they should be largely free of nausea and pain, although they may vomit periodically.[14] Even with regular vomiting, enough fluid and nutrients can often be absorbed to maintain adequate hydration and nutritional status. Foods high in potassium should be encouraged if the patient vomits frequently and likes such foods. Vomiting under these conditions has been described as a sensation similar to that of voiding or defecating—it relieves an uncomfortable fullness.[15,16]

APPROPRIATE THERAPY FOR SYMPTOMS IN TERMINAL ILLNESS

At the end of this chapter is an indispensible table for the dietitian working with terminally ill patients (Appendix 9-A). As a ready reference, it identifies appropriate palliative therapies for terminally ill patients and suggestions for family members. In addition to identifying the dietary therapies for symptoms and disorders, the appendix lists the causes of the symptoms, the usual drug treatment, and the medical and nursing techniques frequently used in palliative care. The appendix is organized for use as a reference table. Therefore, symptoms and disorders are listed alphabetically, using common descriptive terminology.

An understanding of the symptoms that commonly occur with the dying process is important because symptoms form the basis for development of the patient's plan of care. An understanding of the usual medical and nursing palliative care therapies will help you put nutritional problems and therapies into perspective and integrate the nutritional plan of care with the medical and nursing plans of care.

NOTES

1. Joanne Lynn, "Appendix B," in *Deciding to Forego Life-Sustaining Treatment: A Report on the Ethical, Medical, and Legal Issues in Treatment Decisions*, ed. President's Commission for the Study of Ethical Problems in Medicine and Biomedical and Behavioral Research (Washington, D.C.: United States Government Printing Office, March, 1983), 276.

2. Amherst H. Wilder Foundation, Planning and Development Office, *Care for the Dying—Study of the Need for Hospice in Ramsey County, Minnesota*, December 1981, 1–14.

3. Tom Wachtel, Susan Allen-Masterson, David Reuben, Richard Goldberg, and Vincent Mor, "The End Stage Cancer Patient: Terminal Common Pathway," *The Hospice Journal* 4, no. 4 (1988): 43–80.

4. Mary S. Baines, "Control of Other Symptoms," in *The Management of Terminal Disease*, ed. Cicely M. Saunders (Chicago: Year Book Medical Publishers, 1978), 99–118.

5. Carol E. Dixon, A. Wyatt Emery, Jr., and Roberta Smith Hurley, "Nutrition and Patients with a Limited Life Expectancy," *American Journal of Hospice Care* 2, no. 3 (May/June 1985): 29.

6. Shirley Ann Newell Smith and Jeanne M. Veglia, "Hospital Utilization of Laboratory Tests, Procedures, and Special Therapies," *American Journal of Hospice Care* 3, no. 3 (May/June 1986): 33–36.

7. Peter A. Cassileth, "Common Medical Problems," in *Clinical Care of the Terminal Cancer Patient*, ed. Barrie R. Cassileth and Peter A. Cassileth (Philadelphia: Lea & Febiger, 1982), 16–17.

8. Ernest L. Mazzaferri, Thomas M. O'Dorisio, and Al F. LoBuglio, "Treatment of Hypercalcemia Associated with Malignancy," *Seminars in Oncology* 5 (1978): 141–153.

9. Andrew F. Stewart, "Therapy of Malignancy-Associated Hypercalcemia: 1983," *American Journal of Medicine* 74 (1983): 475–480.

10. J. Andrew Billings, *Outpatient Management of Advanced Cancer: Symptom Control, Support, and Hospice-in-the-Home* (Philadelphia: J.B. Lippincott Co., 1985), 134.

11. Arthur B. Schneider and Louis M. Sherwood, "Calcium Homeostasis and the Pathogenesis and Management of Hypercalcemic Disorders," *Metabolism* 23 (1974): 975–1007.

12. Gregory R. Mundy and T. John Martin, "The Hypercalcemia of Malignancy: Pathogenesis and Management," *Metabolism* 31 (1982): 1247–1277.

13. Billings, *Outpatient Management of Advanced Cancer*, 52.

14. Mary Baines, D.J. Oliver, and R.L. Carter, "Medical Management of Intestinal Obstruction in Patients with Advanced Malignant Disease. A Clinical and Pathological Study," *Lancet* 2 (1985): 990–993.

15. Robert E. Enck, "Management of Malignant Intestinal Obstruction," *American Journal of Hospice Care* 4, no. 2 (March/April 1987): 8–9.

16. Robert T. Osteen, Sigrid Guyton, Gleen Steele, Jr., and Richard E. Wilson, "Malignant Intestinal Obstruction," *Surgery* 87, no. 6 (June 1980): 611–615.

Appendix 9-A

Appropriate Therapy for Symptoms in Terminal Illness

Symptoms and Causes of Symptoms	*Drug Management*
ANEMIA	
Hemorrhage from many and varied bleeding sites, secondary to	Packed red blood cells and/or platelets if hemoglobin is less than 8 g/dL
intravenous lines and gastrostomy tubes	
lung disease with severe coughing	Anabolic steroids, such as DecaDurabolin, if no gastrointestinal bleeding
brain tumor or metastases with severe cerebral edema	
head and neck cancer	Antacids if gastrointestinal bleeding
Thrombosis	Anti-anxiety drugs as needed
Decreased red blood cell and platelet synthesis	
Gastrointestinal bleeding often due to medications, such as steroids and nonsteroidal anti-inflammatory agents	
alcohol abuse	
anxiety	
stress	
ANOREXIA	

Tumor effects: pelvic/abdominal mass, liver metastases, abdominal compression, constipation	Appetite stimulants:
	   prednisone
	   amitriptyline
	   beer or wine or sherry
	   Thorazine
	   antidepressants
	   Periactin
	   Megace

Treatment effects: postsurgical stasis or small stomach, drug treatment, chemotherapy, radiation therapy, mouth and esophageal pain, dental problems, loss of teeth	
Taste changes: early satiety, unappetizing food, too much food offered, food aversions	Nutritional supplements or complete nutritional replacements, including tube feedings or parenteral nutritional support
Systemic illnesses: infection, hepatitis, pancreatitis, malodorous ulcer, endocrinopathies	Zinc, niacin and vitamin B complex supplements may improve appetite if malnourished

Dietary Management	*Other Management*
If gastrointestinal bleeding, avoid methyl xanthines (coffee, tea, and chocolate).	Avoid tobacco.
Avoid foods causing abdominal pain, such as alcohol, carbonated beverages, acidic foods or spices; if patient refuses to avoid alcohol consumption, discourage consumption of alcohol on an empty stomach.	Have red towels available if major vessel bleed is expected and transfusions or hospitalization are not planned.
Avoid foods that may decrease lower esophageal sphincter pressure, especially high-fat foods, chocolate, peppermint, spearmint, and alcohol.	Reduce stress and anxiety by meeting patient's physical, emotional, social, and environmental needs as appropriate. Stress reduction techniques may be helpful.
Try small frequent meals, avoiding food 2 hours before bedtime.	
For general bleeding, allow multivitamin-mineral supplement if patient desires; avoid megadose vitamins, especially vitamin C.	
Do not nag patients to eat. A gentle positive attitude is helpful in encouraging patients to eat. Allow patients to be in charge of their situation; do not criticize them if they eat poorly. If the patient does not eat, remove the food without undue comment.	Avoid routine weighing of the patient. Place little emphasis on weight loss. Encourage the patient to wear clothes that fit.
Serve small servings. A small plate will make the foods more attractive and the serving sizes look smaller and may increase amount of food eaten.	Be sure the patient takes medications appropriately to relieve pain, depression, anxiety, constipation, nausea and vomiting, diarrhea, systemic infections, and biochemical imbalances that may contribute to anorexia.
Feed the patient when hungry. Note patient's best meals (usually breakfast is better than supper) and make these the	Encourage mild exercise and relaxation techniques; they may overcome fatigue and sleep problems and improve appetite.

continues

Symptoms and Causes of Symptoms	*Drug Management*

ANOREXIA (Cont'd)

Biochemical effects: hyponatremia, dehydration, hypercalcemia, uremia

Psychogenic effects: anxiety, depression, fear of vomiting

Physical complications: fatigue, pain, shortness of breath, chronic obstructive pulmonary disease

Acquired immune deficiency syndrome (AIDS)

Food and fluid viewed by the patient as a burden instead of a benefit

Natural consequences of dying

BELCHING

Swallowed air usually due to anxiety or regular, constant pain	Anxiety-relieving drugs, such as Vistaril Atarax Benadryl
	Antacids, such as Rolaids Gelusil Maalox Maalox Plus Mylanta
	Pain medications, such as narcotics if needed

Dietary Management	*Other Management*

largest meals. Change traditional mealtimes if needed.

Provide the patient's favorite foods.

Contain smells in the kitchen if they cause nausea, vomiting, or anorexia.

Encourage high-calorie foods, including eggnog, milkshake, custard, pudding, peanut butter, cream soups, cheese, fizzy drinks, pie, sherbet, cheesecake. Patients particularly like fresh oranges and freshly prepared lemonade if their mouth is not sore.

Make mealtimes enjoyable; dress to eat, eat at the table, and vary the place of eating.

Consider transfusions for anemia, which may reduce fatigue and improve appetite.

Consider dental relining if needed and prognosis warrants.

Ameliorate social consequences and physical complications of cachexia. An old photo of the patient without cachexia will help caregivers see the patient as human. A new photo of the cachectic patient with family and friends will help caregivers see the patient as still having a place in the family. A new set of clothes that fit the patient will improve self-esteem.

Eat solids at mealtimes.

Drink liquids between meals and not with solid foods.

Keep mouth closed when chewing and swallowing.

To determine if specific foods cause belching, suggest avoiding gas-producing foods, especially alcohol, beer, carbonated beverages, dairy products if lactose intolerant, yeast, nuts, high-fat foods, beans, onions, peas, corn, mushrooms, cucumbers, cabbage, broccoli, Brussels sprouts, spinach, radishes, and cauliflower. Allow the patient to make the final choice of foods to eat and avoid.

Avoid chewing gum.

Avoid sucking through straws.

Avoid eating quickly and reclining immediately after eating. Relax before, during, and after meals.

Avoid chewing tobacco.

Avoid snoring with open mouth.

Avoid regular and constant pain.

Symptoms and Causes of Symptoms   *Drug Management*

CACHEXIA

Failure to eat

Maldigestion and malabsorption:
pancreatic insufficiency, bile
insufficiency, bowel infiltration,
ulceration, fistulas, postsurgical gastric
stasis, diarrhea, steatorrhea, enteritis,
obstruction, protein-losing enteropathy,
vomiting, hemorrhage, AIDS

Malutilization: increased host energy
expenditure, tumor metabolism, steroid
effects on nitrogen wasting,
hyperglycemia, hormonal changes

CONSTIPATION

Personal habits, including	Use laxatives, including
inattention to urge to defecate	bulk formers:
physical inactivity	Metamucil
	stool softeners:
Weakness in straining and difficulty	Colace
getting to toilet	Pericolace
	Senokot-S
Dietary habits, including poor intake of	Surfak
fluids, food, and fiber	Doxidan
	Doxinate
Drugs, including	lubricants:
narcotics and opiates	mineral oil
aluminum and calcium antacids	stimulants:
iron supplements	Pericolace
tricyclic antidepressants	Colace
phenothiazines	Doxidan
anticholinergics	Senokot
	Ex-Lax
Gastrointestinal tumor or stricture	castor oil

Dietary Management	*Other Management*
Socialize and relax before and during meals. Try relaxation techniques before mealtimes.	
Set an attractive table and plate. Garnish foods with parsley, mint, spices, or wedges of lemon, lime, or orange. Remove bedpans and other less-than-appetizing items from the bed and room before bringing in the food tray.	
Use dietary suggestions to overcome dysgeusia, dysphagia, and xerostomia.	
Eat foods high in fiber (bran; whole grains; fruits, especially pineapple, prunes, and raisins; vegetables; nuts; and legumes) if adequate fluid intake can be maintained. Avoid high-fiber foods if dehydration, severe constipation, or obstruction are anticipated.	Try to help the patient establish a consistent pattern of bowel movements and regular physical activity as tolerated.
Increase fluid intake as tolerated; encourage fruit juices, prune juice, cider. Taking 1–2 ounces with the evening meal of a special recipe (2 cups applesauce, 2 cups unprocessed bran, and 1 cup 100% prune juice) has been shown effective and is low in cost.	Be alert to need for manual disimpaction, preceded by pain medication. Give plain mineral oil at bedtime and on an empty stomach; give emulsion mineral oil with meals. Be wary of aspiration any time that mineral oil is given.
Suggest limiting cheese, rich desserts, and other foods that may be constipating.	
Discontinue calcium and iron supplement if contributing to constipation.	

continues

Symptoms and Causes of Symptoms   *Drug Management*

CONSTIPATION (Cont'd)

Metabolic and endocrine problems,
 including
  hypercalcemia
  hypokalemia
  hypothyroidism

hyperosmolar laxatives:
  Milk of Magnesia
  magnesium
   citrate
  Chronulac or
   Cephulac
 miscellaneous:
  Golytely

Use enemas, including
 tap water
 saline
 soap suds
 Fleet
  Phospho-Soda
 Glycerin suppositories
 Dulcolax
 oil

Possible IV fluids and Mithracin for
 hypercalcemia

Potassium replacement for hypokalemia

Thyroid replacement for hypothyroidism

COUGH

Tumor

Infection

Bronchospasm

Aspiration

Congestive heart failure (CHF)

Anxiety

Dehydration

Mouth breathing and excessive secretions

Postnasal drip

For tumor, consider radiation and
 steroids.

For infection, use antibiotics, Xylocaine
 viscous, and expectorants: potassium
 iodide (SSKI) and Robitussin.

For bronchospasm, use antibiotics,
 adrenergic agents, theophylline, steroids,
 narcotics.

For aspiration, use antibiotics and
 steroids.

For CHF, use diuretics and cardiac
 glycosides.

Dietary Management

Other Management

A large fluid intake is essential if bulk-forming laxatives are to be effective. Because these laxatives are unpalatable, mask them in applesauce, mashed potatoes, gravy, orange juice, and nectars.

Maintain good hydration if possible. Sip on ice chips, carbonated beverages, or juices.

Try sour foods, such as sour balls and sour juices. Try other hard candy.

Try tea and coffee to dilate pulmonary vessels.

Avoid milk, chocolate, and other mucus-producing foods if found to be helpful.

Maintain room humidity with vaporizer.

Consider postural drainage if needed and tolerated by patient.

Consult speech therapy and physical therapy for help to stimulate swallowing if needed.

continues

Symptoms and Causes of Symptoms	*Drug Management*

COUGH (Cont'd)

For anxiety, use sedatives.

For dehydration, use narcotics.

For mouth breathing, use antihistamines and cough suppressants: narcotics with or without terpin hydrate, dextromethorphan.

For excess secretions, use atropine.

For postnasal drip, use antihistamines and atropine.

DEHYDRATION

Reduced intake of fluids due to inability to consume liquids: comatose, weakness, inability to swallow

To moisten lips, try Vaseline, Chap Stick, or K-Y jelly.

Excessive fluid losses due to
excess sweating
fever
nausea and vomiting
diarrhea
fistula and ostomy losses
excess urine output
deficiency of antidiuretic hormone

To moisten mouth, use mouth rinses; avoid the drying effects of lemon and glycerin. Remove debris in mouth with frequent dilute peroxide and water rinses.

Treat mouth infections appropriately.

Manage electrolyte imbalance secondary to endocrine problems with hormone replacement and other medications as appropriate.

Electrolyte imbalances due to
kidney failure
catabolism
liver failure

Consider IV fluid replacement.

Treat nausea and vomiting with antiemetics.

DIARRHEA

Postsurgical dumping

Short bowel syndrome

Radiation-induced colitis

Enteroenteric fistulas

Deficiency of pancreatic enzymes or bile salts

Use antidiarrheals:
Kaopectate
Lomotil
Lomodium or Imodium
Paregoric

Cautious increase in narcotic administration may be warranted.

Dietary Management

Other Management

Encourage liquids and favorite beverages, such as ice chips, juices, carbonated beverages, gelatin, sherbet, and broth-based soups.

Encourage milk, milkshakes, creamed soups, and eggnogs if mucus or fever is not problematic.

Be creative: try carbonated beverage ice cubes and popsicles of juice and Polycose.

Discuss goals, expectations, and quality of life issues with patient, family, and health care team when considering tube feedings or parenteral feedings for treatment of dehydration or electrolyte imbalance.

Treat underlying renal failure with dialysis, liver failure with shunts, and catabolism if appropriate.

Reduce ambient room temperature or provide lighter bed clothes and blankets if excessive sweating.

Suggest omission of milk, whole-grain breads and cereals, ice cream, beans, legumes, nuts, greens, raisins, fruits with seeds and skins, fresh pineapple, cider, prune juice, raw vegetables, and gas-forming vegetables if associated with diarrhea.

Provide prophylactic, protective, and emollient ointments to irritated perianal skin.

Use stress-reduction techniques to alleviate diarrhea associated with anxiety.

continues

Symptoms and Causes of Symptoms	*Drug Management*

DIARRHEA (Cont'd)

Zollinger-Ellison (Z-E) syndrome

Drug-induced from antibiotics, laxatives, and/or antacids

Immunosuppression

Fecal impaction

Anxiety

Tumors in the colon and/or rectum

Acquired immune deficiency syndrome (AIDS)

Pancreatin or pancrealipase with meals and snacks if pancreatic insufficiency; parenteral fat-soluble vitamins may also be warranted. Antacids or Tagamet may decrease the inactivation of pancreatic enzymes by gastric acid.

Tagamet may decrease diarrhea caused by Z-E syndrome.

Use antibiotics if definitive; opportunistic infections have been found to cause diarrhea in AIDS patient.

DYSGEUSIA (ABNORMAL TASTE)

Chemotherapy, especially Leukeran, cisplatinum, 5-fluorouracil, nitrogen mustard, Tamoxifen

Acquired immune deficiency syndrome (AIDS) medications, especially amphotericin B, metronidazole, azidothymidine

Cleanse mouth with appropriate compounds, tooth brush, floss, toothettes, and mouthwash.

Dietary Management	*Other Management*

Try refined grains, crackers, pasta, cream of wheat, oatmeal, rice, cooked vegetables, bananas, applesauce, peeled apple, tapioca, and peanut butter.

Encourage high-potassium foods if dehydration is a problem.

Drink liquids an hour after a meal instead of with meals. In general, omit alcohol and caffeine-containing beverages. Try to keep patient hydrated with fluids containing sugar and electrolytes.

Encourage intake of medium-chain triglycerides and a diet high in protein and carbohydrates for the patient with steatorrhea due to pancreatic insufficiency.

Help the patient relax before and after meals.

Aggressive treatment of malnutrition by enteral and parenteral nutritional support in an attempt to treat diarrhea is not a realistic goal except perhaps in the patient with AIDS and a lengthy life expectancy.

In AIDS patients, encourage a high-protein, high-calorie, low-fiber, low-lactose, low-fat diet with supplements if cause of diarrhea is known and treatable. Encourage adequate hydration.

If foods taste bitter, try the following:
   reduce red meat, sour juices, coffee, tea, tomatoes, chocolate
   consume poultry, fish, dairy products, eggs, milk, cheese, legumes
   add wine or beer to soups, sauces, and meats

Obtain a dental consult if needed.

continues

Symptoms and Causes of Symptoms   *Drug Management*

DYSGEUSIA (Cont'd)

Specific tumor-associated food aversions, e.g., proteinaceous foods, such as beef and pork with pancreatic cancer

Poor oral hygiene and dental caries

Uremia

Possible nutrient deficiencies, especially zinc and niacin

**DYSPHAGIA
(DIFFICULTY SWALLOWING)**

Stomatitis, mucositis, xerostomia, and atrophy of salivary glands due to radiation therapy and chemotherapy

Candidiasis in esophagus due to immunosuppression or steroid therapy

For stomatitis, mucositis, and xerostomia, try Dyclone anesthetic, Xylocaine viscous, or Benadryl.

For candidiasis, try Nystatin possibly made into popsicles or Nizoral or Fungizone.

Dietary Management   *Other Management*

marinate meats and poultry in juices
try fruit drinks, carbonated beverages,
  popsicles
increase sugar intake if tolerable; use
  commercial liquid supplements, which
  may be well liked by many patients
add seasonings, herbs, and spices to
  enhance flavors
try microwaving foods or cooking in
  glass or porcelain instead of cooking
  in metal containers; avoid serving
  foods on metal; use plastic or other
  nonmetal utensils
provide oral care before mealtimes to
  refresh the mouth and enhance tastes
if foods taste "old," try adding sugar;
  sour and salty tastes are often not liked

If foods taste sweet, try the following:
  use sour juices
  use tart foods, lemon juice, vinegar,
  pickles, spices, herbs, mint
  use Polycose

If foods have no taste, try the following:
  marinate foods
  add many seasonings, especially lemon
  juice, mint; serve highly seasoned
  foods, such as Italian dishes
  add sugar
  eat foods at room temperature
  consider using a multiple vitamin and
  mineral supplement containing zinc
  and niacin in particular

Provide small frequent meals of soft
  (pureed if needed) consistency.

Add butter, margarine, sour cream, cream
cheese, or half-and-half to liquefy foods
and add color, taste, and calories.

Attempt to retard lumen constriction with
  steroids, laser treatment, radiation
  therapy, and/or dilation as appropriate.

If reduced saliva is due to obstruction, use
  radiation therapy.

continues

Symptoms and Causes of Symptoms	*Drug Management*
DYSPHAGIA (Cont'd)	
Neuromuscular damage due to radiation therapy, surgery, tumor, or metastases	When swallowing is no longer possible, give atropine.
Mechanical obstruction due to tumor or stricture of hypopharynx or esophagus	If reduced saliva, try alum and mouth washes.
Pain	Consider medical nutritional products via oral, enteral, or parenteral routes.
Motor neuron disease	
Psychogenic problems	
DYSPNEA (DIFFICULTY BREATHING)	
Lung cancer or metastases to lungs	For dyspnea with wheezing and bronchospasm, try dexamethasone.
Cachexia with pulmonary muscle weakness	Use sedatives (Vistaril, Benadryl, Valium, Thorazine), narcotics (morphine), bronchodilators (Theodur), expectorants (SSKI and Robitussin) and oxygen therapy.
Inability to cough due to weakness	
Anemia due to cachexia	
Decreased alertness due to anemia	
Congestive heart failure (CHF)	For infection, use antibiotics.
Respiratory infections	For CHF, use cardiac glycosides and diuretics.
Pulmonary edema and pleural effusion	

Dietary Management	*Other Management*
Recommend suitable soft food cook books and recipes.	Consult a dentist and/or speech therapist if needed.
Avoid acidic juices or fruits, spicy foods, very hot or cold foods, alcohol, and carbonated beverages that might irritate the mouth and esophagus.	
Consider tube feeding (esophageal, Celestin, or gastric) or parenteral nutritional support if prognosis and overall goals warrant. If Celestin tube, instruct patients to consume only fluid for 1–2 days, then add semisolids for 3–4 days, then solids. Chew foods twice as long as normal, and sip frequently on carbonated beverages. Avoid foods that might stick in the tube: fish, pithy fruit, legumes with hulls, cheese chunks, chips, fried foods, raw vegetables, fresh bread and toast, hard-boiled eggs, and dumplings.	
If neuromuscular damage or obstruction, sit patient upright when eating.	
See dietary suggestions for xerostomia (dry mouth).	
Encourage methyl xanthines: caffeine, theophylline, and theobromine. Coffee, tea, carbonated beverages, and chocolate are bronchodilators that can increase blood pressure, dilate pulmonary vessels, increase glomerular filtration rate, and thereby break up and expel pulmonary secretions and fluid.	Decrease patient exertion. Position pillows, bed, and chairs to support the patient in an upright position.
	Improve air circulation with fans and open windows. Nasal cannula oxygen is helpful.
Use a soft diet; liquids are usually better tolerated than solid foods; cool foods are generally preferred to hot foods.	Increase the humidity in the patient's room to reduce dry airway passages or thick secretions.
	Reduce the patient's anxiety with relaxation techniques.

continues

Symptoms and Causes of Symptoms	*Drug Management*

DYSPNEA (Cont'd)

Acquired immune deficiency syndrome (AIDS)

For excess secretions, use mucolytic agents.

For death rattle, use atropine or Transderm Scop.

Consider steroids to improve appetite.

FEVER

Tumor-induced fever often caused by
  rapidly growing tumor
  Hodgkin's disease
  non-Hodgkin's lymphoma
  disseminated breast or pancreatic cancer
  with metastases to the liver

Dehydration

Infection and sepsis, including acquired immune deficiency syndrome (AIDS) secondary to increased basal metabolic rate and bacterial overgrowth; infection due to malnutrition or patient's own normal gastrointestinal flora

Excessive ambient room temperature or excessive bed clothes and coverings

Adrenal insufficiency

Anti-inflammatory agents, such as
  aspirin
  ibuprofen
  Indocin

Corticosteroids

Pro-Banthine for night sweats

Broad-spectrum antibiotics or specific antibiotics for infection if condition warrants

FLUID ACCUMULATION

Lack of normal muscular activity that facilitates venous and lymphatic return of fluids from the periphery to the central circulation

Hypoalbuminemia due to malnutrition, tumor effects, malabsorption, infection,

Use thiazide or furosemide diuretics for fluid accumulation; avoid vigorous diuresis.

Use Aldactone with secondary hyperaldosteronism.

Dietary Management	*Other Management*
Serve small and frequent meals. Cool liquids should be sipped frequently.	Use deep coughing, postural drainage, and suctioning only if they do not cause pain.
Provide ice chips and popsicles, which are soothing to the patient's mouth.	
Consider oral or tube feeding use of Pulmocare, a disease-specific commercial supplement high in fat and low in carbohydrates that can increase caloric intake, decrease carbon dioxide production, and improve ease in breathing.	
Increase fluid intake, especially with cold beverages, ice chips, and popsicles. (See dehydration recommendations.)	Lower the ambient room temperature.
Consider IV fluids for severe dehydration if prognosis warrants.	Use light bed clothes and coverings.
Increase caloric intake. (See anorexia recommendations.)	Use tepid baths or sponge baths with water or a water-alcohol mixture.
Restrict salt to 4 g sodium daily as maximum restriction for terminally ill patients unless the patient requests less.	Elevate edematous extremities as appropriate. Compression therapy is helpful for lymphedema.
Do not restrict fluid intake unless significant hyponatremia develops.	Increase bed rest or encourage gentle exercise as appropriate.

continues

Symptoms and Causes of Symptoms	*Drug Management*

FLUID ACCUMULATION (Cont'd)

hepatic failure, protein loss from loss of protein-rich fluids	Use antitussive agents for pleural effusion.
Venous or lymphatic obstruction due to tumor	Use IV albumin or plasma expanders only if untimely death would otherwise occur.
Peripheral venous disease	
Cardiac, renal, or liver failure and hypertension	
Sodium and water accumulation from administration of corticosteroids, estrogens, and/or nonsteroidal anti-inflammatory agents, such as Indocin	

FUNGATING TUMORS (ULCERATING WOUNDS)

Bacterial growth in moist necrotic tissue, especially	Topical antiseptic agents (Betadine)
breast cancer	Wet-to-dry gauze dressings
neck cancer secondary to radiation	Oral Flagyl
deep chest wound	Plain yogurt or buttermilk applied directly to wound; capsules of Lactobacilli may be opened and the powder sprinkled on the wound
uterine wound	
	Devrom

HALITOSIS

Putrefaction in the mouth, pharynx, nose, nasal sinuses, or lungs	Use nystatin, Nizoral, or Fungazone for candidiasis.
Toxic conditions of the alimentary canal	Use gargles, mouthwashes, and antibiotics as needed.
Sepsis or uremia	
Excretion of volatile substances from the lungs or in the saliva	Use Xerolube or other artificial salivas if mouth is dry.
Smoking	
Ingestion of foods, such as garlic, onions, alcohol, and other odor-forming foods	
Poor mouth care	

Dietary Management	*Other Management*
Provide adequate dietary potassium and protein if possible. Use of aggressive nutritional support to increase protein and caloric intake sufficient to raise blood albumin level rarely achieves its purpose.	Consider thoracentesis or chest tube insertion and sclerosing and radiation therapy for pleural effusion in patients who will benefit with increased quality and quantity of life. Consider paracentesis or LaVeen shunt or nephrostomy if prognosis warrants.
Encourage foods that the patient enjoys. Use of aggressive nutritional support to heal wounds is rarely effective, but may be desired by the patient and family when the goal is quantity of life. See use of yogurt under Drug Management column.	Add deodorants (e.g., Banish) to ostomy bags. Place odor-absorbent dressings over the wound. Place baking soda between bandage layers to reduce odor. Place charcoal near bedside. Provide psychosocial support for the disheartening problems of open ugly wounds.
Avoid foods causing bad breath, such as alcohol, fish, eggs, garlic, onion, asparagus, peas, beans, cabbage, broccoli, and turnips. Maintain adequate fluid intake.	Maintain good oral and dental hygiene, such as 10% hydrogen peroxide gargles on waking, after meals, and at bedtime. Consult dentist if appropriate. Culture sputum if lung sepsis.

Symptoms and Causes of Symptoms	*Drug Management*

HEARTBURN

Reflux of acidic gastric contents into esophagus

Increased abdominal pressure due to ascites, obesity, sleeping flat, or constricting abdominal garments

Smoking

Anticholinergic usage

A diet high in fat or containing excessive alcohol, carbonated beverages, and mint

Provide Reglan to increase lower esophageal sphincter pressure; also give antacids and Tagamet or Zantac.

HICCUPS

Diaphragm and/or phrenic nerve irritation

Intraperitoneal metastases

Hepatic metastases

Gastric dilation

Uremia

Central nervous system (CNS) tumor

Psychological illness

Try antipsychotics, including Compazine, Thorazine, or Haldol.

Try Valium.

If gastric distention, try Reglan, Mylanta, Maalox Plus, or nasogastric tube intubation.

Try Decadron for hiccups caused by diaphragm irritation secondary to metastases to liver.

Try Dilantin and Tegretol for hiccups of CNS origin.

HYPERCALCEMIA

Hypercalcemia caused by
   tumor on parathyroid gland
   tumor elaborating parathormone
   multiple bony metastases
   dehydration
   demineralization of bone secondary to
   limited physical activity

Hydration

IV saline with loop diuretic (furosemide)

Mithracin

Steroid therapy

Fleet Phospho-Soda

Dietary Management	*Other Management*
Avoid coffee, tea, alcohol, chocolate, fat, fried foods, mint, fizzy drinks, gum, and hard candy that lower the lower esophageal sphincter pressure. Eat small meals. Avoid lying down after eating.	Avoid smoking or constricting garments. Correct ascites if possible. Avoid anticholinergics.
Avoid overeating. Drink sugar water, or swallow quickly a large spoonful of dry granulated sugar. Add peppermint to water to decrease gastric distention. Consider alcoholic beverages.	Rebreathing into a paper bag. Nasopharyngeal stimulation with cotton swab Carotid pressure Pressure over eyeballs Phrenic nerve block (rarely needed)
Push fluids as tolerated. Caution against calcium and vitamin D supplementation. Do not restrict high-calcium foods; it is rarely helpful. Encourage carbonated beverages containing phosphoric acid.	Encourage physical activity if possible.

Symptoms and Causes of Symptoms	*Drug Management*
INCONTINENCE (URINARY)	

Overflow incontinence caused by
    bladder outlet obstruction
    loss of normal bladder contractility
    anticholinergic drugs
    metabolic problems: hypercalcemia,
      diabetes insipidus
    congestive heart failure with diuretic
    administration; large fluid intake	

Stress incontinence caused by
    low bladder outlet resistance
    pelvic relaxation
    incompetent bladder sphincter
	For stress incontinence, use ephedrine,
	phenylpropanolamine, tricyclic anti-
	depressants.

Detrusor instability caused by
    bladder infection
    radiation therapy
    chemotherapy
    stones
    tumor
    neurogenic bladder
	For detrusor instability, treat infection,
	provide local anesthetic, try anti-
	cholinergic drugs and tricyclic
	antidepressants.
	
	Use Belladonna and opium or Thorazine
	to help bladder spasm.

Continuous incontinence caused by
    bladder surgery
    radiation therapy to bladder
    bladder tumor	

Uncontrolled diabetes mellitus	For uncontrolled diabetes, use oral hypoglycemic agents or insulin as appropriate.
Urinary tract infection	For urinary tract infections, use Bactrin, Septra, or Amoxicillin (if allergic to sulfa drugs). Acidify the urine with cranberry juice or vitamin C (1,000 mg po qid) plus administration of urinary antiseptic, methenamine hippurate (Hiprex), to reduce incidence and severity of catheter- induced urinary tract infection.

Dietary Management	*Other Management*
For overflow incontinence, decrease fluid intake and methyl xanthine intake, especially during evening hours.	For overflow incontinence, encourage a regular voiding regimen. Create ease in reaching the commode, bedpan, or urinal. Stop or decrease anticholinergic drugs. Decrease smoking in evening hours.
	For stress incontinence, encourage a regular voiding regimen. Encourage exercises to strengthen pelvic musculature. Use pessary or penile clamp.
	For detrusor instability, try perineal or lower abdomen stimulation.
	For continuous incontinence, use incontinence pads, indwelling Foley catheter, urinary diversion procedures, and condom catheter at night.
For diabetes mellitus, allow the patient to eat as desired; control blood sugar with medications.	

Symptoms and Causes of Symptoms   *Drug Management*

JAUNDICE AND HEPATIC ENCEPHALOPATHY

Tumors of liver, biliary tract, pancreas,   Try Neomycin or Cephulac.
and abdomen or other malignancies that
have metastasized to the liver

Drug toxicity

MENTAL DISORDERS

Central nervous system process due to   Neuroleptic drugs, including
  brain tumor or metastases, especially   Haldol
  breast, lung, renal cell, and melanoma   Mellaril
  radiation toxicity   Thorazine
  seizure disorders   Ativan
  encephalitis or abscesses   Serax
  cerebral bleeding or increased pressure   Valium
  trauma   Librium
  hypoxia, hypercapnia   Phenergan

Adverse reactions to medications,   Steroids for brain tumors, metastases, or
  including   cerebral edema

  sedatives, antipsychotics (often used for   Concommitant antacid or Tagamet
  antiemetic effect), and antidepressants   administration is essential to minimize
  narcotics   HCl secretion
  anticholinergics
  anticonvulsants   Anticonvulsants for seizures, including
  hormones   Dilantin
  steroids   Tegretol
  stimulants, especially caffeine,   phenobarbital
  amphetamines, and theophylline
  alcohol   Antiparkinsonian drugs to control
  withdrawal from barbiturates, chloral   extrapyramidal twitching-like effects of
  hydrate, alcohol, stimulants, steroids   Haldol, including
                                         Cogentin
                                         Artane

Dietary Management	*Other Management*
Theoretically a protein-restricted diet may be appropriate, but dietary restrictions are usually not desired by the patient and are generally not effective.	Consider radiation therapy or stent insertion for internal or external biliary drainage if quantity of meaningful life can be achieved.
Diet should reflect patient preference and should be generally high in carbohydrates.	
Specialized commercial nutritional products for tube feedings or IV administration are generally ineffective in terminally ill patients.	
Ascertain if the patient's dietary intake of alcohol, caffeine, theophylline or theobromine could contribute to anxiety, sleep deprivation, or depression.	For comatose or advanced stupor patients, advise the family of the importance of good mouth and skin care for the patient. Help the family and caregivers accept the patient's need for more comfort and other supportive measures.
Ascertain if uncontrolled diabetes mellitus, uremia, and hepatic encepholopathy should be treated by dietary intervention.	For patients with cerebral metastases, consider radiation therapy to the brain, oxygen if the patient is hypoxemic, or shunting if feasible. Brain radiation therapy, brain implants, or intrathecal chemotherapy may be appropriate with cerebral metastases. Lymphoma and testicular cancer are considered radiosensitive; intermediate-sensitivity tumors include lung, breast, and ovarian cancers; nonradiosensitive tumors include melanomas and carcinoma of bowel and kidney.
Remember that, although malnutrition and frank vitamin and mineral deficiencies are theoretical causes of mental deterioration, these have not been studied in the terminally ill patient and are probably rarely the cause of mental disorders.	
When the patient is drowsy and apathetic, help the family and caregiver adapt to the new responsibility of feeding the patient. Help the family identify and choose the patient's best-liked foods, usually in soft form to serve with a spoon or for the patient to handle (if possible), such as small pieces of fruit, small bites of sandwich or small cookies. Help the family protect the patient and others from the patient by shutting off or removing	Use oxygen therapy for hypoxemic patients.
	Consult psychologist/psychiatrist if needed.
	Counsel family members against self-blame and patient-blame for patient's

continues

Symptoms and Causes of Symptoms	*Drug Management*

MENTAL DISORDERS (Cont'd)

Metabolic and endocrine problems, including	Benadryl to control acute dystonic reactions
liver failure	
renal failure	Elavil for depression
circulatory failure	
respiratory failure	Maximum treatment for pain and mental
fluid and electrolyte imbalance, especially acidosis; alkalosis; high or low levels of serum sodium, potassium, or magnesium; hypo- and hyperosmolality	problems in the evening and at night is essential to help the patient and family sleep.
hypo- and hyperglycemia	
vitamin B deficiencies, especially thiamin, pyridoxine, and vitamin B_{12}	
sepsis and pneumonia	
Other factors, including	
sleep deprivation	
stress, fear, anxiety, depression	
pain	
debility	
syphilis	

Dietary Management   *Other Management*

knobs from stoves, removing matches,   bizarre personality and unseemly
and locking doors to cabinets or closets   behavior when caused by illness or
that contain poisons, alcohol, or   treatment and not a willful misbehavior.
medications. Put away electrical
appliances, such as mixers, food
processors, can openers, and waffle
irons. Unplug microwave ovens.

For comatose or advanced stupor patients,
  help the family and caregiver accept the
  patient's need for less food intake.
  Counsel family and caregivers that
  semistarvation and dehydration are not
  painful to the patient, that IV nutrition or
  tube feedings are generally worthless in
  comatose or stuporous patients and may
  result in less comfort than not feeding,
  and that support and love can be best
  shown in ways other than feeding.

For the agitated and confused patient,
  caution family and caregivers about hand
  feeding the patient. Patients may bite or
  strike others if combative. Feed with a
  spoon and avoid opportunities for the
  patient to injure self or others by not
  allowing the patient to handle feeding
  utensils, plates, glass, etc. Tell the
  patient what meal is served, what time of
  day it is, and what foods are served.
  Remind the patient that the foods served
  are favorites. Reminisce about former
  favorite foods and special dinners in the
  distant past that the patient is most likely
  to remember. Minimize discussion or
  comments if the patient appears
  frightened or confused. Do not wake the
  patient for feeding even if it is mealtime.
  Keep the bed free of crumbs or food that
  can contribute to the development of bed
  sores. Warm milk is anecdotally heralded
  by many patients to be effective in
  inducing sleep.

Symptoms and Causes of Symptoms	*Drug Management*
NAUSEA AND VOMITING	
Gastric and high intestinal obstruction	Try Reglan and steroids.
Small intestine and colonic obstruction, constipation, ileus	Try steroids.
Gastric irritation or ulcers from corticosteroids, aspirin, nonsteroidal anti-inflammatory agents, alcohol	Try antacids: Tagamet Reglan Carafate Zantac
Psychogenic (fear, pain, anxiety)	Try sedatives: Vistaril Atarax Benadryl Phenergan
Pharyngeal stimulation, cough	Try antitussives with narcotics and local anesthesia.
Increased intracranial pressure	Try steroids and diuretics.
Motion and position disturbance	Try Antivert, Dramamine, and Transderm Scop.
Metabolic, hormonal, and system failure, including uremia, ketosis, hyponatremia, hepatic failure, renal failure	Try Compazine, Thorazine, Haldol, Inapsine, and Reglan.
Drug induced: narcotics, aspirin, chemotherapy, digitalis, radiation therapy, steroids, alcohol	

Dietary Management	*Other Management*
Seek out possibility that nausea and vomiting is a "conditioned behavior" to thought, smell, and sight of foods.	For gastric and high intestinal obstruction, alleviate pressure by inserting a nasogastric or gastric tube; the gastric tube may be open to straight drain.
Do not let the patient eat when nauseated. Avoid eating at all if nausea or vomiting is anticipated.	For small intestine and colon obstruction, consider tolerating infrequent vomiting; correct constipation.
Serve cool nonodorous foods, such as fruit juices, gingerale, carbonated beverages, lemonade and other fruit juices, popsicles, gelatin, sherbet, hot or dry cereal, dry toast, soda crackers and other salty foods, potatoes, tapioca, cold broth, skim milk soups.	For gastric irritation, avoid known gastric irritants, including tobacco.
	For psychogenic causes, provide emotional support, relaxation techniques, imagery, and hypnosis; change the environment if possible.
Provide small meals. Make plates attractive with foods the patient likes. Do not let the patient overeat, and encourage the patient to eat and drink slowly. Provide a pleasant atmosphere and companionship at mealtimes.	For pharyngeal stimulation and cough, consider radiation therapy.
	For increased intracranial pressure, raise the head of the patient's bed and consider lumbar puncture.
Avoid nausea-precipitating foods, such as overly sweet foods, alcohol, odorous foods, spicy foods, and tobacco with meals.	For motion and position disturbance, encourage the patient to rest and lie flat; avoid sudden head motions and body movements.
Avoid fatty, greasy, or fried foods as a trial.	For metabolic, hormonal, and systems failure, treat the underlying cause if possible.
Avoid mixing hot and cold foods at the same meal.	Stop or decrease nausea-producing drugs; give drugs with food if drugs induce nausea and vomiting.
Avoid high-bulk meals.	

continues

Symptoms and Causes of Symptoms   *Drug Management*

NAUSEA AND VOMITING (Cont'd)

Tumor position and pain

Try morphine and Vistaril, Atarax, Benadryl, and Phenergan.

OBSTRUCTION (INTESTINAL)

Presence of tumor, especially abdominal, ovarian, and colonic

Postoperative stricture and/or adhesions

Chemotherapy with vinca alkaloids may cause paralytic ileus

Drugs, including
  narcotics
  anticholinergics
  antidepressants
  antihistamines
  corticosteroids
  belladonna alkaloids
  neuroleptics
  anticoagulants
  antacids

Massive ascites

Hepatomegaly, "squashed stomach syndrome"

Inadequate therapy to prevent constipation and possible obstruction

Prevent by vigorous bowel regimens with enemas or stool softeners, such as Colace, Doxinate, Peri Colace.

For high obstruction and "squashed stomach syndrome," use Reglan and Maalox Plus.

For low severe obstruction, use stool softeners.

For colicky pain, use Lomotil or Imodium.

For obstruction due to peritoneal carcinomatosis, use dexamethasone to reduce inflammation and edema.

For complete obstruction, use narcotics with atropine (Lomotil) or antiemetics with antihistamine (Benadryl).

Dietary Management	*Other Management*
Do not let the patient prepare own food.	For tumor position and pain, consider radiation therapy.
Encourage the patient to relax before and after meals; alcohol before meals may help the patient relax. Avoid physical activity and lying flat for 2 hours after eating.	
When oral intake is not contraindicated, eat small meals.	For high obstruction, consider radiation therapy and surgery (dilation or bypass).
Avoid high-fiber and high-residue foods. Blenderized and strained foods or low-residue commercial supplements may be needed.	For low obstruction, consider gastric or nasogastric suctioning.
Avoid nausea-producing foods, such as overly sweet foods, alcohol, and odorous foods. Do not eat or drink rapidly.	For total distal colonic obstruction in patient with several months life expectancy, consider colostomy.
Eat largest meal early in the day.	
Many patients prefer to eat their favorite foods, enjoy large meals, and then vomit frequently. Vomiting is often preferable to nasogastric suctioning, restrictive diet, or surgery. If patients vomit frequently, encourage high-potassium foods. A gastric tube, open to straight or intermittent drain, may alleviate need for regular vomiting.	
If complete obstruction, minimize fluid and food intake.	
With "squashed stomach syndrome," eat small frequent meals, and avoid nausea-producing foods, odorous foods, gas-producing foods, high-fat, and fried foods. Limit fluid with meals, taking fluids 45 minutes before and after meals.	

Symptoms and Causes of Symptoms	*Drug Management*

**PRESSURE SORES
(ALSO SEE FUNGATING TUMORS)**

Inability to protect against daily trauma of lying, sitting, moving on bed or chair, due to
  coma, immobility
  mental confusion
  restlessness, friction
  malnutrition, hypoalbuminemia
  dehydration
  edema
  venous stasis
  ischemia
  anemia
  steroid administration
  urine, stool, sweat on skin
  obesity
  poorly controlled diabetes mellitus
  infection
  poor hygiene
	Wound ointments and dressings, such as
	  Stomahesive
	  Duoderm
	  Op-Site
	  Tegaderm
	
	Bacteriostatic agents, such as Betadine
	
	Antibiotics as needed

PRURITIS

Frequently associated with the following diagnoses:
  lymphoma
  leukemia
  myeloma
  liver failure
  renal failure
  gallbladder disease
 	
Drug reactions or toxicity of aspirin or opiates
 	
Drug withdrawal
 	
Psychogenic causes
 	
Skin diseases, such as
  xerosis
  urticaria
  candidiasis
  local irritation
  open wounds
  allergy reactions
	For metastatic disease, try steroids, aspirin, Motrin, Indocin, Benadryl, Zantac, and Tagamet.
	
	For gallbladder disease, uremia, and hepatological malignancies, try Questran.
	
	For psychogenic causes, try Valium or Librium.
	
	For skin diseases, try antihistamines (Benadryl, Atarax, Periactin, Chlortrimeton), anesthetics (phenol with methanol or camphor, Benzocaine, Calamine lotion), steroids (dexamethasone, prednisone), H_2-blocking antihistamines (Tagamet, Zantac), serotonin blockers (Periactin).
	
	Remove offending irritants.
	
	Apply topical creams, including lanolin, Alpha-Keri, and hydrocortisone.

Dietary Management	*Other Management*

Consider providing multiple vitamin-mineral supplement, including zinc and vitamin C.

If feasible, correct elevated blood glucose levels to decrease chance of infection.

Encourage caloric and protein intake equal to needs if patient desires and is able.

Do not treat cachexia, obesity, or anemia by diet imposition unless prolonged life expectancy is anticipated.

Cleanse with soap or detergents. Debride necrotic tissue with wet-to-dry dressings, enzymes, or oxidizers. Place gauze over irrigated deep wounds.

Place baking soda between bandage layers to reduce odor.

Use sheepskin guards, blankets, pads, or special egg crate mattresses or cushions to reduce trauma to skin.

Turn and position patient as often as appropriate. Consider use of a Clinitron bed.

Avoid methyl xanthines, including coffee, tea, cocoa, carbonated beverages with caffeine, and alcohol that can cause vasodilation and itching.

Avoid known allergy foods.

Encourage fluid intake in patients receiving antihistamines.

Mix Questran with applesauce or pureed tart fruit to improve palatability.

Avoid smoking unless smoking reduces anxiety.

Avoid dry skin. Increase humidity, avoid hot and frequent baths, use bath oils and tepid baths, avoid drying soaps, use Alpha-Keri and emollients.

Trim nails to avoid excoriation.

Symptoms and Causes of Symptoms	*Drug Management*
STOMATITIS	
Monilia: thrush may be due to immunosuppression, broad-spectrum antibiotics, steroids, diabetes mellitus, esophageal motor disorder	Dyclone gel anesthetic
	Xylocaine viscous
	Milk of magnesia
Herpes	Antacids
Aphthous ulcers	Kaopectate and Benadryl
Caries, gingivitis	Hydrocortisone for aphthous ulcer
Vitamin B deficiency or large weight loss	Nystatin for monilia
Drugs, including methotrexate and aspirin	Clean mouth routinely with saline mouthwash; avoid drying and irritating commercial products (including lemon-glycerin swabs) or dilute these products. Try sodium bicarbonate, mint-flavored foam sticks or hydrogen peroxide diluted to tolerance.
Radiation therapy	
Reflux esophagitis	
Poor oral hygiene	
Poorly fitting dentures	
Acquired immune deficiency syndrome (AIDS)	Treat reflux esophagitis with Maalox Plus, Mylanta, Tagamet, and other antacids.
WEAKNESS	
Neurogenic causes, including central nervous system lesion peripheral nerve injury possibly due to vitamin B_{12} or thiamin deficiency, alcoholism, diabetes mellitus, ischemia, or medications	Steroids, including testosterone
	Dantrium and Lioresal for spasticity
	Flexeril and Robaxin for muscle spasms
	Ritalin to treat lethargy
	Packed red blood cells to correct anemia
Muscular causes, including malnutrition and weight loss inactivity, prolonged bed rest	Sedatives to overcome anxiety
Neuropsychiatric causes, including confusion, depression pain insomnia	
Systemic causes including fluid and electrolyte imbalance, particularly potassium, calcium, magnesium, phosphate hyperglycemia	

Dietary Management	*Other Management*
Try blenderized foods and cold foods; popsicles may be well tolerated.	Avoid smoking.
Add sugar, honey, or corn syrup to tone down acidic and salty foods.	Use soft toothbrush and floss or toothettes; avoid mouthwash with alcohol.
Serve bland creamy foods, gravies, and soups; they may be very appealing.	Consult dentist as needed.
Increase caloric intake with eggnog, cream pie, cheesecake, half-and-half, macaroni and cheese, stews, casseroles, and blenderized cold soups.	
Avoid acidic, spicy, rough, hot, and high-salted foods and alcohol.	
Try to control mouth pain before mealtimes.	
Provide multivitamin-mineral supplement with additional iron, vitamin B_{12}, and folate.	Treat underlying causes, especially if systemic or neuropsychiatric.
Encourage high-potassium foods if patient is hypokalemic or vomits often.	Save energy for important events and chores. Use energy-saving aids. Plan strategic rest periods during day.
Rarely restrict dairy products to treat hypercalcemia.	Delegate responsibility or obtain assistance as needed.
Save energy in chewing by providing soft foods and liquids; use large-bore flexible straw and other aids for eating in bed.	Avoid prolonged bed rest. Encourage reasonable exercise. Occupational therapy or physical therapy consult may be helpful.
Provide a warm non-caffeinated drink at bedtime to help patients sleep.	Plan diversional activities as appropriate.
Note that weakness is rarely improved through aggressive nutritional support.	Consider radiation therapy or neurosurgery if appropriate.

continues

Symptoms and Causes of Symptoms   *Drug Management*

WEAKNESS (Cont'd)

dehydration
anemia
renal, hepatic, cardiovascular,
 cardiopulmonary failure
infection, fever
acquired immune deficiency syndrome
 (AIDS)

XEROSTOMIA (DRY MOUTH)

Drugs, including
 anticholinergics
 phenothiazines
 antihistamines
 tricyclic antidepressants
 opiates
 diuretics
 antispasmodics
 belladonna alkaloids
 oxygen therapy

Mouth-breathing

Dehydration and poor oral intake

Local radiation therapy and decreased
 saliva or diseased buccal mucosa

Connective tissue disease (Sjögren's
 syndrome)

Aging

Poor oral hygiene

Mineral oil

Saliva substitutes by applicator or spray
 (Xerolube or MoiStir)

Cleaning solution: ½ teaspoon baking
 soda and 1 teaspoon hydrogen peroxide
 in a glass of water
  or
equal parts hydrogen peroxide, glycerin,
 Cepacol, and saline.

After mouth is clean, treat with mint-
 flavored foam sticks

Urecholine

Nystatin or Nizoral for monilia

Petroleum jelly for lips

Dietary Management

Other Management

Try frequent sips of water, juice, ice chips, popsicles with Polycose (wrapped in gauze), ice cream, fruitades, or slushy-frozen baby foods mixed with fruit juice.

Suck on candy; cinnamon balls, sugarless candy, sugarless gum, or lifesavers to stimulate saliva.

Try sour foods, lemon drops, and pineapple, melon, or papaya juice; tart, sour, acid, or spicy foods may not be tolerated, especially if stomatitis is also present.

Eat moist foods, including high-caloric liquids, milk and instant breakfast, milkshakes, gravies, soups, and casseroles.

Puree foods if needed. Consider medical nutritional products as needed.

Dip foods into gravy, broth, melted butter, or margarine.

Avoid dry or crisp foods, especially bread, nuts, chips, and fresh fruits or vegetables unless softened.

Avoid extremely hot or cold foods; moderately cold foods are usually preferred.

Avoid alcohol.

Consult a dentist as needed.

Irrigate the mouth with bulb syringe.

Keep lips and mouth moist; a room humidifier will help.

Brush the teeth frequently (use an electric toothbrush for sensitive gums) and use dilute mouthwashes frequently. Avoid alcohol-containing or lemon-glycerin mouthwashes that may irritate or dry out the oral cavity.

Take Nizoral after eating to reduce gastric irritation.

Beware of aspiration when mineral oil is used.

Avoid tobacco.

continues

Symptoms and Causes of Symptoms   *Drug Management*

XEROSTOMIA (Cont'd)

Dietary Management	*Other Management*

Hold breakfast until mucus is removed from mouth. Meat tenderizer, papain, or papaya juice may help loosen thick oral secretions. Try soybean milk if milk causes mucus.

Mix Nystatin with cherry Kool-Aid and freeze as popsicles or cubes for monilia.

REFERENCES FOR APPENDIX 9-A

Allman, Richard M., Laprade, Carol A., Noel, Linda B., et al. "Pressure Sores among Hospitalized Patients." *Annals of Internal Medicine* 105 (1986): 337–342.

Baines, Mary J. "Control of Other Symptoms." In *The Management of Terminal Disease*, edited by Cicely M. Saunders, (London: Edward Arnold Ltd., 1978), 99–118.

Baines, Mary, Oliver, D.J., and Carter, R.L., "Medical Management of Intestinal Obstruction in Patients with Advanced Malignant Disease. A Clinical and Pathological Study." *Lancet* 2 (1985): 990–993.

Behm, Roberta Mathiesen. "A Special Recipe to Banish Constipation." *Geriatric Nursing* 6, no. 4 (July/August 1985): 216–217.

Billings, J. Andrew. "The Management of Common Symptoms." In *Outpatient Management of Advanced Cancer: Symptom Control, Support and Hospice-in-the-Home*, edited by J. Andrew Billings (Philadelphia: J.B. Lippincott Co., 1985), 40–138.

Bohnet, Nancy L. "Symptom Control." In *Nursing Care of the Terminally Ill*, edited by Madalon O'Rawe Amenta and Nancy L. Bohnet, (Boston: Little, Brown & Co., 1986), 67–80.

Brennan, Murray R. "Total Parenteral Nutrition in the Cancer Patient." *New England Journal of Medicine* 306 (1981): 375–382.

Cassileth, Peter A. "Common Medical Problems." In *Clinical Care of the Terminally Ill Cancer Patient*, edited by Barrie R. Cassileth and Peter A. Cassileth (Philadelphia: Lea & Febiger, 1982), 15–52.

Colburn, Louise. "Pressure Ulcer Prevention for the Hospice Patient: Strategies for Care to Increase Comfort." *American Journal of Hospice Care* 4, no. 2 (March/April 1987): 22–26.

Collins, Candy L. "Nutrition Care in AIDS." *Dietetic Currents* 15, no. 3 (1988): 11–16.

Daeffler, Reidun Juvkam. "Oral Care." *The Hospice Journal* 2, no. 1 (Spring 1986): 81–102.

DeWys, William D., and Kubota, Thomas T. "Enteral and Parenteral Nutrition in the Care of the Cancer Patient." *Journal of the American Medical Association* 246, no. 15 (9 October 1981): 1725–1727.

Dolan, Marion B. "If Your Patient Wants to Die at Home." *Nursing '83* 13, no. 4 (April 1983): 50–55.

Doll, Donald C., and Doll, Kinder J. "Malodorous Tumors and Metronidazole (Letter)." *Annals of Internal Medicine* 94 (1981): 139–140.

Dornan, Valerie. "Diet in Terminal Illness." *Nursing Mirror* 160, no. 8 (20 February 1985): 38–41.

Dwyer, Johanna T., Bye, Rancy L., Holt, Pamela L., and Lauze, Scott R. "Unproven Nutrition Therapies for AIDS: What is the Evidence?" *Nutrition Today* 23, no. 2 (April 1988): 25–33.

Enck, Robert E. "Management of Malignant Intestinal Obstruction." *American Journal of Hospice Care* 4, no. 2 (March/April 1987): 8–9.

Enck, Robert E. "Anorexia and Cachexia." *American Journal of Hospice Care* 4, no. 5 (September/October 1987): 13-15.

Enck, Robert E., and Hogan, Catherine M. "Management of Nausea and Vomiting." *American Journal of Hospice Care* 4, no. 4 (July/August 1987): 17–19.

Engleman, Edgar G., Lankton, James, and Lankton, Barbara. "Granulated Sugar as Treatment for Hiccups in Conscious Patients." *New England Journal of Medicine* 285, no. 26 (1971): 1489.

Fowler, Evonne M. "Pressure Sores." *Long Term Care Currents* 6, no. 4 (October/December 1983): 15–18.

Green R.F. "Subclinical Pellagra and Idiopathic Hypogeusia (Letter)." *Journal of the American Medical Association* 218, no. 8 (22 November 1971): 1303.

Henkin, Robert I. "Prevention and Treatment of Hypogeusia Due to Head and Neck Irradiation (Questions and Answers)." *Journal of the American Medical Association* 220, no. 6 (8 May 1972): 870–876

Levy, Michael H. "Symptom Control Manual." In *Clinical Care of the Terminal Cancer Patient*, edited by Barrie R. Cassileth and Peter A. Cassileth (Philadelphia: Lea & Febiger, 1982), 214–262.

Lynn, Joann. "Supportive Care for Dying Patients: An Introduction for Health Care Professionals (Appendix B)," In *Deciding to Forego Life-Sustaining Treatment: A Report on the Ethical, Medical, and Legal Issues in Treatment Decisions*, edited by the President's Commission for the Study of Ethical Problems in Medicine and Biomedical and Behavioral Research (Washington, D.C.: United States Government Printing Office, 1983), 275–297.

Mazzaferri, Ernest L., O'Dorisio, Thomas M., and LoBuglio, Al F. "Treatment of Hypercalcemia Associated with Malignancy." *Seminars in Oncology* 5 (1978): 141–153.

Mundy, Gregory R., and Martin, T. John. "The Hypercalcemia of Malignancy: Pathogenesis and Management." *Metabolism* 31 (1982): 1247–1277.

Nixon, Daniel W., Lawson, David H., Kutner, Michael, et al. "Hyperalimentation of the Cancer Patient with Protein-Calorie Undernutrition." *Cancer Research* 41 (1981): 2038–2045.

Osteen, Robert T., Guyton, Sigrid, Steele, Gleen, Jr., and Wilson, Richard E. "Malignant Intestinal Obstruction." *Surgery* 87, no. 6 (June 1980): 611–615.

Poland, Joseph M. "Xerostomia in the Oncologic Patient." *American Journal of Hospice Care* 4, no. 3 (May/June 1987): 31–33.

Poland, Joseph M. "Stomatitis and Specific Oral Infections of the Oncologic Patient." *American Journal of Hospice Care* 4, no. 4 (July/August 1987): 27–30.

Poland, Joseph M. "Oral Thrush in the Oncologic Patient." *American Journal of Hospice Care* 4, no. 5 (September/October 1987): 30-32.

Resler, Susan S. "Nutrition Care of AIDS Patients." *Journal of the American Dietetic Association* 88, no. 7 (July 1988): 828–832.

Reuben, David B., and Mor, Vincent. "Nausea and Vomiting in Terminal Cancer Patients." *Archives of Internal Medicine* 146 (1986): 2021–2023.

Russell, Robert M., Cox, Michael E., and Solomons, Noel. "Zinc and the Special Senses." *Annals of Internal Medicine* 99 (1983): 227–239.

Scalzo, Ginny. "Nutritional Management of the Patient with AIDS-related Complex: Case Study," *RD* 8 (1988): 10–11.

Schneider, Arthur B., and Sherwood, Louis M. "Calcium Homeostasis and the Pathogenesis and Management of Hypercalcemic Disorders." *Metabolism* 23 (1974): 975–1007.

Slowie, Linda A., Paige, Myrna S., and Antel, Jack P. "Nutritional Considerations in the Management of Patients with Amyotrophic Lateral Sclerosis (ALS)." *Journal of the American Dietetic Association* 83, no. 1 (July 1983): 44–47.

Stewart, Andrew F. "Therapy of Malignancy-Associated Hypercalcemia: 1983." *American Journal of Medicine* 74 (1983): 475–480.

Tchekmedyian, N. Simon, Tait, Nancy, Moody, Mark, and Aisner, Joseph. "High-Dose Megestrol Acetate. A Possible Treatment for Cachexia" *Journal of the American Medical Association* 257 (1987): 1195–1198.

Tucker, Bennett D., Jr. "The Hospice Patient—Dental Aspects: Indications, Contraindications, and Limitations." *American Journal of Hospice Care* 1, no. 3 (Summer 1984): 21–24.

Zerwekh, Joyce V. "Symptom Control." In *Hospice and Palliative Nursing Care*, edited by Ann G. Blues and Joyce V. Zerwekh (Orlando, Fla.: Grune & Stratton, 1984), 108–146.

Chapter 10

Pain Management in Terminally Ill Patients

Pain is a burden, and to be in pain and to be dying at the same time poses a double burden. Because pain is a major fear of terminally ill patients, its control is of paramount importance to palliative care professionals who are trying to help the dying patient and the patient's family live a meaningful and enjoyable life until death occurs.

> One cannot adequately help a man to come to accept his impending death if he remains in severe pain, one cannot give spiritual counsel to a woman who is persistently vomiting, or help a wife and children say their goodbyes to a father who is so drugged that he cannot respond.[1]

Unlike the acute, intermittent pain that most healthy persons experience, terminally ill patients often experience chronic, continuous pain. Chronic pain is demoralizing and devastating. It wears the body down and causes patients to withdraw from life because of constant anxiety and lack of sleep. Patients often groan and whine. They appear helpless and defeated. Chronic pain takes control of patients' every senses and leaves them with little or no desire or energy for living.

Margo McCaffrey has proposed a clinically useful and workable definition of pain: "Pain is whatever a person says it is, existing whenever he says it does."[2] This definition identifies the attributes of pain with which palliative care professionals must deal, namely that[3]

- Pain is personal and private.
- Pain is unique to the person experiencing it.
- Pain is physical, subjective, and emotional.
- Reactions to pain vary among persons and within the same person from time to time.
- The patient is the authority on his or her pain; only the patient knows when and if pain is being experienced.

Pain is not a prerequisite for dying. Robert Twycross has shown that pain will be difficult to control in only about 10 percent of terminally ill cancer patients.[4] Arthur G. Lipman is even more optimistic, believing that over 95 percent of terminally ill patients can be pain-free if the causes of pain are correctly identified.[5] Of course, "Not only 1 per cent but one person is a relevant statistic if it happens to be you or someone you love."[6]

COMPONENTS OF PAIN

Pain has physical, psychological, social, emotional, spiritual, and financial components. Most pain experienced by cancer patients is due to physical pain caused by the disease itself. Although they do not cause pain directly, fear, depression, anxiety, and family, financial, and spiritual problems can lower the threshold for pain, thereby intensifying the total pain experience.

Lipman reports that one in three terminally ill patients has four or more causes of pain, whereas one-half to two-thirds of patients have two to three causes of pain.[7] Multiple causes of pain require multiple workup procedures, and multiple professionals are often needed to diagnose and treat total pain. Without a correct etiology of pain it is virtually impossible to choose the correct treatments. In addition, pain must be continually reassessed due to its propensity for change.

The interrelationship between physical and psychosocial pain is not often adequately recognized. Physical pain often causes anxiety, which in turn can produce hostility, sleep disturbances, and depression. Hostility breeds loneliness. Sleep disturbance and loneliness manifest themselves as depression, which lowers the threshold for physical pain. Thus, an unending cycle is created that feeds back on itself, ultimately resulting in spiraling pain (Figure 10-1).

Too often, medications are administered for each of these separate problems, with no recognition of their interrelatedness and potentially common cause. For example, a narcotic may be given for physical pain, a sedative for hostile behavior, and a tranquilizer for insomnia. If physical pain is at the root of each of these psychosocial problems, administration of an adequate narcotic alone may be all that is needed to control the psychosocial symptoms. Ultimate pain control can only be reached both by alleviating physical pain and by gaining the confidence of the patient that pain can be controlled.

INDIVIDUAL REACTIONS TO PAIN

Individuals react differently to pain as a result of many factors. It appears from reports of pain and the amounts of analgesics needed to treat it that pain varies with the setting and significance of the wound but not necessarily with the extent of the

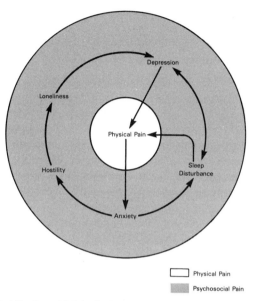

Figure 10-1 Physical-Psychosocial Pain Cycle

injury. Henry K. Beecher, an army surgeon treating soldiers who were wounded in the beach assault on Anzio during World War II, found that minimal or no analgesics were required to treat wound pain. These same soldiers, however, complained about the pain of inept venipuncture attempts. Civilians with similar wounds were found to require more analgesia. The difference could be that, for the soldiers, wounds meant a ticket home, away from war. To the civilians, injuries and surgeries meant disruption in their usual lives and routines, as well as other less desirable changes.[8,9]

Although it would seem that pain control would be desired by everyone, such is not always the case. Many patients gain attention by complaining of pain. In some families and in some cultures, complaining serves a social purpose and is part of a long-standing stable pattern of family and cultural behavior. (See Chapter 8 on ethnic considerations in palliative care.)

Men and women react differently to pain. Men since boyhood are admonished not to show pain: "Big boys don't cry." Women traditionally experience fewer societal constraints, but most people have been taught that "only babies cry." And indeed, society is more tolerant of a wailing child than a whimpering adult who is thought to be old enough to exhibit self-control.

Some people may have seemingly bizarre views of pain. For example, to some people, pain means punishment for past transgressions. A woman suffering from uterine, cervical, or breast cancer may view her pain as penance for past sexual promiscuity. A man with chest pain and lung cancer caused by tobacco abuse may feel ashamed to tell his doctor about his pain because he did not take his doctor's advice to stop smoking 40 years earlier. To others, increased pain may signify the death knell of growth and spread of cancer. In contrast, increased pain is valued by some people because to them it means "I'm still alive!."

PHYSIOLOGY OF PAIN AND PAIN CONTROL

A theory to explain the physiology of pain was formulated in 1965 by two research psychologists Ronald Melzack and Patrick Wall.[10] In their gate control theory they proposed that there are two pain pathways in the body: the limbic system pathway that transmits emotional pain and a second system that transmits physical pain from the spinal cord to the brain.

According to the gate control theory, pain impulses travel from the nerve receptor at the site of the pain's origin to synapses in the gray matter of the dorsal horns of the spinal cord. The synapses act as gates that either close to keep the impulses from reaching the brain or open to allow the impulses to ascend. Whether these gates are opened or closed depends on what other kinds of sensory impulses are simultaneously bombarding the gates. Impulses on thick mechanoreceptor fibers (which detect touch or pressure) close the synaptic gates to impulses on thin thermoreceptor fibers (mild temperature change detectors) or nociceptor fibers (irritation detector) and keep them from reaching the brain, thereby preventing the patient from perceiving pain. When impulses on thin fibers predominate, the gates open, allowing pain impulses to reach the brain and be felt by the patient.

It has been known for some time that the brains of animals contain many specific sites on which opiate analgesics, such as morphine, can attach. These sites are also present in the hypothalamus and amygdala, parts of the limbic system that regulate emotions. They are present as well in the gray matter in the midbrain, believed to be the origin of descending control pathways that modify incoming sensory impulses, and in the dorsal horns of the spinal cord. The abundance of opiate receptors in the areas of the brain associated with emotions supports the assumption that opiates relieve pain by altering the perception of pain, rather than by actually preventing it.

Reasoning that the brain would not have receptors for an exogenous plant alkaloid, such as morphine, unless it also had natural chemicals that used those receptors, researchers began to search for an endogenous chemical in hopes of finding a safe, effective natural analgesic.[11] In 1975, a compound called beta-endorphin, isolated from the pituitary gland and brain of animals, was shown to have a protective effect against pain. Endorphins are now known to be the body's naturally produced morphine-like pain-relieving substances.

When released onto the opiate receptors of the afferent pain neuron, endogenous and exogenous opiates are thought to act by preventing the perception of pain. By blocking the pain message across the synapse, no pain message is transmitted to the brain, and pain is not perceived. Opiate narcotics are most effective against high intensity or "sharp" pain. In contrast, aspirin and similar analgesics have their primary actions outside the central nervous system and are effective against the "dull" pain of low to moderate intensity associated with inflammatory tissue damage.

PHARMACOLOGICAL MANAGEMENT OF PAIN

Narcotics are the mainstay of management of chronic pain. A dosage that is too low leaves the patient in pain; too high doses produce sedation or clouded sensorium. Between these two "analgesic zones" is a zone where pain is abolished. The appropriate dose provides adequate pain relief without sedation.

Several naturally occurring and synthetic narcotics are available for relief of pain. Morphine is the most often used narcotic during terminal illness. As a whole, narcotics are highly effective, and each has similar side effects.

Dose Schedule

Narcotic administration in the terminally ill patient should be on an "around-the-clock" schedule. Too often, analgesics are administered on an "as needed" basis (prn). The prn order is inappropriate for the patient with chronic pain because it means that the patient must experience pain before asking for a pain medication, and usually at least 30–60 minutes will elapse before the medication is given, absorbed, and begins to work. This leaves the patient in pain between every dose, thereby causing him or her to spend considerable time preoccupied with the regular recurrence of pain.

Instead of waiting for pain to occur, analgesics should be given before pain begins, on a regular (e.g., every 3-, 4- or 6- hour) basis. When pain is treated prophylactically, the anxiety associated with recurring pain can be avoided, and the total daily dose of narcotics needed to control pain can be minimized.

Giving narcotics, especially around-the-clock, is foreign to many people's thinking and brings to mind the ideas of tolerance and dependence. Tolerance is the phenomenon whereby narcotics become less effective when used for a long period of time. If tolerance occurs, the narcotic dose merely needs to be increased slightly so that pain is abolished. Most terminally ill patients are maintained in good pain control on quite low doses of narcotics. Stronger pain-killing effect is always available if needed.

Fears of dependence (formerly called addiction) are unfounded for the terminally ill patient. The incidence of dependence among patients who receive narcotics for pain is probably not greater than 0.1 percent.[12,13] If dependence develops, it can be physical, psychological, or both. Physical dependence parallels tolerance and is treated by slightly increasing the amount of narcotic administered. If narcotics are withdrawn from terminally ill patients who have received them for many months, mild discomfort frequently results. Patients, however, do not experience the turbulent effects often seen in narcotics abusers who have gone "cold turkey." Addiction in terminal illness is primarily a myth.

Route of Administration

Narcotics can be given orally, subcutaneously, intramuscularly, intrathecally, and rectally. Although oral medications require longer to take effect than parenterally administered narcotics, they wear off slower and more often produce longer periods of sustained relief than parenterally administered medications. Parenterally administered medications act rapidly, have increased likelihood of causing brief toxicity, and wear off quickly.

Individualizing narcotics administration in terminally ill patients requires time and many adjustments. Different patients respond to narcotics differently. Physiological variations among patients occur due to the bioavailability, distribution, and clearance of these drugs. In managing chronic pain, the interval of time between doses may need to be as short as 2 hours or as long as 12 hours, depending on patient response, the medication chosen, route of administration, and amount of medication required for pain control.

Table 10-1 lists various narcotics and the equivalent oral and parenteral doses. Several often quoted references were used to compile the table.[14-20] Table 10-2 indicates the usual duration of effectiveness of these common narcotics.

Analgesic Regimen

Mild to Moderate Pain Regimen

Mild to moderate pain can be treated with the following simple regimen:

- acetaminophen (Tylenol) orally (po) or rectally (pr)
- aspirin po or pr: taken with meals, with antacid, or in buffered or enteric coated form
- codeine with aspirin or acetaminophen po
- oxycodone (Percocet, Percodan, Roxicet) po

Adjunct Medications–Nonsteroidal anti-inflammatory drugs (NSAIDs), such as salicylates (aspirin), phenylbutazone (Butazolidin), indomethacin (Indocin),

Table 10-1 Approximate Equivalent Narcotic Doses for Treatment of Chronic Pain

Drug	Oral/Rectal Dose	Equivalent Parenteral Dose
Codeine	200 mg q 3–4 h	130 mg SC q 3–4 h 120 mg IM q 3–4 h
Meperidine* (Demerol)	300 mg q 3–4 h	75 mg IM q 2–3 h
Hydromorphone (Dilaudid)	4–6 mg q 3–6 h	1.5 mg IM q 3–6 h
Levorphanol (Levo-Dromoran)	4 mg q 3–8 h	2 mg SC q 3–8 h
Methadone	20 mg q 3–6 h	10 mg SC/IM q 3–6 h
Morphine sulfate	20-30 mg q 3–4 h	10 mg SC/IM q 3–4 h
Oxycodone (Percodan, Percocet, Roxicet)	30 mg q 3–6 h	15 mg IV q 3–6 h

NOTE: SC— subcutaneously
IM — intramuscularly
IV — intravenously

*Demerol is not recommended in management of chronic pain.

ibuprofen (Motrin), and naproxen (Naprosyn), are helpful therapy for treating inflammatory pain such as bone pain and soft tissue pain. These drugs or co-analgesics can also be added to narcotics, thereby decreasing the amount of narcotic needed for pain control. Aspirin is the first discovered and most commonly used drug in this class and probably is the most effective and efficacious overall.

NSAIDs have several significant side effects. They cause gastric irritation and therefore should be taken with a meal or snack, along with an antacid. They are also sodium-retaining, nephrotoxic, and platelet-inhibitory. Therefore, they should not be taken by patients with thrombocytopenia or those who are on coumadin therapy.

Steroids are helpful in treating pain associated with tissue swelling, especially swelling from a CNS mass. Steroids are also effective against pain caused by liver distension, nerve compression, pelvic tumor with metastases, and refractory bone

Table 10-2 Likely Duration and Effects of Common Narcotics

Drug	Hours of Effectiveness Per Method of Administration		
	Orally (po)	Intramuscularly (IM)	Intravenously (IV)
Morphine sulfate	4	3	2
Methadone	6–8	4–6	4–6
Levorphanol (Levo-Dromoran)	6–8	4–6	4–6
Meperidine* (Demerol)	3–4	2–3	2
Hydromorphone (Dilaudid)	3–4	3–4	2

* Demerol is not recommended in management of chronic pain.

pain. They are a secondary analgesic, working at the cyclic adenosine mono-phosphate (cAMP) level. Prednisone is the primary steroid used in nerve edema pain, and dexamethasone is used for cerebral edema pain.

Increased appetite and improvement in mood are characteristic side effects of steroids. Other side effects include gastric irritation (therefore, Tagamet and/or antacids should be taken between meals and at bedtime), oral candidiasis, edema, moon facies, agitation, insomnia, and more florid psychiatric disturbances.

Exhibit 10-1 shows common uses for steroids in terminally ill patients.

Moderate to Severe Pain

Morphine is the best narcotic to use with moderate to severe pain. It and codeine are naturally occurring substances extracted from opium found in the poppy plant. Oxycodone is a semisynthetic narcotic made from codeine with some structural modifications. Pain can be controlled in 80 percent of patients with a morphine dose of 30 mg po every 4 hours. In palliative care patients, doses of 150 mg po every 4 hours are not uncommon. Because of its disagreeable taste, morphine is often best taken orally when dissolved in applesauce or a tart juice. Any strength can be devised, and if needed, it can be coated with cocoa butter and given rectally.

Exhibit 10-1 Uses of Steroids in Terminal Illness

- to improve appetite
- to reduce elevated serum calcium
- to decrease hemoptysis
- to enhance feelings of well-being
- to improve strength
- to decrease rectal tumor discharge and treat tumors in the liver, head and neck, and pelvis
- to decrease intracranial pressure
- to decrease nerve and spinal cord compression
- to decrease metastatic arthralgia
- to decrease toxic effects of radiation therapy or chemotherapy
- to decrease superior vena caval obstruction and airway obstruction

Brompton's cocktail is a narcotic mixture developed in Great Britain in the 1920s for pain control. It contains cocaine, alcohol, a phenothiazine, and either morphine or heroin. Cocaine is useful as a local anesthetic, but it is not efficacious when combined with an oral narcotic. Upon consumption, cocaine is quickly metabolized to morphine. Although it is desired by drug abusers due to the fast "buzz" it gives, this side effect is not wanted in terminally ill patients. Alcohol may aggravate pain in patients with an injured mouth, throat, or upper gastrointestinal tract and in those with lymphoma. Heroin, a pro-drug to morphine, is used in Great Britain where its use is legalized. Although it is more potent on a milligram-to-milligram basis than morphine, heroin has no other advantage over morphine.

Hydromorphone (Dilaudid) is a semisynthetic narcotic that is made from morphine with some structural modification. High-potency hydromorphone or Dilaudid-HP provides low-volume, high-potency injections and on a milligram-per-milligram basis is more potent than heroin. The duration of action of hydromorphone is short; therefore, morphine is usually a better choice. Dilaudid is also effective in treating air hunger.

Levorphanol (Levo-Dromoran) is another synthetic narcotic, made to be structurally similar to morphine. It has a long duration of action, causes hallucinations and disorientation, and is frequently not tolerated by elderly patients.

Long-acting morphine (M.S. Contin or Roxanol S.R.) is the newest narcotic in the arsenal against pain. It is designed to be taken by mouth and is slowly released into the blood. Its duration of action is generally from 8–12 hours. Suppositories of long-acting morphine have also recently been developed.

Methadone can be used to treat moderate to severe pain. It is a synthetic narcotic that is structurally similar to morphine. Because it tends to cause significant confusion and disorientation and has a high rate of toxicity due to its long half-life, it is not recommended for treatment of elderly or debilitated patients. Methadone is also hepatotoxic and should not be used in patients with pre-existing liver damage.

Several drugs are not recommended in the management of chronic pain. Demerol is not an efficacious drug because of its very short half-life and the accumulation of its metabolite, normeperidine. Repeated doses can cause convulsions. Talwin has no place in chronic pain control because of the high incidence of dysphoria. Darvon has been proven less efficacious than placebo and produces all the negative side effects of narcotics.

Terminally ill patients who are both depressed and in pain are best treated with an antidepressant. Tricyclic antidepressants are helpful in treating chronic pain by acting to change monoamine function. By enhancing the efficacy of narcotics, they decrease the amount of narcotic needed to achieve pain relief. Tricyclic antidepressants should only be used with neuritic pain or with patients with first-generation depression.

Anxious patients need anxiolytic medication, such as diazepam (Valium), at bedtime to reduce agitation and insomnia. Valium may also be helpful in treating muscle spasm pain. Phenobarbital, an anxiety-relieving drug, is excreted through the kidneys and therefore should not be given to renal failure patients. A diuretic is a recommended co-analgesic treatment for lymphedema pain. Metronidazole or Clindamycin is recommended for pain associated with an infected malignant ulcer.

The large arsenal of narcotics available for use and the wide range of dosages necessary to control pain in terminally ill patients requires that medication regimens be individualized. It is important to note that a placebo helps reduce pain in 30-35 percent of patients.

Side Effects of Narcotics

Despite the positive effects of narcotics, they also cause negative side effects. Constipation, a major side effect of narcotic use, can be effectively treated prophylactically with stool softeners or laxatives, such as Colace or Dulcolax. Prune juice and hydration are also helpful, especially in dehydrated patients (see Chapter 9 on symptom control). Nausea and vomiting are other major side effects of narcotic use. The pathophysiology of vomiting is complex, but is fairly well defined. Its treatment is discussed in Chapter 9.

Narcotics cause dehydration, dry mouth, and hypotension with dehydration. Neuropsychiatric effects of narcotics include dysphoria, hallucinations, shakiness, and strange dreams. Urinary retention is also common.

Finally, yet of major importance, narcotics affect the respiratory system by decreasing respirations, which increases the blood carbon dioxide level. Hypoxia results in confusion. Significant respiratory depression rarely poses a problem unless the patient has severe respiratory impairment or is often highly overmedicated. It is easier to overmedicate and cause decreased respiratory function with intravenous narcotic administration than with oral administration. If the patient has a life-threatening respiratory depression secondary to narcotic administration, Nubane or naloxone (Narcan)–opiate antagonists–are indicated. Such stimulants as Ritalin or dextroamphetamine can also be given.

OTHER MEASURES FOR PAIN CONTROL

Many measures, other than administration of narcotics and other medications, are useful in pain control in terminally ill patients and are acceptable when palliation is the goal. These include chemotherapy, radiation therapy, and surgery. Other noninvasive methods for pain control include physical therapy, such as heat-cold application, massage, and immobilization, and relaxation therapies, such as hypnosis and biofeedback.

Chemotherapy

Chemotherapy can be an effective palliative treatment in controlling pain. If chemotherapy decreases the tumor size, the resulting diminished pressure on pain-sensitive tissue, such as nerves or the periosteum, can yield a noticeable decrease in total pain. Hormones may be used in the terminally ill patient, such as Tamoxifen for breast carcinoma, Provera for endometrial cancer, and diethylstilbestrol (DES) for prostate cancer.

Before administering chemotherapy, the issue of quality of life must be addressed and, with it, a discussion of the negative side effects of chemotherapy. These side effects should be weighed against the possible benefit of pain control. Chemotherapy can detract from the patient's ability to function in the last few months of life. It often causes nausea and vomiting that can sap a patient's strength and desire for living. Chemotherapy also causes several less-than-dignified side effects, including loss of hair. Certainly, the patient must be included in the decision-making process. For the majority of terminally ill patients, the side effects of active chemotherapy do not warrant its application.

If chemotherapy is administered, the initial goals for doing so must always be kept in mind, and discontinuation of the drugs should occur if these goals are not being met. Continuation of chemotherapy in the face of disease progression without other beneficial side effects only enhances morbidity and is not justifiable.

Radiation

Radiation therapy may be effective palliative therapy in some terminally ill patients. Effective palliation can sometimes be achieved in a single treatment, but usually several treatments over a period of 2–3 weeks are best. Radiation in terminally ill patients should not cause side effects, and the benefits should be carefully balanced against the price the patient and family have to pay in terms of the time and trouble involved.

The management of painful bone metastases is the most common reason for the use of radiation therapy. Bone metastases stem primarily from lung, breast, and prostate tumors. Seizures and headaches associated with brain metastases can be helped by radiation. Radiation should be preceded and augmented by dexamethasone therapy. Other possible palliative uses for radiation therapy include treatment of (1) moderate hematemesis from esophageal or gastric carcinoma, (2) hemorrhage from pelvic tumors, and (3) airway obstruction, chest pain, shortness of breath, and hemoptysis associated with lung cancer.

Surgery

Palliative surgery may also be appropriate therapy in some terminally ill patients. These conditions might include (1) diverting enterostomy for painful intestinal obstruction, (2) "toilet" mastectomy for advanced fungating breast masses, (3) bypass procedure for painful esophageal obstruction, (4) transhepatic catheter insertion for biliary colic and painful obstructive hepatomegaly, and (5) palliative neurosurgery via percutaneous procedures of rhizotomy, cordotomy, or stereotactic ablations.[21]

SUMMARY

Mark Twain is reported to have said, "No ship can outsail death. . . . When I seem to be dying, I don't want to be stimulated back to life. I want to be made comfortable to go."[22] Indeed, patients in pain will not be able to assist you in performing a nutritional assessment or in remembering to use intervention techniques that you may suggest for treating bothersome symptoms. On the other hand, patients in good pain control can answer questions with accuracy and will remember practical advice that they perceive is in their best interest. The following nutrition-related questions will help you assess important pain characteristics:

- Can you enjoy a meal without pain?
- Do you notice increased pain when you eat? After you eat?
- Does eating ever decrease your pain?
- Are you afraid to eat?
- Does pain limit your eating, drinking, and enjoyment of food?

It is important for dietitians and palliative care professionals to understand that pain is not only the presence of a negative physical sensation, it is also the absence of enjoyment. Therefore, in addition to controlling physical pain, it behooves us to try to create an enjoyable living environment for the patient and family. People, objects, activities, and places play an important role in how the patient perceives pain. Whether the patient is cared for at home, in a long-term care facility, or in an inpatient palliative care facility, the place of residence should have a warm, homelike, and cheerful atmosphere. Patients should be made to feel secure, their self-esteem should be maintained, and they should be granted as much personal control and sense of identity as possible. To achieve these goals, terminally ill patients should be encouraged to wear their own clothes, rather than institutional gowns. They should be allowed to surround themselves with personal possessions, administer their own medications if possible, participate in cooking, be given foods they like, and be entertained with pets, children, friends, television, music, and hobbies as they desire.

The ability to control chronic pain has been at the root of the reputation and success of the palliative care movement worldwide. Miracles or secret formulas are not required for success. Application of knowledge in the areas of pharmacology, psychology, and common-sense environmental management is the key to pain control.

NOTES

1. Mary Baines, "The Principles of Symptom Control," in *Hospice: The Living Idea*, ed. Dame Cicely Saunders, Dorothy H. Summers, and Neville Teller (London: Edward Arnold Ltd., 1981), 93.

2. Margo McCaffrey, *Nursing Management of the Patient with Pain* (Philadelphia: J. B. Lippincott Co., 1979), 10–21.

3. Nancy L. Bohnet, "Assessment of Pain," in *Nursing Care of the Terminally Ill*, ed. Madelon O'Rawe Amenta and Nancy L. Bohnet (Boston: Little, Brown & Co., 1986), 81–83.

4. Robert G. Twycross, "Relief of Pain," in *The Management of Terminal Disease*, ed. Cicely M. Saunders (Chicago: Year Book Medical Publishers, 1978), 66–92.

5. Arthur G. Lipman, "Pharmacological Needs of a Hospice Program" (Presentation at the First Annual American Conference on Hospice Care, Boston, 9 June 1985).

6. Gillian Ford, "Terminal Care in the National Health Service," in *The Management of Terminal Disease*, ed. Cicely M. Saunders (London: Edward Arnold Ltd., 1978), 169.

7. Lipman, "Pharmacological Needs of a Hospice Program."

8. Henry K. Beecher, "Pain in Men Wounded in Battle," *Annals of Surgery* 123 (1946): 96–105.

9. Henry K. Beecher, "Relationship of Significance of Wound to the Pain Experience," *Journal of the American Medical Association* 161 (1956): 1609-1613.

10. Ronald Melzack and Patrick Wall, *The Challenge of Pain* (New York: Basic Books, 1983), 221–239.

11. B. Anne West, "Understanding Endorphins: Our Natural Pain Relief System," *Nursing 81* 11 (February 1981): 50-53.

12. Russell R. Miller and Hershel Jick, "Clinical Effects of Meperidine in Hospitalized Medical Patients," *Journal of Clinical Pharmacology* 18 (1978): 180–189.

13. Jane Porter and Hershel Jick, "Addiction Rare in Patients Treated with Narcotics," *New England Journal of Medicine* 302, no. 2 (1980): 123.

14. Raymond W. Houde, "Systemic Analgesics and Related Drugs," in *Advances in Pain Research and Therapy* (vol. 2), ed. John J. Bonica and Vittorio Ventafridda (New York: Raven Press, 1979), 263–273.

15. Raymond W. Houde, "The Use and Misuse of Narcotics in the Treatment of Chronic Pain," in *Advances in Neurology* (vol. 4), ed. John J. Bonica (New York: Raven Press, 1974), 527–536.

16. Jerome H. Jaffe and William R. Martin, "Opioid Analgesics and Antagonists," in *Goodman and Gilman's The Pharmacological Basis of Therapeutics* (7th ed.), ed. Alfred Goodman Gilman, Louis S. Goodman, Theodore W. Rall, and Ferid Murad (New York: Macmillan Publishing Co., 1980), 491–531.

17. William T. Beaver, "Management of Cancer Pain with Parenteral Medication," *Journal of the American Medical Association* 244 (1980): 2653–2657.

18. Cicely M. Saunders and Mary Baines, *Living with Dying: The Management of Terminal Disease* (New York: Oxford University Press, 1983), 55–65.

19. Nancy L. Bohnet, "Management of Pain," in *Nursing Care of the Terminally Ill*, ed. Madelon O'Rawe Amenta and Nancy L. Bohnet, (Boston: Little, Brown & Co., 1986), 93–95.

20. Michael H. Levy, "Symptom Control Manual," in *Clinical Care of the Terminal Cancer Patient*, ed. Barrie R. Cassileth and Peter A. Cassileth (Philadelphia: Lea and Febiger, 1982), 223–230.

21. Ibid., 230–231, 233.

22. "Mark Twain," in *How Did They Die?*, ed. Norman Donaldson and Betty Donaldson (New York: St. Martins, 1980), 373.

SUGGESTED READINGS

Angell, Marcia. "The Quality of Mercy." *New England Journal of Medicine* 306, no. 2 (14 January 1982): 98–99.

Melzack, Ronald. "Current Concepts of Pain." In *Hospice: The Living Idea*, edited by Dame Cicely Saunders, Dorothy H. Summers, and Neville Teller, London: Edward Arnold Ltd., 1981, 76–92.

Ruch, Gerard A. "Endorphins: Pharmacologic and Physiologic Implications for Pain Control." In *Clinical Care of the Terminal Cancer Patient*, edited by Barrie R. Cassileth and Peter A. Cassileth, Philadelphia: Lea and Febiger, 1982, 91–107.

Chapter 11

Planning

THE PROBLEM LIST AND PLAN OF CARE

The data base from which is derived the assessment of the patient and the patient's family is assembled from the initial intake session, subsequent visits with the patient and family, and interdisciplinary team meetings during which the patient and family are discussed. After the information in the data base is assessed, a problem list is delineated and a palliative plan of care is developed.

The problem list focuses on factors that the patient, family, and palliative care team members identify as deterrents to achieving a comfortable and dignified death. Any team member can add an identified problem to the list. The list is continually updated, and as new problems are identified, the date of identification is recorded. When a problem is resolved, this date is also noted.

Labeling of problems is sometimes made difficult by the jargon used by different disciplines. For example, the same problem may be labeled in these ways:

- The physician may identify a problem as "dysphagia due to radiation therapy secondary to recurrent buccal cancer."
- The nurse's diagnosis may read "impaired swallowing and pain due to oral candida."
- The dietitian's assessment may show "mouth blindness and inability to chew and swallow solids only; no knowledge of food assistance programs available in the community."
- The social worker may describe the problem as "anger over inability to provide self-care; refuses to discuss potential aid from community resources."
- The patient may say, "Everything I eat tastes the same. It makes me mad that I can't get meat soft enough to swallow. A man can't live this way for long."

The goals and the appropriate palliative therapies that are planned to treat each problem are written in the plan of care. The care plan is individualized to the patient and family, negotiated with those affected, and modified as needed based on ongoing assessment and negotiation. As is the problem list, the plan of care is recorded in the patient's medical record and updated regularly.

The medical record of the terminally ill patient serves several functions. It serves as a channel of communication between members of the palliative care team, a tool for the team's recording and review of patient and family observations, the record of the plan developed and implemented, and an evaluation tool by which team members evaluate the achievement of palliative care.

Yet, the patient's medical record is even more; it is also a legal document and a record for certification, accreditation, and quality assurance review. As a means of documenting responses to palliative measures, the medical record serves as a research tool. Medical records become tools through which the efficacy of new techniques can be evaluated and subsequently recommended or not recommended for future practice.

The responsibility of the dietitian in updating the nutritional information in patients' medical records cannot be overemphasized. Generally, palliative care policies and procedures state that any contact (telephone call or visit in the home, nursing home, hospital, free-standing building, or day care center) with patients and their families must be summarized in the medical record within 48 hours.

The medical record in palliative care programs usually includes the following five sections:

1. data base and assessment form
2. problem list
3. care plan
4. progress notes
5. discharge summary

Specific forms assist the team members in recording pertinent information in the medical record. The data base and assessment form is usually completed by the palliative care nurse and includes such information as diagnosis and medical history, family situation and coping ability, physical examination, review of systems, and pain level. It is from this form that the dietitian can complete the patient summary and nutritional screening form shown in Chapter 7 (Exhibit 7-2).

A completed problem list and plan of care form for a 91-year-old female diagnosed with cancer of the stomach is shown in Exhibit 11-1.

Palliative care team members use progress notes to record their observations of the patient and the patient's family, document what care was rendered, and evaluate the care given along with the acceptance of the help offered. Progress notes can be written on flow sheets, but frequently are written on discipline-

Exhibit 11-1 Problem Sheet and Plan of Care Form

HOSPICE AT RIVERSIDE   PATIENT NAME _____ *Mrs. M.* _____   HAR _00087_

1. MEDICATIONS: 2. ALLERGY: _____ *NKDA* _____   3. SPECIAL NOTE: *Takes Meds with Apple sauce*

DATE	MEDICATION PRESCRIPTION	DOSE	RT	FREQ.	DATE	MEDICATION PRESCRIPTION	DOSE	RT	FREQ.
		CURRENT					CURRENT		
9-17-88	Pepto Bismol	1 tsp	po	prn					
9-17-88	Haldol *Titrate as needed*	0.25cc	po	q4 prn.					
9-17-88	Atropine *Terminal choking*	0.4 mg	IM	prn					
9-17-88	Carafate *Slurry*	1 gm	po	qid					

4. Equipment, supplies, treatments, diet:
1) Do not resuscitate
2) Skin care of choice
3) Enema of choice
4) Diet as tolerated
5) #16 F. 5cc Foley to straight drain, prn
6) Irrigate Foley with N/s prn
7) Equipment as needed

5. Disciplines Involved & Freq. Visits
[√] RN _3x/WK_   [√] VOL _prn_
[√] MD _prn_   [ ] PT _____
[ ] PSYCH _____   [ ] OT _____
[√] CHAP _prn_   [ ] HM/HHA _____
[√] SW _prn_   [√] OTHER _RD. prn_

6. PROBLEM	GOAL	PLAN	DISCIPLINE
Constipation - Impaction	Pt. will receive relief within 2 wks. of symptom identification.	Titrate meds as needed. Modify diet as needed. Use enema prn.	MD, RN / RD, RN / RN
Burning in esophagus	Pt. will achieve relief within 2 wks. of symptom identification.	Titrate meds within limits of Rx. Encourage pt. to prop up on pillow. Modify diet as needed.	MD, RN / RN / RD, RN
Cough	Pt. will achieve relief of symptom within 2 wks.	Encourage increased fluid intake. Use vaporizer. Use Haldol if gags.	MD, RN
Weakness; needs assist with ADL	Pt. will maintain safety and hygiene.	Instruct daughter on how to move and turn pt. safely.	MD, RN
Coping of pt. and daughter	Pt./dau. will maintain emotional integrity.	Assist dau. to augment 24 hr. care. Provide active listening and support.	RN / RN, SW

7.
_____ Director Patient Services   Date   _____ Staff Nurse   Date   _____ Social Worker/Counselor   Date

_____ Volunteer Coordinator   Date   _____ Medical Director   Date

I HEREBY APPROVE THE PLAN OF CARE.   _____ Attending Physician   Date

Source: Courtesy of Hospice at Riverside, Columbus, Ohio.

specific pages. However, flow sheets usually take less time to complete and are useful in documenting the ongoing status of the patient and the patient's family and their response to the intervention.

The dietitian has several options for recording information in progress notes. The SOAP format and the narrative format are most frequently used. The SOAP format is most appropriate for documenting the initial nutritional assessment and plan. In this format, the subjective (*S*) information about the patient and family is recorded first; the objective (*O*) data, observed by the dietitian, is recorded next, followed by the clinical assessment or analysis (*A*). The plan (*P*) of care, which completes the SOAP format, documents the stated outcomes and interventions to be implemented. In the interest of brevity, it may be more desirable to use SOAP on several problems at once instead of each problem separately. The narrative format is particularly helpful when a patient's status changes often, resulting in frequent modification of the care plan. Exhibit 11-2 is a completed example of a progress note on the same 91-year-old terminally ill patient, which shows the initial assessment and plan of care written by the dietitian.

During the planning phase of providing nutritional care to terminally ill patients and counseling their families, the dietitian has two major responsibilities: (1) to suggest nutritional techniques that will be helpful in symptom and pain control and (2) to anticipate the most likely problems and to guide the patient and the patient's family in making plans to prevent these problems from occurring.

TECHNIQUES FOR SYMPTOM CONTROL

When developing an individualized nutritional care plan for the patient and the patient's family that can appropriately and effectively meet their needs, keep these factors in mind:

- the patient's and family's ongoing capacity for caregiving: their knowledge, motivation for self-help, strengths, and limitations

- the results of the nutritional assessment

- the overall goals for patient and family care that were agreed upon by the patient, the patient's family, and the palliative care team

Incorporated into the nutritional care plan should be nutritional intervention techniques that have been proven helpful in overcoming symptoms commonly affecting terminally ill patients. Symptom control is an important goal because these patients have numerous symptoms that can be successfully alleviated with adjunctive nutritional therapy. A full chapter in this book is devoted to nutritional therapy in symptom control (Chapter 9). The suggestions that follow, for treatment of anorexia and cachexia, and those made in Chapter 9 are helpful in developing an individualized plan of care.

Exhibit 11-2 Progress Note Form

RIVERSIDE METHODIST HOSPITALS
Columbus, Ohio

HOSPICE AT RIVERSIDE

Contact Form

Patient Name: Mrs. M.   Date: 9/24/88

Type of Contact (home/telephone/hospital/etc.): Home

S: "How can I be impacted; I haven't eaten anything all week?"

O: Dx: 91-year-old thin female with inoperable metastatic stomach cancer, S/P partial
              gastrectomy
       Sx: (1) Constipation, impaction; no bowel movement x 7 days since enema
             (2) Burning in esophagus with reflux, following meals and when anxious
             (3) Cough; vomits occasionally secondary to gagging

A: (Sx1) Discussed causes of constipation and impaction with patient and daughter.
              Patient's diet history (provided by daughter) includes three small meals daily
              and an evening snack. Foods eaten daily include hot cereal, toast, egg, milk,
              fruit juices, small amounts of chicken and fish, small amounts of cooked
              vegetables, ice cream, sherbet, and tea. Patient's intake of fiber is low, and
              total fluid intake daily equals 500–1,000 ml. Encouraged patient to drink 1/2
              cup prune juice at breakfast and eat 1/4 cup applesauce at lunch and dinner to
              increase fiber. Encouraged patient to consume additional fluids daily, trying
              for 1,000–1,500 ml if possible. Showed daughter how to measure ml of liquids
              and calculate total ml consumed daily.
       (Sx2) Discussed causes of esophageal burning with patient and daughter. Patient
              notes increased burning with juices, but no effect of milk or tea. Patient drinks
              no alcohol. Encouraged patient to avoid acidic juices (orange, grapefruit,
              cider) and substitute with less acidic juices, milk, and dilute tea. Encouraged
              patient to sit up after every meal for 30 minutes and relax before and after
              meals.
       (Sx3) Discussed poor fluid intake as one cause of cough. Patient appears to have no
              thirst sensation, and daughter places fluids at bedside but does not encourage
              patient to drink. Encouraged patient to drink 1/4 cup fresh liquid every hour in
              addition to beverages at meals.

P: Phone patient and daughter regarding patient progress in 48 hours; left R.D. phone
       number if daughter has additional questions or plan of care needs modification prior
       to 48 hours. Visit prn. Suggest consideration of second enema and round-the-clock
       use of non-bulk-forming laxatives to treat constipation and minimize impaction.

Signature:

Title:

Anorexia and Cachexia

In 1985, the staff of *The American Journal of Hospice Care* conducted a telephone survey of 100 hospices across the country on the topic of nutrition. The major nutritional problem of patients identified by hospice teams was anorexia or loss of appetite (60 percent of patients).[1]

The survey revealed some additional interesting findings. Twelve percent of the programs did not force-feed patients but did allow "gradual dehydration" to occur in those patients who did not want to eat. Only in 10 percent of the programs surveyed was a dietitian assigned to each patient to be sure that the patient received some form of nutrition. Over half (53 percent) of the programs surveyed used some form of enteral feeding.

Cachexia, a hallmark of cancer malnutrition, is indicated by loss of body weight, lean muscle mass, and adipose tissue; glucose intolerance; and fluid-electrolyte imbalance. It occurs primarily with bronchogenic and gastrointestinal cancers but affects an average of 30 percent of all cancer patients when all types of malignancies are combined. Suggested causes include abnormal host metabolism of protein, carbohydrate, fat, hormones, fluids, and electrolytes; nitrogen trapping by the tumor; tumor elaboration of cachexia-inducing toxins; and debilitating effects of surgery, chemotherapy, and radiation therapy.

Cancer-related anorexia and cachexia are poorly understood phenomena. Any tumor in the gastrointestinal tract region appears to result in anorexia, which is caused by early satiety (especially with stomach and pancreatic tumors), specific food aversions (particularly to proteinaceous foods, such as beef and pork often with pancreatic cancer), nausea and vomiting (especially with liver cancer or metastases to the liver), and decreased interest in foods (particularly with any external tumor compression or partial obstruction of any part of the gastrointestinal tract). Although weight loss in the cancer patient is a worrisome sign, treatment does not necessarily improve the patient's well-being or survival.[2,3]

Establishing Goals of Treatment

Although anorexia and cachexia commonly occur with advanced cancer, they are not always problems to the patient and family. One task of the palliative care dietitian is to ascertain whether anorexia and cachexia are of significant concern to the patient and family. When anorexia and cachexia are problems it is important to identify whether the problem is the patient's, the family's, or both. Often anorexia and cachexia are more problematic for the family than the patient. One reason why cachexia is such a problem for patients and families is that they do not understand what causes it or how it occurs. Therefore, tell patients and their families that, contrary to the popular misconception, cancer does not cause loss of body weight by eating away body parts like a worm eats a leaf. Hearing this from the dietitian can help alleviate the fear that something ugly is happening inside the body.

The goal of the dietitian with the advanced cancer patient is to enhance the comfort and enjoyment of the patient whose food preferences and tolerances may be altered by the disease and its treatment. Treatment is best directed at ameliorating social consequences such as embarrassment of the patient at his or her gaunt appearance and physical complications. Answering the patient and family's concerns about diet and weight loss and treating the common symptoms of advanced disease are important parts of nutritional counseling.

If anorexia is due to correctable causes and the patient has a predicted life expectancy of several months, the correctable causes should be treated aggressively if desired by the patient. Likewise, treatment should be aggressive if the patient's anorexia appears to be an isolated symptom and the suspected consequence is malnutrition that could compromise both the quality and quantity of the patient's remaining days. Supplements, tube feedings, or total parenteral nutrition may be warranted.

On the other hand, if the patient is terminally ill (advanced tumor or late stage of disease) and life expectancy is measured in weeks or days, enteral and parenteral nutrition support is generally best avoided. Aggressive nutritional support techniques should be implemented only after the goals to be accomplished have been considered and the expected benefits and burdens have been analyzed.

The Patient Who Can and Wants To Eat

For patients who want to eat and who can be helped to eat better, the importance of improving appetite and enabling them to eat as normally as possible cannot be overestimated. In some patients, the loss of the ability to eat and to enjoy food is a major problem, and the resultant weight loss is devastating to both patient and family. Trying to improve patients' appetites with small portions of food that they like is important.

Medications can be administered to improve appetite and mood. Steroids, alcohol as an aperitif, tricyclic antidepressants (such as Sinequan and Elavil po at bedtime), Periactin (30 minutes po before meals), Thorazine, and megestrol acetate[4] stimulate appetite. Zinc has been proposed as a treatment for anorexia caused by hypogeusia after radiation treatment, although toxicity and gastric irritation may occur with large oral ingestion.[5,6] Niacin has also been proposed as a treatment for hypogeusia, primarily because pellagra has been associated with taste disorders.[7] Like zinc, large niacin intake can cause toxicity and gastric irritation.

Improving a poor self-image can also improve a patient's appetite. Good self-image can be enhanced in many patients by their wearing clean, well-fitting street clothes instead of bed clothes during the day. Regular appointments with a barber or hairdresser will make most patients feel better. Often, these professionals make home visits.[8]

A visit with the family dentist can help restore a patient's self-image. A dentist should be summoned when the patient has such mouth problems as sores, dryness, and taste changes, when dentures do not fit well, or when a toothache occurs. Dentists can also be found who will make home visits. Many dental treatments do not require office calls and are capable of being performed in the patient's home.[9]

The Patient Who Cannot or Will Not Eat

The dietitian, in working with an anxious family with a patient who cannot or will not eat, should attempt to diminish the effects of the no-win situation. Teaching the family about the effects that the disease and dying process have on eating is important. The family's anxieties can be diminished and the patient can be freed from the pressure to eat when you help the family shift attention from maintaining the patient's nutritional status to enhancing patient comfort through providing small appetizing meals. Sometimes it is most appropriate to offer the patient no food unless the patient requests it. Although this shift may be difficult at first for the family, it brings considerable relief to both patient and family in the long run.

Helpful phrases in discouraging the "he must eat or he will die" syndrome include the following:

- "When his illness is this far along, he doesn't use very much energy."
- "Just give him a little of what he wants."
- "His system is so sick, he can't digest much anyway."
- "Giving him only fluids will be fine."
- "It's okay if he doesn't meet his needs; he can't use food appropriately anyway."
- "Pushing him to eat will only make him more uncomfortable."
- "He's sick. Feed him if he wants food or will take it, but don't force him. He'll still be sick even if he eats."
- "He really doesn't want to eat. He can live a long time even if he eats or drinks only a little bit each day."
- "His illness controls his appetite. Don't trouble him with eating, but let him sit with you during meals and enjoy your company."
- "It's important to show him you love him in ways other than through food."
- "Try not to worry that he doesn't eat much. It's not a major problem and it doesn't seem to bother him."

If the dietitian convinces the patient's family not to push food, family members often shift their attention to other physical aspects of caring for the patient. For example, they may push medications by placing an undue emphasis on timing of medications and absolute pain control; frequently they insist on providing impeccable care for bed sores. By alleviating a feeding problem, a nursing problem may thus be created. Communication between the dietitian and nurse is critical so that plans can be made in anticipation of this situation.

Aggressive Nutritional Support through Oral Intake

When the dying patient is cared for in a nursing home, day care center, hospital, or free-standing palliative care facility, the institution's dietary department can be instrumental in stimulating the patient's appetite and oral food intake. The following ten suggestions should be considered:

1. Serve food attractively. Consider serving the patient's food on trays set with embroidered tray cloths and pretty china or stoneware, rather than on traditional paper underliners and dishes. Allow the patient's personal china and utensils from home to be used if feasible.
2. Consider serving foods from a hot trolley instead of or in addition to allowing patients to choose their meals in advance.[10]
3. Consider soup and soft sandwiches for midday meals. Soups are foods especially enjoyed by older people.
4. Provide supplemental foods, such as sandwiches, custards, puddings, ice cream, eggnog, and milkshakes, for those who prefer them at any time during the day or night.
5. Try to supply as much variety in food selection as possible, including regional favorites.
6. Provide lipped dishes for those patients who have arm and hand weakness. Use rubber grips on ordinary cutlery for those with a weak grip.
7. Have a separate kitchen area available, complete with utensils and equipment, for the patient and family to prepare favorite foods when desired.
8. Have a dining room available, with a home-like atmosphere, where the patients can eat and patients and families can eat together. Allow the family to eat with the patient in the patient's room if desired.
9. Have staff available to feed patients who are unable to feed themselves. Family members should be encouraged to feed patients if desired. Mealtimes should be as enjoyable as possible. Do not hurry patients to eat.
10. Liberalize diets as much as possible. Rarely are diabetic or low-sodium diets essential, but if they are, consider low simple sugar foods and no regular salt packets instead of more restricted diets.

When the terminally ill patient is able to take food orally, it has been the experience of the author that special nutritional supplements rarely offer much advantage over carefully prepared foods that the patient likes. Powdered instant breakfasts mixed with milk and homemade milkshakes are often preferred by patients to commercial liquid supplements. On the other hand, family members often appreciate medical nutritional products because they feel that they provide "something special" or "extra nourishment." Generally, commercial supplements are best used as additional sources of nutrition, rather than as meal replacements. Exceptions include the patient who receives nourishment via tube feedings and the patient who cannot prepare foods at home and for whom commercial products are more convenient.

Aggressive Nutritional Support through Tube Feedings

Enteral tube feedings are sometimes needed in terminally ill patients. Liquid commercial nutritional products are usually administered from a small-bore, flexible catheter that in most terminally ill patients is passed through the nose into the stomach or upper small intestine, or directly into the stomach through the abdominal wall. Most formulas are isotonic solutions. Depending on the patient's ability to tolerate the solution, feedings should be started with a continuous drip at half or full strength if isotonic solutions are used, or at quarter or half strength if hypertonic solutions are used. An appropriate beginning rate is usually 50 ml/hr. Within each 24- to 48-hour period, the infusion rate can be increased 25 ml/hr (up to a final rate of 100–125 ml/hr), or the concentration can be increased (quarter to half to three-quarter to full strength), depending on patient tolerance and nutritional goals. In theory, administration of 100–125 ml/hr of full-strength (1 kcal/ml) solution is the maximum amount needed if weight maintenance is the goal (2,400–3,000 kcal) for terminally ill patients. In practice, however, only 1,000–1,800 kcal/day (continuous drip for 10–15 hours) is generally needed to achieve satiety and comfort. Greater amounts frequently cause complications in terminally ill patients, including fluid overload, cramps, diarrhea, reflux, and aspiration. Raising the head of the patient's bed 30 degrees helps prevent reflux and aspiration. Unless commercially prefilled bags are used, formula should hang no longer than 4–6 hours and the tubing should be changed daily; commercially prefilled bags and tubing can be hung for 24 hours.

Many patients and families prefer intermittent tube feedings to continuous drip because that method seems more like a meal than drip delivery via pump. An additional advantage of intermittent feedings is the cost savings because a pump and extra tubing are not required. (When tube feeding is deemed essential to palliative care, the palliative care program must often bear the financial cost of the feeding, depending on the patient's third party payer coverage.) Regardless of the method of administration, the patient and family must be taught how to administer the feeding safely and how to handle the formula and tubing in a sanitary manner. The administration of tube feedings by the family in the home setting can be a source of satisfaction when it is performed properly, is appreciated by the patient, and is acknowledged by the palliative care team.

Aggressive Nutritional Support through Total Parenteral Nutrition

Total parenteral nutrition (TPN) is possible but difficult at best to administer in the home setting. Parenteral regimens generally should begin in the hospital, and home administration should be under the supervision and close monitoring of a home care TPN team. Disease-specific enteral and parenteral formulas are available for a variety of nutrition-related problems, such as renal failure, hepatic encephalopathy, and pulmonary disease, and they can be helpful to certain patients. Terminally ill patients with pulmonary disease for example, frequently experience less respiratory distress when Pulmocare, a commercially-prepared enteral medical nutritional product, is consumed as their sole source of nutrition or as a supplement to other food intake.

Careful consideration must be given when deciding to use parenteral feedings. Parenteral feedings rarely reduce the distress of anorexia and cachexia. Instead, they often seem to subject the patient to new problems that are more distressing and to prolong suffering that would not have been faced had parenteral feedings been foregone.[11]

ANTICIPATORY GUIDANCE

The nutritional care plan for a terminally ill patient and the patient's family should provide anticipatory guidance to them. When teaching them to manage the symptoms associated with dying, you anticipate those problems most likely to occur and guide them in making plans to handle them, thereby alleviating their fears of future problems. In addition, you need to reassure the patient and the patient's family of your availability at any time the need arises.

Information about diet and nutrition that is generally part of their anticipatory guidance includes the following:

- how the disease process and the process of dying can affect the patient's desire for food
- how changes in a patient's appetite and ability to eat can cause changes in food intake, bodily appearance, and bodily function
- specific dietary measures for symptom control
- relief measures that will be available as the patient's condition deteriorates
- the availability of community nutrition and food resources
- how to reach the dietitian when questions arise and nutritional assistance is needed

The usefulness of anticipatory guidance can easily be demonstrated by discussing two types of patients as examples. You can be of tremendous service to the terminally ill patient with cardiopulmonary disease by anticipating that the patient will at some point develop shortness of breath and the fear of choking to death on solid foods. Therefore, assure the patient that nutritious liquids can be consumed without causing him or her to choke or to experience increased shortness of breath.

For the patient with a sluggish colostomy and a belly full of growing tumor, you can provide assurance that there is no need to quit eating because the colostomy (or gastrostomy tube) fails to perform adequately and that, in fact, eating favorite foods can be enjoyed. Teach the patient to expect that mild vomiting may occur a few minutes or hours later but that the sensation will be similar to the normal feeling that comes with defecating.

In the past, it was thought that, if patients and their families were given anticipatory information, an increase in the incidence of symptoms would occur due to the "power of suggestion." However, such information has not been found to lead to the increased incidence of symptoms; rather, it has helped the patient and family make sense of the experiences that may occur. Such information empowers them to act rationally on present and future experiences. Patients state that having such knowledge contributes to a sense of control and security, which they appreciate.

OUTCOME CRITERIA

The nutritional care plan should include patient outcome statements that identify the performance standards the patient and the patient's family should meet. Examples of outcome criteria that might be appropriately written by the dietitian for patient and family follow. The patient and the patient's family should be able to

- describe the dietary measures that will help the patient alleviate [symptom] (such as nausea and vomiting)
- identify those foods that contribute to the patient's [symptom]
- verbalize their decision and rationale regarding whether to forego aggressive nutritional support if the question should arise (recognizing that this decision can change with a variety of situations)
- identify appropriate community and personal resources that can help the patient and the patient's family meet their food and nutritional needs

Identification of such criteria as these serves to focus the dietitian's efforts in patient-family counseling. When included in the medical record, these outcome criteria also serve as identifiable goals that other palliative care team members can help meet or reinforce. A dietary plan of care for a terminally ill patient residing in a nursing home has been written on a typical nursing home form (Exhibit 11-3) and includes patient and family outcome statements. The patient used in this example is a 69-year-old smoker with chronic obstructive pulmonary disease (COPD), shortness of breath (SOB), and organic brain syndrome (OBS).

EFFICACY OF DIETARY MODIFICATIONS

It is important for the dietitian to be realistic in developing a nutritional care plan. Strict dietary restrictions are rarely needed or appropriate with the terminally ill patient, unless specific foods or habits induce significant pain and symptoms that decrease patient comfort. For terminally ill congestive heart failure patients, for example, a severe sodium restriction is probably not only useless, but may decrease their quality of life, especially when their appetite is minimal and intake is poor.

Similarly, aggressive nutritional therapy is rarely needed or appropriate for terminally ill patients unless it will improve the quality of their lives without prolonging a painful end. Usually when aggressive nutritional therapy is implemented, the purpose is to reduce weakness or prolong life until after a meaningful event has occurred, such as the wedding or graduation of a family member or friend. If nutritional support is begun in an effort to reduce weakness, the feeding should generally be stopped in about 10 days if the weakness does not lessen. When the end of life appears near, only comfort measures need to be taken. Food and drink have little if any meaning to a patient who is near death, and therefore they should not be required.

UNORTHODOX NUTRITIONAL THERAPIES

Palliative care dietitians are often asked questions about unorthodox nutritional therapies or claims that have not undergone or withstood empirical scientific validation. Typical questions relate to the use of desiccated body parts, laetrile, or large doses of vitamin C or zinc, and the increased consumption of fruits and vegetables, particularly those containing vitamin A and beta-carotene. Out of ignorance, hope, and fear of abandonment, many people cling to nutritional claims that have no proven basis and in fact have often been disproven. It is hard for the medically unsophisticated, the undiscriminating, and the desperate to sort scientifically valid treatments from spurious ones. What does a dietitian say when a patient is taking 10 g of vitamin C daily in hopes that it will provide him or her added days of life?

The first goals of the dietitian are to understand the patient's point of view and then to acknowledge the patient's concern as real. After identifying the patient's

Exhibit 11-3 Dietary Plan of Care Example

DATE IDENTIFIED	CLIENT PROBLEMS	OUTCOME CRITERIA (GOALS, FREQUENCY)	INTERVENTION, ACTION PLAN	RESPONSIBLE PERSON OR DISCIPLINE
11-2-88	Shortness of breath due to chronic obstructive pulmonary disease.	Patient will eat greater than 75% of each of 3 meals a day without shortness of breath by 1-2-89.	1) Call physician to request diet change from regular to regular with pureed meats. 2) Serve patient food preferences; substitute if less than 75% of food is eaten each meal. 3) Instruct patient to relax prior to meals. 4) Instruct patient to eat slowly. 5) Consider Pulmocare® if intake is less than 75%.	Registered dietitian Dietary manager
11-2-88	Inability to feed self without assistance due to organic brain syndrome.	Patient will feed self 1 finger food each meal every day by 1-2-89.	1) Provide 1 finger food per meal. 2) Instruct nursing to encourage patient to hold food and serve self 1 bite of finger food after each sip of beverage. 3) Advance toward independence in feeding if possible.	Registered dietitian Dietary manager Nursing staff
11-2-88	Depression due to lack of family visitation and limited activities of daily living.	Patient will participate in 1 weekly activities function where food is served, and will self-serve 1 finger food during activity.	1) Ensure patient receives food preference at each activities function. 2) Encourage patient to self-feed the finger food. Praise patient for each success. 3) Encourage family to bring 1 food patient likes each visit and explain purpose in overcoming patient depression and improving self-help.	Registered dietitian Dietary manager Activities director Social worker

concerns, you must deal with the patient's ignorance, fear, or other less constructive feelings in a caring manner. It is very important to confirm that the patient will not be abandoned by the palliative care team. Be willing to discuss the treatment fully and to outline the pros and cons dispassionately and in a nonjudgmental way.

Although it may be appropriate to do so, there is no obligation on the part of the dietitian to dispel the last hopes of a patient, unless what is being practiced is harmful or unless the costs outweigh the benefits. Try to identify whether the unorthodox practice is producing a positive psychological effect. If so, then the cost-to-benefit ratio can be determined and a decision whether to discuss the practice with the patient can be made somewhat objectively. If the practice is producing harmful effects or not allowing positive experiences to happen, intervention may be warranted. In choosing whether to condone or disapprove the patient's practice, consider whether the end result of providing or sanctioning false hope is the erosion of time that could be better used to develop and enjoy relationships or a supportive and nurturing environment. Above all, your practice must be consistent with the Code of Ethics of the American Dietetic Association,[12] which states that under no circumstances should the dietitian provide untrue nutritional advice.

Not all so-called unorthodox therapies must be condemned. Given their sheer numbers, now and again one should statistically prove to be helpful. Therefore, keep up with the "unorthodox remedy of the day," but in so doing, heed Clark Glymour and Douglas Stalker's warning[13] that "while keeping our minds open, we should not let our brains fall out."

Finally, dietitians should discuss with patients and the patients' families any thoughts they may have that they caused the patient's terminal illness. These thoughts are wrong, and not to dispel them is to leave in place an inhumane weight of guilt that may be weighing on both the patient and the patient's family.[14,15] Sick people feel guilt for several reasons, some realistic, others fantasized. The dietitian's goal is to comfort them—any inducement of blame is inconsistent with this goal.

NOTES

1. Joseph Simonetti, "Nationwide Survey Conducted by American Journal of Hospice Care," *American Journal of Hospice Care* 2, no. 5 (September/October 1985): 12.

2. William D. DeWys and Thomas T. Kubota, "Enteral and Parenteral Nutrition in the Care of the Cancer Patient," *Journal of the American Medical Association* 246, no. 15 (9 October 1981): 1725–1727.

3. Daniel W. Nixon, David H. Lawson, and Michael Kutner, et al., "Hyperalimentation of the Cancer Patient with Protein-Calorie Undernutrition," *Cancer Research* 41 (1981): 2038–2045.

4. N. Simon Tchekmedyian, Nancy Tait, Mark Moody, and Joseph Aisner, "High-Dose Megestrol Acetate. A Possible Treatment for Cachexia," *Journal of the American Medical Association* 257 (1987): 1195–1198.

5. Robert I. Henkin, "Prevention and Treatment of Hypogeusia Due to Head and Neck Irradiation (Questions and Answers)," *Journal of the American Medical Association* 220, no. 6 (8 May 1972): 870–871.

6. Robert M. Russell, Michael E. Cox, and Noel Solomons, "Zinc and the Special Senses," *Annals of Internal Medicine* 99 (1983): 227–239.

7. R.F. Green, "Subclinical Pellagra and Idiopathic Hypogeusia (Letter)," *Journal of the American Medical Association* 218, no. 8 (22 November 1971): 1303.

8. Marion B. Dolan, "If Your Patient Wants to Die at Home," *Nursing '83*, 13, no. 4 (13 April 1983): 50–55.

9. Bennett D. Tucker, Jr., "The Hospice Patient—Dental Aspects: Indications, Contraindications, and Limitations," *American Journal of Hospice Care* 1, no. 3 (Summer 1984): 21.

10. Valerie Dornan, "Diet in Terminal Illness," *Nursing Mirror* 160, no. 8 (20 February 1985): 40.

11. J. Andrew Billings, *Outpatient Management of Advanced Cancer: Symptom Control, Support, and Hospice-in-the-Home* (Philadelphia: J. B. Lippincott Co., 1985), 68.

12. The American Dietetic Association, "Code of Ethics for the Profession of Dietetics," *Journal of the American Dietetic Association* 88, no. 12 (1988): 1592–1593.

13. Clark Glymour and Douglas Stalker, "Engineers, Cranks, Physicians, Magicians," *New England Journal of Medicine* 308, no. 16 (1983): 960–963.

14. O. Carl Simonton, "Unproven Methods of Cancer Management," *Ca-A Cancer Journal for Clinicians* 32 (1982): 58.

15. Barrie Cassileth, Edward J. Lusk, David S. Miller, Lorraine L. Brown, and Clifford Miller, "Psychosocial Correlates for Survival in Advanced Malignant Disease," *New England Journal of Medicine* 312, no. 24 (1985): 1551–1555.

Chapter 12

Ethical and Legal Considerations in the Nutritional Support of the Terminally Ill Patient

The ethical and legal issues that surround nutritional support of terminally ill patients are myriad. A position statement entitled "Issues in Feeding the Terminally Ill Adult," published in 1987 by The American Dietetic Association,[1] assists the dietitian in dealing with these issues. The concepts delineated in the position statement are useful in helping dietitians make right and good decisions—a fundamental task of all health care professionals. This chapter discusses in depth the ethical and legal issues surrounding nutritional support of terminally ill patients.

ETHICS

Ethics is a branch of philosophy that deals with moral actions or values. Ethical inquiry is concerned with questions of what is right, good, desirable, and worthy. Ethical questions present themselves as dilemmas, which are difficult problems that demand choices among several alternatives, none of which may appear to result in a satisfactory resolution.

The palliative care dietitian and interdisciplinary team experience dilemmas daily. What does the dietitian do when a terminally ill chronic renal failure patient refuses hemodialysis and wants to hasten death by eating a meal with high potassium foods? What does the dietitian recommend to family members of a dying patient about the Medicare hospice benefit when the patient is receiving expensive nutritional support not covered in the Medicare option? Would the dietitian's advice be different if placing the patient on the option could financially strap or literally bankrupt the palliative care program? Does the program's survival (for the purpose of providing service to many) ever supercede the needs of an individual patient?

Ethical questions that must be considered in feeding the terminally ill patient, and that are currently being debated with fervor on both sides are posed as follows:

- Is it ever permissible to permit a patient to die from lack of nourishment?
- Is it ever permissible to discontinue nutritional support with the intent to cause a patient's death?
- Is artificial feeding ethically different from artificial respiratory support?
- Is a nasogastric tube or an intravenous tube for feeding a "medical treatment," or is it obligatory palliative care?

The palliative care team and family caring for a terminally ill patient often must decide whether to continue, withhold, or terminate treatments. Such decisions are difficult at best. As difficult as it is, however, setting treatment limits in terminally ill patients is an obligation, not an option.

Feeding and hydration became ethical issues when advances in medical technology enabled us to provide food and fluid by means other than by bread and water. There is often a thin path between implementing treatments that are overzealous and not implementing treatments that could denote neglect. Neglect is often judged to occur by family members or others who are not involved in the patient's care when they do not understand that treatment would accomplish very little. On the other hand, the family and palliative care team may overzealously treat a patient because "doing everything" appears easier than denying treatment. Overzealous treatment often occurs when the patient's wishes are unknown or unable to be expressed, when family members disagree regarding what is appropriate, and when the team is threatened with a lawsuit if "everything is not done." Just as patient neglect is unthinkable, to do more than necessary because the technology is available is not medically sanctioned.

There are usually no right or wrong solutions to dilemmas. Ethical theories and reasoning do not solve ethical problems. Rather, they suggest ways of structuring and clarifying them. It is the responsibility of the persons involved or their surrogate decision makers to strive for ethically and legally "acceptable" solutions to dilemmas. Decisions must be made based on the achievement of specific, definable, and realistic goals.

BIOETHICAL PRINCIPLES IN MEDICINE

Bioethics simply means "the ethics of life." Medical ethics, often used interchangeably with bioethics, is the study of human values as they apply to the practice of medicine. According to Edwin H. Cassem[2] three medical ethics principles apply when making decisions about treatment and setting treatment limits in patients with a terminal illness.

1. Good must be done and evil avoided or first do no harm or palliate everything, exacerbate nothing.
2. Let the will of the patient, not the health of the patient, be the supreme law.
3. Stopping a treatment is ethically no different from never starting it.

The Hippocratic Oath or Normalfeasance

The first principle identifies the good that a physician and palliative care team should strive for—to restore health and relieve suffering. Ethical concerns arise when these two duties conflict, as when restoring health with available and appropriate treatments causes the patient increased suffering.[3] This first principle requires that the physician and palliative care team discuss with the patient and the patient's family those treatments that are available and their probable benefits, risks, and costs.

The code of ethics of the American Medical Association states that "[A] physician shall be dedicated to providing competent medical service with compassion and respect for human dignity."[4] The code does not specify a duty to prolong life, which suggests that the respect for human dignity is the primary obligation when it conflicts with prolonging life.

Autonomy

The second principle ensures that all competent patients over the age of 18 years have the right to accept or reject any or all medical treatments and medical recommendations after comparing their risks and benefits.[5,6] Moreover, the refusal of life-sustaining treatment is not suicide so long as the patient's death, when it occurs, results from an underlying disease or disorder that is not of the patient's own doing.[7-13]

Legally, a competent adult has the right to refuse medical treatment in most circumstances. The right of the patient to refuse treatment is supported by two important laws.

1. Ancient common law doctrine of battery (unauthorized touching) protects people from unwanted treatments or procedures whether they are life-saving, life-prolonging, curative, or not.
2. The first amendment to the Constitution of the United States guarantees the right of privacy. Legally competent and incompetent adults are guaranteed the right, within broad limits, to control their own destinies and to dispose of their own bodies in any way that they wish.

Both laws warn health care professionals against intrusive probing, either physically, mentally, or emotionally.

Despite these two laws, the patient does not always have the legal right of self-determination. The state may exert its power to limit the patient's right on the basis of four other concepts: (1) the state's interest in preservation of life, (2) the state's interest in prevention of suicide, (3) the state's interest in protecting innocent third parties, and (4) the state's interest in protecting the ethical integrity and professional discretion of medical professionals.

Cassem[14] notes the following four factors that may impair the patient's ability to choose competently:

1. intense pain and other physical symptoms that impair the patient's ability to make rational decisions
2. mental depression that may also impair the patient's ability to identify his or her true wishes
3. an emergency in which a patient cannot express his or her opinion
4. conditions, such as delirium, dementia, and/or coma, that render the patient incompetent

The presence of one or more of these conditions requires additional thought and decisions to be made by the palliative care team and family. For example, when there is intense pain or mental depression, the pain, symptoms, and depression should be treated aggressively and relieved before the patient's potentially irrational statements concerning the withholding or the implementation of treatment are carried out. In an emergency, the physician and team are obligated to act in accordance with the patient's best interests. When the patient is incompetent, the next of kin or designated other is obliged to judge what the patient would want done.

Most everyone knows the basic facts of the Karen Quinlan case. In this precedent-setting case of 1976, the Supreme Court of New Jersey held that it was legally acceptable to withdraw artificial life-support measures from a comatose patient who had suffered severe, irreversible brain damage and who could not reasonably be expected ever to return to a "cognitive, sapient state." The court gave Karen's adoptive father, Joseph Quinlan, the right to make the decision to terminate treatment based on the belief that he was choosing what the patient would choose for herself if she were able to formulate and express her choice.

Joseph Quinlan's decision to terminate treatment was not disputed by any major Western religion. In fact, in 1957, 20 years before the Quinlan case, Pope Pius XII declared that prolonging the dying process by extraordinary medical measures was not required. Extraordinary measures were defined as those that added excessive expense, pain, or other inconvenience or that, if used, would not offer a reasonable hope of benefit. The Pope recognized the complex psychosocial aspects of terminal illness when he observed that not only the needs of the patient but also the economic and emotional impact of prolonged dying upon the family and attending staff should be considered in such cases.[16,17]

Most states have enacted Natural Death Acts that authorize the use of "living wills." The living will is a statement made by a mentally competent adult of his or her wish to be allowed to die and not be kept alive by artificial means or heroic measures. It indicates that palliative treatment (or lack of heroic measures) does not constitute suicide. Such a signed document authorizes others to decide to terminate treatment should the adult at some future time be unable to decide. Living wills, although morally binding, are not valid in states without legislation authorizing their enforcement. By 1986, all states (with the exception of Kentucky, Massachusetts, Michigan, Minnesota, Nebraska, New Jersey, New York, North Dakota, Ohio, Pennsylvania, Rhode Island, and South Dakota) had declared "living wills" legally binding.

Only recently have living wills been applied to artificial feeding and hydration. Yet, as of 1986, the Natural Death Acts of 16 states explicitly exclude nourishment and hydration from care that may be withdrawn or withheld through a living will. These states are Arizona, Colorado, Connecticut, Florida, Georgia, Illinois, Iowa, Maine, Maryland, Missouri, New Hampshire, Oklahoma, Tennessee, Utah, Wisconsin, and Wyoming. Indiana requires provision only of "appropriate" nutrition and hydration.[18]

In states that have enacted Natural Death Acts, if living wills are not honored, persons giving unauthorized treatment could be charged with battery, and the caregiver could recover some compensation for the pain, suffering, and expense caused by the unauthorized treatment. Eleven states (including four that have no living will legislation—Massachusetts, Minnesota, New Jersey, and New York) have recognized, through court action, the right of patients to refuse treatment even if it is known to result in death.

Starting and Stopping Treatment Are Equivalent

The third principle looks ethically and legally, but not emotionally, at the act of stopping a treatment once it is implemented. Legally and ethically, the decisions to stop and start a treatment are equivalent. This means that if a treatment is beneficial to the patient, it is justified; if and when a treatment ceases to be beneficial, it ceases to be justified and should be discontinued. Emotionally, however, it is much harder to stop a treatment, especially if it means probable death, than it is to start it. In real-life situations, the patient's and family's emotions often prevent appropriate use of this principle.

Elements of an Ethical Decision-Making System

Dietitians and all health care professionals have a responsibility to make ethical decisions. An ethical decision-making system can help us refine or clarify values and issues and make reflective rather than emotionally reactive judgments. Because there is no such thing as a "unified ethical theory," differences in ethical opinions will necessarily exist.

Ethical analysis must be distinguished from professional codes of ethics. Codes of ethics are simply norms for professional behavior and are not designed to help the dietitian make ethical decisions. For example, the code of ethics of the American Dietetic Association[19] states that "The dietetic practitioner maintains the confidentiality of information." Yet, if a patient tells the dietitian a secret that has anything to do with a criminal act, the dietitian is legally bound to share it with the authorities.[20] If patients ask the dietitian to keep secrets, the dietitian must advise them about this requirement. The dietitian must also inform patients that if they say something that the dietitian deems necessary to share with the palliative care team for the good of the patient, the dietitian is legally and ethically bound to do so.

We act ethically when we have analyzed our decisions in light of our standards of "right" and "good." Ethical analysis engages the whole person in a process of self-reflection and critique of action. A code of ethics alone does not guarantee that ethical decisions will be made.[21]

Madalon O'Rawe Amenta identifies the following eight elements of an ethical decision-making system that individuals and palliative care teams should address when confronted with the need to make decisions about ethical issues:[22]

1. values
2. problem and facts
3. rights, obligations, and priorities
4. alternatives
5. consequences
6. available resources
7. shared decision making and community accountability
8. documentation

The more people who are involved in delineating the problem and choosing the solution, the safer the ground on which the decision rests. Discussing the decision with the patient, the patient's family, other caregivers, the physician, team members, ethics committees, and appropriate others is important. Being able to write out the decision comfortably in the patient's medical record is a good rule of thumb to support the safety of the decision. Several professional health care groups have made recommendations and suggested guidelines for nutritional support of terminally ill patients.[23–27] The suggested readings at the end of this chapter will help dietitians develop an ethical decision-making system.

ETHICAL ISSUES IN NUTRITIONAL SUPPORT OF TERMINALLY ILL PATIENTS

Today's dietitian is at the threshold of new developments on the ethical and legal issues of feeding the terminally ill patient. Before tackling these sensitive issues, it is useful to examine the history of the movement toward allowing refusal of food and drink by terminally ill patients.

Change through Consensus

In the United States, change is usually achieved through consensus first and laws second. We have within the past several years seen a public consensus against suicide, for informed consent, for "do not resuscitate" orders for persons who are diagnosed as brain dead, and for "living wills." Consensus has not yet been reached, however, on abortion, care for comatose or brain injured persons who are not terminally ill, and whether to withhold nutrition and fluid in any patient, especially those who are not terminally ill.[28]

Resuscitation is defined as "the ability to rescue people from the brink of death by restoring life-giving heartbeat and breathing."[29] It is a series of procedures aimed at restarting the heart beat and maintaining adequate circulation of oxygenated blood. Begun immediately after the occurrence of a cardiac or pulmonary arrest, resuscitation typically includes (1) cardiac massage, (2) chest compression, (3) electrocardiogram, (4) oxygen through endotracheal tube into the lungs, (5) intravenous line for medications and heart stimulation, (6) defibrillator and electrical shock, and (7) pacemaker.

Resuscitation was initially developed for healthy persons whose heartbeat and breathing had failed suddenly and unexpectedly due to such events as shock, asphyxiation, surgery, or near-drowning. It was not originally meant to be used on everyone with heart or respiratory arrest. Now, however, it is used for virtually anyone with cardiac or respiratory arrest when the procedure can be administered. Cardiopulmonary resuscitation is rarely successful in terminally ill patients.

"No code" and "do not resuscitate" mean that useless technology will not be used to keep the patient alive if the heart and/or lungs stop working. However, it does not automatically preclude other aggressive medical interventions, such as parenteral nutrition, unless specifically requested by the patient. "No code" and "do not resuscitate" orders can be revoked if the patient experiences a sudden and unexpected improvement in condition and desires to revoke the orders.

Patients with irreversible cessation of all functions of the brain are considered medically and legally dead. No further treatment is required when a patient has been diagnosed as brain dead in accordance with accepted medical standards.

However, comatose patients can recover. The judicial council of the American Medical Association in March 1986 ruled that it is not unethical for physicians to withhold all means of life-prolonging medical treatment, including food and water, from patients in irreversible comas, even if death is not imminent.[30] It is not believed that during the coma state the patient experiences pain of dehydration or hunger.

A patient in a persistent vegetative state has no hope for recovery because the neocortex of the brain is largely and irreversibly destroyed, although some brain-stem functions persist. A 6-week trial, using aggressive cardiopulmonary and nutritional support techniques, is a moral obligation after which the techniques can be ethically discontinued if no benefits accrue. It is believed that patients in the persistent vegetative state do not experience pain, including the pain of dehydration or hunger.

Consensus is reached in the United States through discussion and debate by the public and professional community. This debate is conducted in television and newspaper articles and public response, group meetings, public health and medical discussions, federal and state commission studies, and statements by professional societies, such as the American Medical Association, the Institute of Society, Ethics and the Life Sciences (Hastings-on-Hudson, New York), and the Society for the Study of Medical Ethics (London). Consensus is influenced by the direct involvement of patients and health care professionals in ethical and legal dilemmas. Health care professionals should be wary if legal consensus, based on a few cases, moves rapidly ahead of public consensus.

The question of whether to discontinue food and fluid to terminally ill patients emerged in the early 1980s. The question arose because we now have the technology to hydrate and maintain patients artificially for an indefinite period of time if necessary. In fact, nutritional support techniques are capable of keeping a patient physically alive much longer than a meaningful life can be maintained. Opinion, but not consensus, has swung in favor of discontinuing food and fluid in many cases. Several members of the lay public, as well as health care professionals and ethicists, have expressed the opinion that nutritional support should be viewed in the same manner as other medical technologies, such as respirators and dialysis, and the considerations of "death with dignity" and cost containment should be weighed in making the decision whether or not to feed.

According to the laws of most states, competent adults can choose before the fact whether they desire nutritional support should they become terminally ill and unable to choose for themselves. In addition, some states have laws that allow terminally ill patients, who have no chance for return to a life of meaning, to be removed from an artificial feeding system or not to be connected to one even though death from starvation or dehydration would ensue in the future.

Some groups of people are vulnerable to having nutritional support discontinued or not initiated unless their situations are given special consideration. These groups include (1) patients who are not terminally ill but who are unable to care for themselves, (2) patients who may be unable to indicate what they want, such as the elderly, mentally retarded, comatose, or senile patient, and (3) patients who have never told anyone else what they want should they not be able to decide for themselves at some future time.[31,32]

Mark Siegler and David L. Shiedermayer[33] state their fear that if legal opinions move ahead of public consensus on when withholding of food and fluid is allowable, a feeding conflict with "Grandpa Doe" (as happened in the abortion conflict with "Baby Doe") may emerge. A second fear is well expressed in their identification of "a dangerous alliance: death with dignity and cost containment." They lament that if nutritional support is discontinued for persons in the vulnerable categories noted above, it may then become financially advantageous to recognize not only a patient's "right to die" but also their "duty to die." This morally repugnant idea must certainly be guarded against.

Ordinary and Extraordinary Care

Terms, such as "ordinary" care and "extraordinary" care, are used in the care of terminally ill patients. Historically, ordinary care has meant a procedure or treatment that is simple, natural, common, and "human"-sized. Such procedures or treatments are tube feedings, antibiotics, and intravenous lines for hydration. Extraordinary care or "heroic" treatment, on the other hand, has traditionally meant the complicated, unnatural, infrequent, and "mechanical" or "artificial" procedures or treatments used to sustain life.

Whether a treatment is ordinary or extraordinary depends on the situation under review. For example, respirators may be ordinary to nurses on pulmonary units at acute care hospitals, but tube feedings may be extraordinary to laypersons. The New Jersey Supreme Court has ruled that there is no ethical, religious, legal, or medical distinction between a respirator and a feeding tube when they are considered as life-sustaining devices.[34]

In 1984 the National Hospice Organization reported the results of a survey on ordinary and extraordinary treatments conducted by its Ethics Committee.[35] Respondents identified these treatments as both ordinary and extraordinary—oxygen therapy, blood transfusions, antibiotics, nasogastric tube feedings, intravenous lines, nasogastric suctioning, radiation therapy, chemotherapy, and surgery. The only treatment consistently identified to be extraordinary and curative was hyperalimentation.

Frank J. Repka deplores the use of the words "ordinary" and "extraordinary," stating:

> [the] degree of nutritional support should be considered a continuum
> from supplemental voluntary food intake, through enteral nutrition by

tube, to total intravenous hyperalimentation. Interjecting considerations of ordinary versus extraordinary treatment on this continuum makes logical decisions on nutritional intervention difficult and diverts such considerations away from the central issue of proportionate benefit to the patient.[36]

Recently the terminology of whether a treatment is "ordinary" or "extraordinary" has changed to whether a treatment is a "benefit" or a "burden," or "proportionate" or "disproportionate." Such a change in terminology reflects an increased emphasis of the impact that the intervention has on the patient's total welfare as opposed to its physiological effect.

An example of benefit versus burden can be seen in the legal case of Mary Hier, a marginally conscious person who continually pulled out her gastrostomy enteral feeding tube.[37,38] In her case, the expected benefits (increased nutrient intake to correct malnutrition) were determined to be less than the potential burdens (surgical risk, diarrhea, and discomfort caused by the feeding apparatus). In another legal case, the Barber opinion asserts that

> Even if a proposed course of treatment might be extremely painful or intrusive, it would still be proportionate treatment if the prognosis was for complete cure or significant improvement in the patient's condition. On the other hand, a treatment course which is only minimally painful or intrusive may nonetheless be considered disproportionate to the potential benefits if the prognosis is virtually hopeless for any significant improvement in condition.[39]

Making decisions about patient care on the benefit versus burden basis argues in favor of the "humanity" of the patient, rather than of the "life" of the patient. This argument suggests that death may be the benefit, and a speedy and painless death may be in the best interest of the patient.

TO FEED OR NOT TO FEED

As with other methods of treatment, whether to feed or not to feed requires that the dietitian and palliative care team ask the following eight questions posed by Bernard Lo and Albert R. Jonsen:[40]

1. Is the purpose of the proposed treatment palliative or curative?
2. Will the treatment achieve remission or a satisfactory period of "quality time"?

3. Will the discomfort and cost justify the benefits of the treatment?
4. Is the patient competent and the decision a product of clear and uncomplicated informed consent?
5. If not, is an advance directive from the patient available or the substituted judgment valid?
6. Will the proposed course of action harm others?
7. Are there legal considerations that might make caregivers or surrogate decision makers liable for manslaughter, negligence, or other charges?
8. What are the opinions and needs of the family?

Substituted judgment permits another person (a surrogate or guardian) to make choices for the patient when the patient is unable to make choices. Substituted judgment cases include (1) those in which the patient's specific wishes are known and are stated by a substitute and (2) those in which the patient's specific wishes are not known, but a family member, presumed to be a reliable spokesperson for the patient, is requested to make the decision on the patient's behalf. It becomes the responsibility of the appointed person to make the decision as he or she thinks the patient would have made it, regardless of what that person or others believe is in the patient's best interest.

Durable power of attorney, initiated by a competent adult, provides the adult with the opportunity to designate one or more agents to make decisions on his or her behalf in the event of subsequent incapacity. Durable power of attorney is effective everywhere in the United States, except in the District of Columbia. It may be revoked by the initiator at any time.

"What good will it accomplish for the patient?" is the underlying question that must be answered. Exploring the question with the patient and the patient's family while the patient is competent to express personal wishes is in the patient's best interest and of utmost help to the family and palliative care team.

Too often, questions regarding whether to feed the terminally ill patient via the enteral or parenteral route arise after the patient loses consciousness or becomes comatose. It then falls to the palliative care team and the patient's family to decide whether feeding the patient will result in increased benefit or increased suffering. The team must assure the patient's family that only the best is wanted for the patient. If the team feels that it is best not to feed the patient artificially, a phrase such as "I am opposed to tube feeding or force-feeding him because it will probably cause him only more suffering" is a sympathetic and direct way to communicate the team's recommendation to the family.

Joanne Lynn and James F. Childress list the following three conditions when nutritional support might result in disproportionate burden to the patient: (1) when nutritional support would be a futile treatment, (2) when no possibility of benefit could occur with nutritional support, and (3) when the burden outweighs the benefit.[41]

In working with patients and families who may consider the use of aggressive nutritional support, the dietitian's role is to

1. listen carefully to the patient and family
2. clarify options
3. provide pros and cons of aggressive nutritional support
4. support the patient-family choice
5. encourage deliberative palliative care team decisions that are consistent with patient and family wishes

When Force-Feeding Constitutes a Burden

There are instances when forcing nutrition and fluids via tube feedings, total parenteral nutrition, or simple intravenous solutions of normal saline or dextrose and water constitutes a burden to terminally ill patients. Five most important reasons not to force-feed via tube feedings are identified in Exhibit 12-1.[42,43]

Tube feeding of elderly individuals who are in the terminal stage of a progressive, neurological disease is often associated with aspiration and subsequent development of pneumonia. I. Campbell-Taylor and R. H. Fisher[44] therefore advise against tube feeding patients with amyotrophic lateral sclerosis (ALS), Alzheimer's disease, Huntington's chorea, multi-infarct states, multiple sclerosis, other dementias, or Parkinson's disease; those who are noncommunicative or recumbent most of the time; and those who have aspirated liquids and pureed foods. Reasons against force-feeding via total parenteral nutrition and intravenous lines are identified in Exhibit 12-2.[45-48]

Exhibit 12-1 Potential Physical Burdens of Enteral Nutritional Support in Terminally Ill Patients

1. Nasogastric tubes are irritating to most patients, outright painful to many, and always painful upon insertion.
2. Nasogastric feedings cause uncomfortable distension, nausea, diarrhea, dehydration, and hyperosmolality in many patients.
3. A gastrostomy or jejunostomy tube requires surgery, although it might result in increased comfort compared to use of nasogastric tubes.
4. Vomiting, aspiration, and subsequent pneumonia commonly occur in terminally ill patients fed via nasogastric tubes or gastric tubes. These problems are most common when the patient is recumbent and noncommunicative and has reduced oral and hypopharyngeal sensation, dysphagia, reduced competence of upper and lower esophageal sphincters, reduced esophageal peristalsis, delayed gastric emptying, and reflux exacerbated by a supine position.
5. Excess stomal leakage and wound dehiscence with enterostomy feedings occur, especially if the abdominal tumor is large and exerts pressure on the tube in the stomach or jejunum.

Exhibit 12-2 Potential Physical Burdens of Parenteral Nutritional Support in Terminally Ill Patients

1. Intravenous fluids can be distressful and painful, especially in patients with scarred and collapsed veins.
2. Patients' activities are usually restricted with parenteral feedings because they are tethered to the infusion apparatus.
3. Sepsis frequently occurs in malnourished patients receiving total parenteral nutrition (TPN) and is an unnecessary and uncomfortable complication.
4. Fluid overload, ascites, peripheral edema, pulmonary edema, and pressure symptoms from edematous masses can occur with TPN and intravenous (IV) solutions.
5. The cost of TPN can be excessive for family and palliative care programs.
6. TPN might exacerbate the patient's disease.
7. Thrombosis is a potential result of TPN and IV solutions used in terminally ill patients.
8. Lung puncture is an unnecessary risk of TPN in terminally ill patients.
9. Increased urine flow with TPN and IV fluids may cause the need for catheterization in those patients too weak to void large volumes.
10. Increased gastrointestinal secretions may require nasogastric suctioning.
11. Increased pulmonary secretions may require suctioning.
12. Death rattle with accumulating pharyngeal secretions is more likely to occur with increased fluid.

To the physical burdens of enteral feedings (Exhibit 12-1) and parenteral feedings (Exhibit 12-2), can be added other burdens. Use of either type of artificial feeding tends to divert attention from the care and support of the patient as a human to the view of the patient as a fluid and electrolyte balance case.[49] The risks of prolongation of suffering and a focus on technological rather than human needs cannot be overemphasized.

Before tube feedings or TPN can safely be recommended for home care, capable family members must be available and willing to administer and monitor the formula or solution. One liter tube feeding or intravenous fluid daily is less likely to cause problems than 2 or 3 liters of fluids daily. According to Ann G. Blues and Joyce V. Zerwekh, home intravenous lines are managed easiest with a heparin lock with fluid running for 6–8 hours. A Hickman line is the most reliable to maintain. Private duty nursing coverage should be recommended, and many insurance companies will pay for this level of skilled care.[50]

When Force-Feeding Constitutes a Benefit

When considering whether to feed aggressively the terminally ill patient, the questions, "What benefits can accrue?" and "Would lack of feeding harm the patient?," should be asked.[51] Indeed, lack of nutritional support may harm some patients, and nutritional support does have potential benefits in some terminally ill patients. Some potential benefits of tube feedings, TPN, and IV lines are identified in Exhibit 12-3.

Exhibit 12-3 Potential Benefits of Enteral and Parenteral Feedings in Terminally Ill Patients

- Correcting fluid and electrolyte imbalance may
  1. increase mental alertness
  2. decrease nausea
  3. stabilize cardiac arrhythmias
- Added calories and other nutrients may prolong life, giving the patient and family more time to get their psychosocial and material affairs in order.
- Aggressive nutritional support may
  1. add to the patient's and family's confidence that "everything is being done" to decrease cachexia and to help the patient live as long as possible
  2. provide emotional support to the patient and family by reducing their fear of abandonment
  3. improve the patient's overall sense of well-being; cosmetic benefits may improve self-esteem
  4. improve patient and family interrelationships
- Nutritional therapy is obligatory if it alleviates discomfort from malnutrition.[52]

Improvement in the quality of life is often mentioned as a benefit of nutritional support. "Quality of life" is a concept that eludes a precise definition. It can only be described and measured in individual terms and depends on the patient's present life-style, past experiences, hope for the future, dreams, and ambitions.[53] Quality of life for the terminally ill patient is measured according to the dimensions of self-perceptions of general well-being and feelings of discomfort. Perceptions of well-being relate primarily to independence in self-care, desire for food, and the patient's overall assessment of his or her condition. Discomfort is evaluated in large part by pain and difficulty in sleeping.

Measurement of quality of life is difficult. If it is based on nutritional parameters, such as weight gain of lean body mass or reversal of negative nitrogen balance, we will have great difficulty accomplishing it in the terminally ill cancer patient. Indeed, although nutritional support may have positive effects on the outcome of patients receiving curative cancer therapy, it cannot change the destiny of the terminally ill patient.

Dehydration

Dehydration, as a natural course of events, may be preferred to aggressive nutritional support if feeding causes discomfort. Reductions in gastrointestinal fluid, vomiting, edema and tumor pressure, need to void, pulmonary secretions resulting in less coughing, fear of choking and drowning, and rattling secretions may be achieved by foregoing aggressive therapy. The technological problem of safely keeping a gastrointestinal or intravenous line open and running is also avoided.

Is dehydration painful? Conscious people with dehydration indicate it is uncomfortable, and unlike the sense of hunger, uncomfortableness associated with dehydration does not disappear with narcotics. Dehydration has been called a natural anesthesia for terminally ill patients, however, because it appears to decrease the patient's perception of suffering by reducing the level of consciousness. The concomitant dry mouth effect associated with dehydration can be relieved through ice chips and lubricants and other simple suggestions (see Chapter 9).

For some patients the procedures required in order to avert malnutrition and dehydration are so onerous that the benefits are inconsequential or meaningless. Is not to intervene acceptable, or is it murder? The choice lies in doing what is in the patient's best interests after due consideration by the patient, the patient's family, and competent health care professionals.[54]

According to Joanne Lynn and Marian Osterweiss, most terminally ill patients rarely find any advantage to aggressive nutritional support via artificial means.[55]

Inpatient and home care palliative care programs usually do not use aggressive nutritional support (enteral or parenteral feedings) in treating terminally ill patients. Instead, terminally ill anorectic patients are allowed to eat and drink as desired and are not pushed to do so if they are unable or do not desire to achieve adequate calories for weight maintenance. A previously placed tube for enteral feedings or an intravenous line for TPN is usually not discontinued, however, unless the patient desires it. Yet, even though the feeding tube may be in place, there is no moral reason for using the tube for feeding.[56-58]

When Feeding Is Important: Food as a Symbol

The symbolism of food and feeding is well summarized in the following quote by Daniel Callahan:

> Feeding of the hungry is the most fundamental of all human relationships.
> It is the perfect symbol of the fact that human life is inescapably social
> and communal—it is a most dangerous business to tamper with or
> adulterate so enduring and central a moral emotion.[59]

The act of serving food to a patient, regardless of setting, carries a highly symbolic value. It characterizes the social and community values of "being thy brother's keeper." Bringing a tray to the patient's bedside symbolizes the health care teams' continued care for the patient and, by so doing, provides emotional support for the family. Food also carries with it religious, cultural, and ethnic values that have meaning to patients, families, and health care professionals.

In point of law, the basic duty to provide patients with ordinary food and fluid was made by a New Jersey trial judge in the Claire Conroy case.[60] Mrs. Conroy was an elderly, incompetent, semiconscious woman living in a nursing home who suffered many debilitating diseases, including organic brain syndrome, diabetes mellitus, painful bedsores, and malnutrition. Her nephew petitioned the court to have her nasogastric feeding tube removed. Removal of the tube was allowed, but the court ruled that food and fluids could not be removed if the patient could take them herself or with manual assistance by others. Thus, the court ruled that a distinction existed between providing nourishment as food taken orally and nourishment given artificially (tube or intravenous). The judge ruled that providing food to be taken orally is a basic duty, whereas providing nourishment artificially is considered in the same category as life-sustaining intervention, such as resuscitation, respirators, and dialysis.

The provision of food and fluid has traditionally been viewed as an obligation of health care institutions. These rationales are often provided for not discontinuing medical feeding and hydration:[61-65]

- the obligation to provide "ordinary" care
- the obligation to continue treatment once started
- the obligation to prevent starvation or dehydration from being the unambiguous cause of death
- the obligation to provide symbolically significant treatment
- the obligation to maintain trust between doctor–patient and institution–patient that the patient will receive any and all treatments essential to maintain life

None of these obligations, however, dictates that artificial nutrition and hydration must always be provided. In fact, if nutritional support is used to prolong life, then it must, above all, do no harm. Similarly, even though it seems wrong and outrageous not to provide food and water and thereby to allow a person to die, it is equally wrong and outrageous to argue that to feed or hydrate a person is required on grounds of sentiment and romanticism.

Rebecca Dresser and Eugene Boisaubin[66] identify four conditions that must be met before the decision is made to withdraw nutritional support:

1. Nutritional support should be withdrawn only in the presence of the highest degree of medical certainty that the incompetent patient's condition will not improve to any notable extent. (The issue of whether and how the unconscious patient perceives various approaches to nutritional support needs to be addressed. Physicians assume that comatose patients have no awareness, an assumption that is impossible to prove or disprove at this time. These

patients are presumed to be unable to perceive the sensations of hunger and thirst because they do not respond to deep pain. Additionally, patients who recover from a coma usually have no memory of the experience. If future studies were to suggest the presence of awareness even in deep coma, the reassessment of nutritional support techniques and other support approaches would be required.)

2. A decision to terminate nutritional support should in no way constitute a choice to abandon all care of the patient.
3. If medical evidence suggests that discontinuing nutrition would produce increased pain or discomfort, the patient should be fed.
4. Care must be taken to ensure that the decision is in the patient's best interest.

Mark Siegler and Alan Weisbard provide several compelling reasons why health care professionals might want to move very slowly in arguing for a policy to allow withdrawal of food, fluid, and nutritional support from ill patients:[67,68]

- From the perspective of the patient, health care professionals should argue that they need to protect patients who are highly vulnerable, such as those who are unable to articulate their desires and needs. To feed them may protect them against inadequate treatment and unscrupulous care.

- From the perspective of the physician and others who make clinical judgments, discontinuing food and fluid may force these professionals to make decisions against their own moral standards. To discontinue nutritional support may be felt, especially by nurses, to break the bond between the professional and the patient, thereby exposing them to malpractice suits.

- Also from the perspective of health professionals, to reject the discontinuation of nutritional support may increase the credibility of health care professionals in the eyes of the public. Health care professionals want to be viewed as caring and nurturing servants of humanity. To support the discontinuation of nutritional support could tarnish that reputation if the public viewed the professional to be concerned solely for money rather than the humane treatment of dying patients.

- From the perspective of society, any rapid move to take away the rights of those who are incapable of deciding for themselves should be rejected. Society should not disregard the needs of the mentally retarded, the elderly, the senile, and others.

The Dietitian's Responsibility When the Patient Discusses Suicide or Requests Help To Accelerate Death

Suicide itself is not a crime in most states in the United States. Penalties against the person who committed suicide are rare and are usually limited to the inability of beneficiaries to collect life insurance if the suicide occurs shortly after a policy was purchased.[69] However, it is usually a criminal act to assist in a suicide, and the dietitian may at times be faced with a suicidal patient.[70]

If the dietitian identifies through verbal or nonverbal clues that the patient is considering suicide, the question, "Has it been so bad that you have wanted to kill yourself?" will nearly always be answered honestly.[71] It is imperative that you tell the patient's primary care nurse or physician and document both the patient's statements and your actions in the patient's medical record as soon as possible. If you have any suspicion that a patient's death may be due to medication overdose, you have the legal obligation in most states to report the suspicion.[72]

The author was once asked by a terminally ill chronic renal failure patient, who had discontinued hemodialysis, to help accelerate her death. The conversation went something like this.

> Patient: "I would like you to help me die as soon as possible."
>
> Dietitian: "How?"
>
> Patient: "By identifying foods high in potassium I can eat for my last meal; then I'll have a heart attack and die quickly."
>
> Dietitian: "What does your family think about your idea?"
>
> Patient: "They don't know about it and probably wouldn't like it, but I really don't care what they think."
>
> Dietitian: "I'm sorry you don't want to tell your family about your desire to hasten your death."
>
> Patient: "Why should I? They'd just object, but I'm going to die anyway."
>
> Dietitian: "I'm able as a health professional to recommend foods, or lack of foods, for comfort, but I cannot recommend foods to help hasten your death. Society and the law do not allow me to kill, even out of motives of mercy. Our team's psychologist would be a good person for you to talk to. May I ask her to give you a call?"

As might be suspected, the patient knew what foods were high in potassium before she asked the question. The question was prompted more by her need to talk, to tell her story, and to be listened to than her need to learn about food composition. An astute dietitian would recognize this motivation and would take the time to listen to the patient. However, a first reaction may be to think only of the legal ramifications of the question and the dietitian's responsibilities in the situation.

It is important to remember that illness is bigger than people, and it cannot be wished away. Instead, it must be dealt with, even when doing so requires making uncomfortable decisions. Documentation in the patient's medical record of what happened, what was discussed, and the patient's response is most important. Honesty in medical record reporting is paramount.

SUMMARY

Dietitians have a professional responsibility to uphold ethical principles in planning and delivering nutritional care to terminally ill patients and their families. Several authors have provided helpful recommendations in fulfilling this responsibility.[73,74] Becoming familiar with the basic ethical and legal principles underlying the patient–health professional relationship presented in this chapter is essential. Clarifying personal values related to feeding issues is also of paramount importance because you will inevitably face situations wherein the patient's and your values conflict.

When your ethical beliefs or sense of professional responsibility is in conflict with the wishes of the patient, the patient's family, or the palliative care team, you have several options. After defining and exploring the ethical dilemma and discussing the problem with others, including the program's ethics committee and legal counsel, you can either continue on the case by accepting a different solution to the dilemma or can withdraw from it. If you decide to withdraw from the case, it is incumbent upon you to ensure that the patient will not be abandoned by making arrangements for continuous care by another dietitian. Above all, you must place the interests of the patient above all personal considerations.

Obtaining liability insurance is a wise idea for the dietitian working with terminally ill patients. Choosing an insurance company that is knowledgeable of the responsibilities of the dietitian is important. The liability coverage provided for professionals by the palliative care program should also be known.[75]

Dietitians who work frequently with terminally ill, malnourished, incompetent, or unconscious patients and their families can be of significant assistance to colleagues and the palliative care team by formalizing standards of care and establishing policies and procedures to guide decision making for nutritional care of these patients. Working with the ethics committee of an institution will provide the dietitian with a depth of knowledge that is needed in developing policies and procedures, in defining the goals and appropriate strategies for nutritional intervention, and in clarifying the use of nutritional support in terminal illness.

Despite the current revolution in financing and delivery systems of health care, the ultimate goal of health care remains the same: to benefit as many as possible in the best way and most cost effective way possible. As health care professionals know, it is easier said than done.

> Gazing into the sunken, hollow eyes of a cachectic patient dying of cancer and into the hopeful eyes of his loved ones makes it very obvious that it appears to be easier to write definitive statements and to agree with them in principle than it is to apply them at the bedside.[76]

As health care professionals, dietitians must support those changes that enhance public good and oppose those that decrease it.

NOTES

1. American Dietetic Association, "Position of The American Dietetic Association: Issues in Feeding the Terminally Ill Adult," *Journal of the American Dietetic Association* 87 (1987): 78–85.

2. Edwin H. Cassem, "Appropriate Treatment Limits in Advanced Cancer," in *Outpatient Management of Advanced Cancer: Symptom Control, Support, and Hospice-in-the-Home*, ed. J. Andrew Billings (Philadelphia: J. B. Lippincott Co., 1985), 139–151.

3. Eliot Slater, "New Horizons in Medical Ethics. Wanted—A New Approach," *British Medical Journal* 1 (1973): 285–286.

4. American Medical Association, "Principles of Medical Ethics," in *Contemporary Issues in Bioethics*, ed. Tom L. Beauchamp and Leroy Walters (Belmont, Ca.: Wadsworth Publishing Co., 1982), 122.

5. Schloendorff v. New York Hospital 105 NE 92, 93, (1914).

6. Bernard Lo and Albert R. Jonsen, "Ethical Decisions in the Care of the Patient Terminally Ill with Metastatic Cancer," *Annals of Internal Medicine* 92 (1980): 107–111.

7. In re Quinlan, 355 A2d 647 (NJ 1976).

8. John F. Kennedy Memorial Hospital v. Bludworth, 452 So2d 921 (FL 1984).

9. Tune v. Walter Reed Army Medical Hospital, 602 F Supp 1452 (DC 1985).

10. In re Conroy, 486 A2d 1209 (NJ 1985).

11. In re Colyer, 660 P2d 738 (1983).

12. Application of Lydia E. Hall Hospital, 455 NYS2d 706 (Sup Ct Nassau Co 1983).

13. Lane v. Candura, 376 NE2d 1232 (MA App 1978).

14. Cassem, "Appropriate Treatment Limits in Advanced Cancer," 140–141.

15. In the Matter of Karen Quinlan, an Alleged Incompetent, 70 N.J. 10 at 41.

16. Pius XII, Pope, "Papal Allocution to a Congress of Anesthetists," *Acta Apostolicae Sedia* 45 (1957): 1027-1033.

17. R. Raible, "The Right to Refuse Treatment and Natural Death Legislation" *Medicolegal News* 5 (Fall 1977): 6–7.

18. Barbara Mishkin, "Withholding and Withdrawing Nutritional Support: Advance Planning for Hard Choices," *Nutrition in Clinical Practice* 1, no. 1 (February 1986): 50–52.

19. American Dietetic Association, "Code of Ethics for the Profession of Dietetics," *Journal of the American Dietetic Association* 88, no. 12 (1988): 1592.

20. *Practices* (Springhouse, Pa.: Nursing '84 Books, 1984), 14.

21. David C. Thomasma, "Human Values and Ethics: Professional Responsibility," *Journal of the American Dietetic Association* 75 (1979): 533–536.

22. Madalon O'Rawe Amenta, "Ethical and Legal Considerations," in *Nursing Care of the Terminally Ill*, ed. Madalon O'Rawe Amenta and Nancy L. Bohnet (Boston, Mass.: Little, Brown & Co., 1986), 310–312.

23. The Hastings Center, *Guidelines on the Termination of Life-Sustaining Treatment and the Care of the Dying* (Bloomington & Indianapolis, Ind.: Indiana University Press, 1987), 18–34, 57–62, 158.

24. ASPEN Board of Directors, "Guidelines for Use of Total Parenteral Nutrition in the Hospitalized Adult Patient," *Journal of Parenteral and Enteral Nutrition* 10 (1986): 441–445.

25. Kevin O'Rourke, "The AMA Statement on Tube Feeding: An Ethical Analysis," *America*, 22 November 1986, 321–322, 331.

26. John J. Paris and Richard A. McCormick, "The Catholic Tradition on the Use of Nutrition and

Fluids," *America*, 2 May 1987, 356–361.

27."U.S. Neurologists on Food and Water to PVCs" (Columbus, Ohio: Association for Freedom to Die, 1988), 1.

28. Mark Siegler and David L. Shiedermayer, "Should Fluid and Nutritional Support be Withheld from Terminally Ill Patients?," *American Journal of Hospice Care* 4, no. 2 (March/April 1987): 32–35.

29. President's Commission for the Study of Ethical Problems in Medicine and Biomedical and Behavioral Research, *Deciding to Forego Life-Sustaining Treatment* (Washington, D.C.: United States Government Printing Office, 1983), 231.

30. Claudia Wallis, "To Feed or Not to Feed?," *Time*, 31 March 1986, 60.

31. Mark Siegler and Alan J. Weisbard, "Against the Emerging Stream: Should Fluids and Nutritional Support be Discontinued?," *Archives of Internal Medicine* 145 (1985): 129–131.

32. Daniel Callahan, "On Feeding the Dying," *Hastings Center Report* 13 (1983): 20–22.

33. Siegler and Shiedermayer, "Should Fluid and Nutritional Support be Withheld," 32–35.

34. R. Sullivan, "Right to Die Rule in Terminal Cases Widened in New Jersey," *The New York Times*, 18 January 1985, 1–9.

35. Barbara Mishkin and J. Arras, "Ethical Perspectives for Hospice Care-Givers" (Paper delivered at the Annual Meeting and Symposium of the National Hospice Organization, Hartford, Conn., 11 November 1984).

36. Frank J. Repka, "Ethical Considerations in Nutritional Support of Cancer Patients," *Topics in Clinical Nutrition* 1 (1986): 51.

37. In Re Hier, 464 NE2d 959 (1984).

38. President's Commission, *Deciding to Forego Life-Sustaining Treatment*, 190.

39. 195 Cal. Rptr. 484, 147 Cal. App. 3d 1054 (1983).

40. Lo and Jonsen, "Ethical Decisions in the Care of the Patient Terminally Ill with Metastatic Cancer," 107–111.

41. Joanne Lynn and James F. Childress, "Must Patients Always be Given Food and Water?," *Hastings Center Report* 13 (October 1983): 17–21.

42. Emma L. Cataldi-Betcher, Murray H. Seltzer, Bernadette A. Slocum, et al., "Complications Occurring during Enteral Nutrition Support: A Prospective Study," *Journal of Parenteral and Enteral Nutrition* 7 (1983): 546–552.

43. Rebecca S. Dresser and Eugene V. Boisaubin, "Ethics, Law, and Nutritional Support," *Archives of Internal Medicine* 145 (1985): 122–124.

44. I. Campbell-Taylor and R. H. Fisher, "The Clinical Case Against Tube Feeding in Palliative Care of the Elderly," *Journal of the American Geriatrics Society* 35 (1987): 1100–1104.

45. Susan Hackler Fetsch and Margaret Shandor Miles, "Children and Death," in *Nursing Care of the Terminally Ill*, ed. Madalon O'Rawe Amenta and Nancy L. Bohnet (Boston, Mass.: Little, Brown & Co., 1986), 215–216.

46. Joyce V. Zerwekh, "Should Fluid and Nutritional Support be Withheld from Terminally Ill Patients? Another Opinion," *American Journal of Hospice Care* 4, no. 4 (July/August 1987): 37–38.

47. Joyce V. Zerwekh, "The Last Few Days," in *Hospice and Palliative Nursing Care*, ed. Ann G. Blues and Joyce V. Zerwekh (Orlando, Fla.: Grune & Stratton, 1984), 180.

48. I.L. Cameron and W.A. Pavlat, "Stimulation of Growth of a Transplantable Hepatoma in Rats by Parenteral Nutrition," *Journal of the National Cancer Institute* 56 (1976): 597–601.

49. David Oliver, "Terminal Dehydration (Letter)," *Lancet* 2, no. 8403 (15 September 1984): 631.

50. Ann G. Blues and Joyce V. Zerwekh, *Hospice and Palliative Nursing Care* (Orlando, Fla.: Grune

& Stratton, 1984), 181.

51. William W. May, "Economics and Ethics," *Journal of the American Dietetic Association* 86 (1986): 1356.

52. Charles D. Aring, "Intimations of Mortality: An Appreciation of Death and Dying," *Annals of Internal Medicine* 69 (1968): 137.

53. K.C. Calman, "Quality of Life in Cancer Patients—A Hypothesis," *Journal of Medical Ethics* 10 (1984): 124–127.

54. President's Commission, *Deciding to Forego Life-Sustaining Treatment*, 1–12.

55. Joanne Lynn and Marian Osterweiss, "Ethical Issues Arising in Hospice Care," in *Hospice Programs and Public Policy*, ed. Paul Torrens (Chicago: American Hospital Association, 1985), 205.

56. President's Commission, *Deciding to Forego Life-Sustaining Treatment*, 1–12.

57. Eugene V. Boisaubin, "Ethical Issues in the Nutritional Support of the Terminal Patient," *Journal of the American Dietetic Association* 84 (1984): 529–531.

58. Lo and Jonsen, "Ethical Decisions in the Care of the Patient Terminally Ill with Metastatic Cancer," 107–111.

59. Callahan, "On Feeding the Dying," 20–22.

60. Matter of Claire C. Conroy, 464 A2d 303 (NJ App 1983).

61. Diann B. Uustal, "Ethical Considerations in Specialized Nutritional Support" (Paper presented at the Ohio Dietetic Association Annual Meeting, Columbus, Ohio, 7 May 1986).

62. Patrick G. Derr, "Why Food and Fluids Can Never Be Denied," *Hastings Center Report* 16, no. 1 (February 1986): 28–30.

63. Gilbert Meilaender, "On Removing Food and Water: Against the Stream," *Hastings Center Report* 14, no. 6 (December 1984): 11–13.

64. Willard Green, "Setting Boundaries for Artificial Feeding," *Hastings Center Report* 14, no. 6 (December 1984): 8–10.

65. David W. Meyers, "Legal Aspects of Withdrawing Nourishment from an Incurably Ill Patient," *Archives of Internal Medicine* 145 (1985): 125–128.

66. Dresser and Boisaubin, "Ethics, Law, and Nutritional Support," 122–124.

67. Mark Siegler, "Ethical Dilemmas in Clinical Practice," (Presentation at the 69th Annual Meeting of The American Dietetic Association, Las Vegas, Nev., 30 October 1986).

68. Siegler and Weisbard, "Against the Emerging Stream," 129–131.

69. Arlene Sheskin and Samuel E. Wallace, "Differing Bereavements: Suicide, Natural, and Accidental Death," in *Death, Dying, Transcending*, ed. Richard A. Kalish (New York: Baywood Publishing Co., Inc., 1980), 74–87.

70. Marcia G. Kliban, "Suicide and the Hospice Patient: Procedures to Work with Right-to-Die Wishes," *American Journal of Hospice Care* 4, no. 2 (March/April 1987): 15–21.

71. Colin Murray Parkes, "Psychological Aspects," in *The Management of Terminal Disease*, ed. Cicely M. Saunders (London: Edward Arnold Ltd., 1978), 56.

72. Mishkin and Arras, "Ethical Perspectives for Hospice Care-Givers."

73. M. Rosita Schiller, "Ethical Issues in Nutrition Care," *Journal of the American Dietetic Association* 88 (1988): 13–15.

74. Repka, "Ethical Considerations in Nutritional Support of Cancer Patients," 50–55.

75. Victoria H. Major, "Legal Aspects of Nutrition Support of the Terminally Ill," *Topics in Clinical Nutrition* 1, no. 4 (1986): 45–50.

76. Susan C. Hushen, "Questioning TPN as the Answer," *American Journal of Nursing* 82 (1982): 852, 854.

SUGGESTED READINGS

Curran, William J. "Defining Appropriate Medical Care: Providing Nutrients and Hydration for the Dying." *New England Journal of Medicine* 313 (1985): 940.

Fletcher, Joseph. "Ethics and Euthanasia." *American Journal of Nursing* 73, no. 4 (April 1973): 670–675.

Johnson, Dana E. "Commentary: Life, Death, and the Dollar Sign: Medical Ethics and Cost Containment." *Journal of the American Medical Association* 252 (1984): 223.

Litton, Robert J. *Nazi Doctors*. New York: Basic Publishers, 1986.

Micetich, Kenneth C., Steinecker, Patricia H., and Thomasma, David C. "Are Intravenous Fluids Morally Required for a Dying Patient?" *Archives of Internal Medicine* 143 (1983): 975–978.

Paris, John J. "When Burdens of Feeding Outweigh Benefits." *Hastings Center Report* 16 (1986): 28.

Reidy, Elizabeth Gamble, and Reidy, Daniel E. "Malpractice Law and the Dietitian." *Journal of the American Dietetic Association* 67 (1975): 335.

Special Committee on Biomedical Ethics. *Values in Conflict*. Chicago: American Hospital Association, 1985.

Spencer, Robin A., and Palmisano, Donald J. "Specialized Nutritional Support of Patients—A Hospital's Legal Duty?" *Quarterly Review Bulletin* 11 (1985): 160.

Wanzer, Sidney H., Adelstein, S. James, Cranford, Ronald E., Federman, Daniel D., Hook, Edward D., Moertel, Charles G., Safar, Peter, Stone, Alan, Taussig, Helen B., and van Eys, Jan. "The Physician's Responsibility toward Hopelessly Ill Patients," *New England Journal of Medicine* 310, no. 15 (12 April 1984): 955–959.

Winick, Myron. *Hunger Disease: Studies by the Jewish Physicians in the Warsaw Ghetto*. New York: John Wiley & Sons, Inc., 1979.

RESOURCES

BioethicsLine, National Library of Medicine Data Base. Medlars Management National Library of Medicine, 8600 Rockville Pike, Bethesda, MD. 20209.

BioethicsLine is an online bibliographic database that focuses on questions of ethics and public policy in the fields of health care and biomedical research. It is produced by the Bioethics Information Retrieval Project of the Kennedy Institute of Ethics at Georgetown University. Its scope includes literature in health sciences, law, philosophy, religion, social sciences, and the popular press. Citations date from 1973 to present. Because BioethicsLine is one of the databases comprising the National Library of Medicine's Medical Literature Analysis and Retrieval System (MEDLARS), most large hospitals, medical schools, universities, and government agencies throughout the United States have access to it.

Appendix 12-A

Case Laws Concerning the Issue of Withholding Nutritional Support

Barber and Nejdl v. Superior Court (California)[1]

Patient: Clarence Herbert

Defendants: Mr. Herbert's two physicians, Neil Barber and Robert Nejdl

Charge: Criminal charges of homicide against physicians for terminating intravenous nourishment

Conditions of the Case:

- Patient was comatose, anoxic, incompetent, and unlikely to recover or regain significant cognitive brain function.
- The patient's family concurred with discontinuing intravenous nourishments.

Court Decision: Allow discontinuation of intravenous nourishment; acquittal of physicians.

Court Discussion:[2–6]

- Providing food as "emotional symbolism" is different from providing food as "medical treatment."
- Medical hydration and nourishment are similar to other forms of medical treatment.
- There is no legal duty to continue medical treatments, including nourishment, once they are demonstrated to be ineffective.
- All treatments should be evaluated according to proportionate burdens and benefits.
- Painful and intrusive treatments may be proportionate if they supply a reasonable chance of recovery or significant improvement.

252

- Intravenous nourishment, although minimally burdensome, is disproportionate to benefits when prognosis is hopeless.
- Intravenous feeding is legally required only if the patient is expected to attain a higher level of awareness, not merely to stay alive, nor simply to show respect or concern for the patient.
- The court did not require the appointment of a legal guardian to make the decisions to terminate treatment in this incompetent patient.

Synopsis: If a patient is diagnosed as comatose with a reasonable degree of certainty and the patient's family concurs, nutritional support can be discontinued.

Claire Conroy v. New Jersey Courts[7-9]

Patient: Claire Conroy
Defendant: State of New Jersey
Request: Mrs. Conroy's nephew and legal guardian petitioned to discontinue nourishment

Conditions of the Case:

- Patient was 84 years old, incompetent, semiconscious, demented with severe organic brain syndrome and other serious health problems, including malnutrition. She was not terminally ill.
- Patient weighed less than 50 pounds and was being fed with a nasogastric tube in a nursing home.

Court Decision:

- New Jersey trial court authorized removal of feeding tube.
- Judgment stayed and subsequently reversed on appeal by appellate court. During the interim, the patient died with the feeding tube in place.
- Two years after the patient's death, the New Jersey Supreme Court reversed the decision of the Appellate Court.

Court Discussion:[10–14]

- The Appellate Court ruled that, because discontinuing the tube feeding would cause the patient's death, removing it would constitute homicide or active euthanasia.
- The Appellate Court distinguished nasogastric feeding from medical treatment, designating tube feeding as "routine nursing care."
- The Appellate Court noted that, because the patient was not brain dead, she might experience pain if the tube feeding was removed.
- The Supreme Court held that there was no difference between a feeding tube and a respirator in determining whether to withdraw life-sustaining care for a competent or incompetent patient with a limited life expectancy. The Supreme Court held that artificial feeding can be withheld or withdrawn from incompetent nursing home patients in certain circumstances, such as the following:
  1. When there is clear and reliable evidence (e.g., "living will") that indicates patient choice, treatment can be withheld; this is called a "subjective test."
  2. When there is general indication (e.g., no "living will") that the patient would have refused life-sustaining treatment if competent, treatment can be withheld only if the burdens of continued treatment outweigh benefits of life with or without feeding; this is called a "limited objective test."
  3. When there is no evidence concerning the patient's preference while competent, it is permissible to discontinue treatment if the net burdens of continued life "clearly and markedly" outweigh benefits; this is called a "pure objective test."

Synopsis:

- Nutritional support can be withdrawn or withheld in certain conscious patients who previously expressed the wish to do so.
- Nutritional support can be withdrawn or withheld in patients whose continued life would inflict more pain and suffering than pleasure and other positive experiences, as long as discontinuing nourishment would not increase pain and suffering.

Mary Hier v. State of Massachusetts[15]

Patient: Mary Hier
Defendant: State of Massachusetts
Wish: Discontinue nutritional support
Conditions of the Case:

- Patient was 92 years old, hospitalized, incompetent, actively resisting with psychiatric problems.
- Patient had a gastrostomy feeding tube that she pulled out, refused reinsertion, and refused surgery.
- No family was available to help in the decision-making process.

Court Decision:

- Probate Court determined that if the patient were competent she would reject nourishment.
- Appellate Court affirmed Probate Court decision.

Court Discussion:[16,17]

- The Courts accepted the physician's belief that providing nourishment would result in greater pain and suffering than benefit.
- The Courts believed the patient's refusals of nourishment were important considerations.
- The Courts stated that there was no interest of the State in preventing suicide that outweighed the patient's wishes to discontinue nourishment.

Synopsis: The decision of these Courts may have been different in other states. Was this patient's right to life sufficiently protected? While competent she never expressed the desire not to be fed; while incompetent she never expressed the desire to die, only not to be fed. An alternative decision has been suggested by Rebecca Dresser.[18] Try to feed the patient and give psychotropic drugs to see if competence could be induced. Then try to ascertain the patient's wishes; if competence can not be achieved, or if the patient becomes competent and requests discontinuation of nourishment, then the decision to discontinue nourishment would have significantly more merit. (Subsequent to the court ruling, the patient was given a gastrostomy tube feeding and Thorazine to try to improve competence.)

Bouvia v. County of Riverside, California[19,20]

Patient: Elizabeth Bouvia
Defendant: County of Riverside, California
Wish: Discontinue nutritional support
Conditions of the Case:

- Patient was 26 years old, hospitalized with cerebral palsy, nearly paralyzed.
- Patient sought to prevent hospital staff from force- feeding her while she relied on staff for care and painkillers; patient essentially sought to die from starvation, asking staff members to assist in her planned suicide.
- Hospital objected to patient's plan and sought to force-feed her.

Court Decision:

- Patient's request for suicide with assistance from society was denied while she was nonterminal. Patient was force-fed.
- Two years later, in another hospital, the patient had a feeding tube placed against her will; a lower court upheld the hospital. However, the Court of Appeals reversed the decision. The California Supreme Court decided not to review the decision.

Court Discussion:[21–24]

- With the first and second court's decisions, the State of California protected its interest in preserving the life of a young person and a patient with a life expectancy of 15–20 years.
- The first two Court decisions upheld the ethical standards of the medical professions.
- These courts also ruled that the negative effect of the patient's starvation would have been significant to hospital personnel and other chronically disabled patients.
- The reversal of the first two court's decisions upheld the patient's right of self-decision, stating that, "As in all matters, lines must be drawn at some point, but that decision must ultimately belong to the one whose life is in issue."[25]

In Re Plaza Health and Rehabilitation Center, New York[26]

Patient: J. Miller
Defendant: Plaza Health and Rehabilitation Center, New York
Wish: To die by starvation
Conditions of the Case:

- An 85-year-old ex-college president suffering from several physical problems wished to die by starvation.
- The patient was competent, depressed, not terminally ill, but had a short life expectancy. He had fasted 40 days before the Court's decision; he died after a 45-day fast.
- The patient's family and court-appointed guardian supported the patient's choice, and the patient's physician recommended against force-feeding.

Court Decision:

- The Probate Court refused to order force-feeding when the nursing home asked for clarification of its legal responsibilities.

Court Discussion:

- Due to the patient's competency, support of family and physician, short life expectancy, his constitutional rights, and a State of New York statute that gives competent patients the right to refuse medically necessary treatment, the patient's request was upheld.

Synopsis:

- The Court may have distinguished this case on the basis of age, allowing the state to place less value on the life of an older person compared to a younger one. If so, this may differentiate this case from the Bouvia case. In addition, the State of California (in the Bouvia case) did not have a statute giving competent patients the right to refuse medically necessary treatment.[27]

Brophy v. New England Sinai Hospital, Massachusetts[28]

Patient: Paul Brophy
Defendant: New England Sinai Hospital, Massachusetts
Wish: Removal of feeding tube

Conditions of the Case:

- Patient was a former fireman, living in a persistent vegetative state following a ruptured aneurysm of the brain in 1983.
- Before his illness, the patient had told friends that he would never want to live in a coma and would want to stop life-support systems. His wife asked hospital officials to remove the feeding tube that kept him alive.

Court Decision:

- The Massachusetts Supreme Court ordered removal of the feeding tube. Eight days after it was removed, the patient died.

Court Discussion:[29-31]

- The 4-3 majority of judges deemed feeding tubes too "intrusive," declared that medical advances require a distinction between death as traditionally conceived and "death in which the body lives in some fashion but the brain (or a significant part of it) does not."
- Dissenting judges accused colleagues of consigning the patient to a "gruesome death"; another suggested the court was improperly endorsing mercy killing and suicide.
- Similarly, in the case of *Jobes v. New Jersey Superior Court*, the family of a 31-year-old comatose woman who had been comatose since 1980 as a result of an anesthesia accident asked for the authority to have her feeding tube removed in 1987. The New Jersey Supreme Court granted the family's request. Six weeks after removing the tube, Nancy Ellen Jobes died. The Court ruled that the patient's right to self-determination could supercede the treatment policies of a medical institution.[32]

NOTES

1. 195 Cal. Rptr. 484, 147 Cal. App. 3d 1054 (1983).

2. Rebecca Dresser, "Discontinuing Nutrition Support: A Review of the Case Law," *Journal of the American Dietetic Association* 85 (1985): 1289–1292.

3. Bonnie Steinbock, "The Removal of Mr. Herbert's Feeding Tube," *Hastings Center Report* 13, no. 5 (October 1983): 13–16.

4. George J. Annas. "Nonfeeding: Lawful Killing in CA, Homicide in NJ," *Hastings Center Report* 13, no. 6 (December 1983): 19–20.

5. John J. Paris and Frank E. Reardon, "Court Responses to Withholding or Withdrawing Artificial Nutrition and Fluids," *Journal of the American Medical Association* 253, no. 15 (19 April 1985): 2243–2245.

6. David W. Meyers, "Legal Aspects of Withdrawing Nourishment from an Incurably Ill Patient," *Archives of Internal Medicine* 145 (1985): 125–128.

7. Matter of Conroy, 188 N. J. Super. 523, 457A2d 1232 (Ch. Div. 1983).

8. In re Conroy, 190 N.J. Super. 453, 464A2d 303 (App. Div. 1983). Appeal docketed, No. 21, 642 (N.H. Sup. Ct.).

9. Matter of Conroy, No. A-108 (N.J. Sup. Ct. 17 January 1985).

10. Meyer, "Legal Aspects of Withdrawing Nourishment," 125–128.

11. Dresser, "Discontinuing Nutrition Support," 1289–1292.

12. Annas, "Non Feeding," 19–20.

13. Paris and Reardon, "Court Responses to Withholding or Withdrawing Artificial Nutrition and Fluids," 2243–2245.

14. George J. Annas, "When Procedures Limit Rights: From Quinlan to Conroy," *Hastings Center Report* 15, no. 2 (April 1985): 24-26.

15. No. 84-592 (Mass. App. June 4, 1984).

16. Dresser, "Discontinuing Nutrition Support," 1289–1292.

17. George J. Annas, "The Case of Mary Hier: When Substituted Judgment Becomes Sleight of Hand," *Hastings Center Report* 14, no. 4 (August 1984): 23–25.

18. Dresser, "Discontinuing Nutrition Support," 1289–1292.

19. Bouvia v. County of Riverside, No. 159780 (Cal. Super. Ct. 16 December 1983).

20. Bouvia v. Superior Court of the State of California for the County of Los Angeles, No. B019134, Super. Ct. C583828, filed 16 April 1986, 20.

21. Dresser, "Discontinuing Nutrition Support," 1289–1292.

22. Francis I. Kane, "Keeping Elizabeth Bouvia Alive for the Public Good," *Hastings Center Report* 15, no. 6 (December 1985): 5–8.

23. George J. Annas, "Elizabeth Bouvia: Whose Space is this Anyway?," *Hastings Center Report* 16, no. 2 (April 1986): 24–25.

24. George J. Annas, "When Suicide Prevention Becomes Brutality: The Case of Elizabeth Bouvia," *Hastings Center Report* 14, no. 2 (April 1984): 20–21, 46.

25. Bouvia v. Superior Court, 20.

26. N.Y. Sup. Ct., Onondaga Co. 2 February 1984.

27. Dresser, "Discontinuing Nutrition Support," 1289–1292.

28. Brophy v. New England Sinai Hospital, Inc. Dkt. No. 85 E0009-G1, Mass. Prob. and Family Court, Norfolk Div., (21 October 1985).

29. Richard N. Ostling, "Is it Wrong to Cut Off Feeding?", *Time*, 23 February 1987, 71.

30. George J. Annas, "Do Feeding Tubes Have More Rights than Patients?," *Hastings Center Report* 16, no. 1 (February 1986): 26–28.

31. Robert Steinbrook, and Bernard Lo, "Artificial Feeding—Solid Ground, Not a Slippery Slope," *New England Journal of Medicine* 318, no. 5 (4 February 1988): 286–290.

32. "Comatose Patient Dies, (Briefs)," *Nutrition Forum* 5, no. 1 (January 1988): 5.

Chapter 13

Implementation

When armed with an individualized and appropriate nutritional care plan, you should experience a great deal of satisfaction in implementing the plan. Most generally, the patient and the patient's family are so pleased to be recipients of the dietitian's time and knowledge that their acceptance of your suggestions is enthusiastic. Some patients, on the other hand, may initially view the palliative care dietitian as someone who will restrict food intake. If the patient has been ill for a long time, it is likely that a hospital dietitian has told the patient to avoid certain foods, such as simple sugars because of glucocorticoid therapy, or to adhere to a low-microbial diet to protect against bacterial infection while undergoing induction chemotherapy. Therefore, the palliative care dietitian can bring a breath of fresh air to the dying patient in not restricting foods, but instead promoting them for the enjoyment they bring. This aspect of the palliative care dietitian's job is an enjoyable one.

Implementing a nutritional care plan usually involves counseling to some degree. To be an effective counselor, the palliative care dietitian must have the following information and skills:

- knowledge about what losses mean to patients and their families
- knowledge of the stage of dying of the patient and the individual members of the patient's family
- ability to listen actively
- communication techniques

Let's look at each of these briefly.

THE MEANING OF LOSSES TO PATIENTS AND THEIR FAMILIES

Dying represents a loss. Through the dying process patients suffer losses in the physical, emotional, social, and financial domains, culminating in the ultimate loss—death.

When visiting patients and their families, you will encounter patients and families who have experienced various amounts of losses. Recognize that terminal illness has brought much more loss and suffering than can be identified. Accept and understand these losses and what they mean to the patient and to the patient's family. Not to do so will result in lack of cooperation by the patient and family, which will lead to compromised care.

Examples of losses that patients and families experience and that directly affect the dietitian–patient–family relationship include those identified in Exhibit 13-1.

Demonstrate your understanding that the patient and the patient's family have experienced losses and suffering by asking them such questions as the following:

- If the patient's weight has changed significantly: Does the change in your weight cause you physical discomfort? Feelings of sadness? Does it bother your family? Do you or your family want us to try to do something about your weight if we can?
- To the patient with an ileostomy or colostomy or who uses bedpans: Do you modify what you would like to eat or drink because you don't want your family to have to mess with the bag? Do you limit what you drink so that your family won't have to help you on and off the bedpan?

Exhibit 13-1 Losses That Affect Nutritional Care

Loss of body image caused by
- loss of body weight
- significant weight gain
- loss of hair
- mutilating surgery
- presence of a colostomy or ileostomy

Loss of independence caused by
- dependence on others for financial, emotional, and physical support
- inability to feed self
- inability to make decisions

Loss of self-esteem, dignity, or sense of worth caused by
- inability to feed one's children, spouse, or self
- loss of roles or purpose in life
- loss of relationships with others

Loss of a personal future due to death

- To the dying man who was once a robust, independent, healthy husband and father: Do you find it difficult to allow your wife and children to feed you?
- To the husband of a dying woman: Do you find it overwhelming to shop, cook, and clean up after a meal? Would you like us to find a volunteer who could help with these tasks?
- To a dying mother and wife: Do you find it difficult to allow your husband to shop, cook, and clean up for you and the children? Would you accept volunteer help if we can arrange it for your family?
- To a dying patient: Do you have enough socializing with your family or others? Would making mealtimes more of a social affair help you?

After asking the above questions and listening actively to the responses of the patient and the patient's family, you should provide an empathetic response to their answers. The response should be simple but compassionate, such as "It's tough, isn't it?" Your response will reflect the depth of your personal feelings about death and dying.

Finally, ask the patient and family what they would like you to do for them. Again, listen actively and reflect on what the patient and family say.

THE MEANING OF THE STAGES OF DEATH AND DYING IN PLANNING NUTRITIONAL CARE

The many ways that patients and grieving families react to the imminence of death have been conceptualized as a series of stages by Dr. Elisabeth Kubler-Ross.[1] Her purpose in defining the stages was to suggest a pattern through which many individuals may pass over varying time periods and through which they may move back and forth. The stages were not meant to be consistently sequential. Nor did Dr. Kubler-Ross suggest that all individuals would and should pass through every stage. Indeed, many individuals respond to grief in undefined ways.

In order to counsel dying patients and their families effectively, dietitians need to understand Dr. Kubler-Ross's grief analysis. As we listen to patients and their families express their needs, we can often identify in which stages of grief the individuals are at present. The five stages of grief are (1) denial, (2) anger, (3) bargaining, (4) depression, and (5) acceptance.

Denial

Denial is the avoidance of the truth that death is probable. The imminence of death may be met with a counterattack, "No, it can't be happening to me" or by actions and speech that would suggest that nothing had ever been said about death's likelihood. Numbness and a dazed feeling are common reactions when the psyche is assaulted with the possible loss of self. Recurrent denial usually is supported by whatever attempts had been used in the past to maintain denial. Overweight people usually eat to cope, whereas lean people usually cease or decrease their eating.

Denial may be therapeutic, especially if it allows the patient and family to accept the imminence of death gradually, rather than being initially overwhelmed by it. It would be wrong to try to break through denial and force acceptance of the truth of terminal illness and death. Denial may be the only coping mechanism that a patient has in order to go on living.

Anger

Anger is often the most intensely felt grief reaction of all. It helps the patient obtain some control or mastery over an essentially uncontrollable situation. In the process of grief, anger is often displaced onto the controllable parts of a person's environment, such as onto people or onto food.

The dietitian may be the recipient of displaced anger. When confronted with an irate patient who is complaining about food, we do need to respond to the patient's anger, but to its real rather than its superficial meaning. Assaults should not be dealt with at face value nor taken personally. Rather than reacting to the patient's complaint about food, confront the source of the anger and respond with such phrases as "I know you are angry. I'd be angry too. I'm very sorry you are sick. And, I'll try to get you something else to eat if you'd like."

Learn to recognize and deal with other examples of displaced anger from patients and their families. For example, the following statements of anger and guilt may require a response by the dietitian:

- "I ate red meat all my life. It's the beef industry's fault I have cancer!"

- "I caused him to be sick. I didn't follow the National Cancer Institute's and American Cancer Society's guidelines. Instead, I fed him too few fruits and vegetables. And, I shouldn't have stopped giving him vitamin A and vitamin C supplements."

Anger may still be felt by the patient's family after the death of the patient. Bereavement care is an important part of palliative care, but some bereaved family members never feel they are receiving enough of the team's attention. If visiting the family during this difficult time, be aware of this tendency, especially from demanding families.

Bargaining

Bargaining is an attempt by the patient or the patient's family to postpone death by striking a bargain or two with whoever is thought to be in control, including God, physicians, family, or fate. The purpose of the bargain is to try to change or at least postpone the inevitable. Statements that will indicate that the patient or family members are in the bargaining stage of grief include the following:

- "If I give up alcohol, will my liver cancer stop spreading?"
- "I'm trying to lose weight so my breast tumor will shrink."
- "If I feed him the 'right' foods, do you think he will get better?"
- "Tell me what I can feed him to give him more strength."

Depression

Depression is an emotion that accompanies any great loss. Patients mourn past losses, expected future losses, and their ultimate deaths. Depression is often manifested by silent sadness, loneliness, unresponsiveness, tearfulness, confusion, and lack of concentration or interest.

Depressed patients usually appear anorectic and do not eat. Medications may be needed to help them move past this stage. Steroids and anti-anxiety medications can improve the patient's appetite. It is also important not to nag the patient to eat or make the patient feel guilty if nothing is eaten. Instead, counsel the family to put favorite foods before the patient, to socialize at mealtimes, and to gently encourage the patient to eat. See Chapter 9 for additional suggestions in dealing with this difficult situation.

Acceptance

Acceptance is not the admission of defeat, nor is it "giving up" or resigning, which may be part of depression. It is instead, for the dying person, a peaceful feeling that is often followed by farewells said to all but a few, often leaving only one or two very special persons to whom it is most difficult to say good-bye. During the acceptance phase, the patient contemplates death with quiet expectation. Neither happiness nor emotional pain exist; the patient is almost devoid of feeling. Acceptance may be signaled by an increase in appetite as the patient is relieved of depression, anger, and denial.

To the bereaved person, acceptance is the ability to re-enter life on new terms by accepting the life that is left. It signals that the individual is ready to make new investments of self in others and in the future. The old loss is not forgotten; it is instead remembered—but in a special place and way. Slowly, the bereaved person loses guilt in enjoying life without the deceased.

THE ART OF "ACTIVE LISTENING"

The quality of the data elicited from the patient and the family and the quality of the plan of care individually developed for the patient and family are proportional to the ability of the professional to listen actively and understand what the patient and family have to say.

To listen actively, the professional "must be willing to see the dying patient as a fellow traveler in life, passing down the same final path that will confront us all one day. . . . There is no greater gift you can give a person than to sit down and listen to his or her story."[2] The same can be said for listening to other family members' life stories and views about life and death.[3]

Elements of active listening include those identified in Exhibit 13-2.

COMMUNICATION TECHNIQUES

"Without an adequate understanding of the patient's world and how to communicate within that framework, the most advanced medical knowledge lies powerless."[4] To promote increased patient and family understanding, the following communication techniques have been suggested by Luann Bell:[5]

- Repeat information at least twice.
- Provide all pertinent information in written form.
- Urge patients to write down their questions.
- Include family members as care providers.
- Always be simple and direct; avoid medical or nutritional jargon.
- Make important points first, reduce the length of visits, and make repeat visits as often as possible if the patient has a short attention span.
- Learn to listen to the patient.
- Know when enough has been said.

Many patients and their caregivers, particularly an older couple who live together on their own, enjoy writing down what the patient eats and regularly telling the dietitian about it. These couples also often take copious notes on the dietitian's comments and frequently write down their questions along with the

Exhibit 13-2 Elements of Active Listening

1. Want to listen.
2. Place the patient and family's needs ahead of one's own needs.
3. Be aware of what is said and what is not said.
4. Use nonverbal and verbal behavior with which the patient and family are comfortable in order to encourage them to share thoughts and identify needs; use good eye contact and appear relaxed, open, ready to listen, and accepting of what is said.
5. Be aware of congruence between verbal and nonverbal communication on the part of the patient and family.
6. Use a variety of interviewing techniques—closed-ended questions, open-ended questions, leading phrases, clarification questions or statements, summarizing statements, and reflecting or paraphrasing the patient and family's words—to elicit more information and to provide support and reassurance.
7. Speak judiciously, with a warm yet clearly audible tone of voice, refrain from giving advice, and avoid interrupting the patient and family.
8. Let silence speak for itself.

dietitian's phone number so that they can telephone when an idea or question comes to mind. These patients are often of enormous help, because they tell what works and does not work for them, they develop new recipes and share them, and they derive great satisfaction in sharing their experiences with other patients.

A helpful communication technique is to have the patient, a family member, or caregiver restate the nutritional messages in their own words. This gives you the chance to be sure that what was said was heard correctly and interpreted appropriately and, if not, to clarify it.

In addition, several written materials have been developed by pharmaceutical companies and professionals that are appropriate handout materials to use with terminally ill patients.

CHARACTERISTICS OF A GOOD COUNSELOR

A good counselor

- is involved and concerned with larger, not smaller, meanings
- is self-revealing, rather than concealing
- is a good listener and hearer
- sees the world as the patient sees it
- is altruistic, rather than narcissistic
- is process-oriented, rather than goal-oriented

- is understanding, open, honest, patient, trustworthy, self-confident, and dependable
- is empathetic, rather than sympathetic
- is reassuring and encouraging
- eliminates unnecessary emotional tension on the part of the patient and the patient's family
- is able to supply concrete and specific strategies for behavioral change

This author was once asked to come to the home of a terminally ill patient who was not expected to live longer than a week. The family (not the patient) requested that the dietitian come because conflict existed among family members as to whether to push the patient into eating more than she was consuming at the time. The patient was asleep when the dietitian arrived; at the end of the discussion with the family, the dietitian did not go to the patient's room to meet her. The patient later remarked that she had not met the dietitian and was unhappy that she had not expressed appreciation to the dietitian for the home visit. The lesson was clear: a visit to the patient's room should be the *modus operandi* unless contraindicated or specifically unwanted.

Because there may be nothing that can be done to change the course of the illness, it is important for the dietitian to encourage the family to spend time with the patient, not only to improve the patient's quality of life but also to help the family realize the benefits of providing for the patient until death occurs.

COUNSELING THE TERMINALLY ILL CHILD

Do not be surprised if terminally ill children shock you by their acceptance of death and their forthrightness in discussing it. Children understand and accept a poor prognosis often better than their parents and are often less fearful. Understanding that their parents are afraid, children often try to protect their parents by not discussing their own feelings. They are often heard to say, "I'm not afraid to die, but everyone else will be sad."

As palliative care dietitians, it is not our responsibility to tell a child he or she is dying. Therefore, be sure to find out how much the child knows before visiting a dying child and the child's family. We can give dying children the reassurance that their lives have been important and that their death will be significant to everyone involved. Reinforcing that the child will not be alone at death and that death will not hurt is appropriate. We can also reassure children that their parents will survive emotionally after the child's death.

Nutritional care of terminally ill children is similar to that of dying adults. The effects of dehydration and overhydration become apparent quickly in children because the proportion of body surface area to size is much larger than that of an adult. Children can be encouraged to drink by playing games or using charts that indicate intake, thereby enhancing their sense of accomplishment. It is fun for a child to drink fluids in out-of-the-ordinary ways, such as through a syringe, in small medicine cups, and by eating juice bars or popsicles.

Generally children eat better at home, than at the hospital, because they are more likely to obtain what they want, when they want it, with less routine restrictions. Children at home feel more like eating because they are more relaxed. The home environment is usually less tense and more conducive to improved appetite.

To encourage the appetites of dying children, offer them foods that they like. If such symptoms as sore mouth, nausea, vomiting, diarrhea, and constipation inhibit appetite and food intake, treat them appropriately. Small frequent feedings are usually liked best, and cold foods are generally preferred to hot foods. Some children's appetites improve if they rest before eating.

Parents often place undue emphasis on the child's eating behavior because feeding is an area in which they feel the need to succeed. The child's refusal to eat may leave parents feeling frustrated and guilty. Parents should be relieved of the task of providing hot, nutritious meals each day for a dying child. Instead, they should be encouraged not to feel guilty if the child wants nothing or only wants a fast-food hamburger and fries. Food variety and nutrient adequacy of the dying child's diet should not be overemphasized. If a child seems to live on ice cream or popsicles, the child's parents should be reassured that they are not improperly caring for the child. Often children refuse to eat in order to gain control of a situation in which they are otherwise dependent. When this occurs, the parents should be told why the child is doing this and encouraged to go along with this behavior.

In general, it is best to make meals as pleasant and normal as possible. Remove bedpans and other appetite-depressing items from the child's room at mealtime. Washing the child's hands before the meal is appetite-encouraging. Also, remove toys from the bed if the child is to eat in bed. Turn off the television. Make the mealtime as social as possible. If possible, bring in friends and serve sack lunches on occasion. The child may like foods cut into interesting shapes or made to look like favorite characters.

If the child refuses to eat and the benefits of nutritional support outweigh its burden, dietary supplements, enteral feedings, or parenteral feedings may be important considerations. Gastrostomy tubes are generally preferred to nasogastric tubes by the patient and family if the tube feeding will be required for a lengthy period of time. Total parenteral nutrition is difficult to accomplish in the home setting, and its efficacy in the terminally ill child is questioned by many physicians and nutritionists. When parenteral nutrition is deemed essential, many children can be taught how to care for the catheter and dressing, which gives them some control of the situation.

During bereavement for a deceased child, the dietitian should encourage the survivors to eat reasonably, even if there is no enjoyment in it. It is important that bereaved persons not neglect their health. Normal appetite and sleep patterns will return at a later time. Suggest that the family eat out with friends or that the family consider asking friends over for dinner on occasion. Encourage them not to wait for friends to guess their needs; instead encourage families to discuss their needs with others and to suggest ways that others can help.

COUNSELING THE GRIEVING FAMILY AFTER THE PATIENT'S DEATH

After the patient's death, the dietitian may be asked to counsel members of the bereaved family because of their concern that they are eating poorly. Weight gain or weight loss is not uncommon in grieving persons, and often it is easier to alter improper eating patterns before they become a habit.

Eating problems in bereaved adults and children are often a result of unresolved grief. Eating problems of adults can usually be overcome with counseling. Eating problems of bereaved children are usually self-limiting and correct themselves when the grief resolves; if the grief is unresolved, however, the childhood obesity that can develop at this time tends to carry into adulthood and to last the rest of life.

When assessing a bereaved family, the dietitian may find that several patterns emerge, depending on how well the family has coped with the recent death. For example, if family members cannot acknowledge the patient's death or transfer personal needs to other persons and activities, then they might want the dietitian to do something for them, or want to talk at length over and over with you, or try to feed you at each visit. If family members are unable to get over the need to "give to" the deceased, they may try to give such items as food, recipes, and hand-made "what-nots" to the dietitian. If family members feel significant guilt, they may want to talk or receive permission to eat foods that they might have associated with the patient's illness, such as red meat. Learning at what stage the family members are in with the grief process is important in order to anticipate questions they may have and to know how to answer those questions.

If you suspect that an abnormal grief reaction is occurring, discuss the suspicion with the patient's nurse or physician. Medical and professional psychological help may be needed.

The author once worked with two grieving members of one family—a grand-mother and a 4-year old daughter of a deceased young woman—both of whom needed psychological referral. The grandmother had a history of manic-depressive illness. After her mother's death, the child refused to eat for several days and then one day found one of her old baby bottles in a box in the grandmother's basement. The child began to drink and eat only if the grandmother fed her through the bottle.

The grandmother's psychiatrist and a child psychologist were consulted, and the situations resolved after several weeks of therapy for both.

QUESTIONS THAT THE DIETITIAN CANNOT ANSWER

At times, we may find that a patient or a patient's family is providing information or asking questions that we are unqualified to interpret or answer. When confronted with such information or questions, it is wisest to write them down, and tell the patient they are outside your area of expertise, but that a team member will be located who can deal with the patient's concerns and questions. The next step is to locate this person immediately.

Remember that, for the terminally ill patient, concerns about abandonment and of being overwhelmed are second only to fears of pain. The actual moment of death is not usually as feared as the process of dying. Therefore, when team members say they will do something for the patient, it should be done when they said it would be done. Not to do so is to reinforce the patient's concern and negative feelings about abandonment.

SUMMARY

Dietitians who counsel bereaved families should keep in mind the following helpful tips:

- Listen conscientiously.
- Accept nonjudgmentally the perceptions and beliefs of the bereaved.
- Share, but do not legislate, your religious beliefs.
- Share your personal experience of death with the bereaved person, acknowledging the painful nature of separation.
- Allow the bereaved to express anger, despair, and guilt; assure the bereaved person that it is okay to laugh and enjoy life again.
- Remember that honesty is the "best" and "only" policy; avoid half truths, fairy tales, and indirect, trite expressions.
- Make referrals to other supportive health care professionals, especially clergy, psychologists, and social workers who can help bereaved persons meet their needs.
- Remember that the height of depression occurs 6 months after death.
- Touch the bereaved person as appropriate and allow emotions, such as tears, to occur naturally.

NOTES

1. Elisabeth Kubler-Ross, *On Death and Dying* (New York: Macmillan Publishing Co., Inc., 1969), 38–137.

2. Joyce V. Zerwekh, "Understanding the Patient Experience," in *Hospice and Palliative Nursing Care*, ed. Ann G. Blues and Joyce V. Zerwekh (Orlando, Fla.: Grune & Stratton, 1984), 30.

3. Jeri Willen, "The Skills of Listening: A Review of Helpful Communication Techniques," *American Journal of Hospice Care* 3, no. 4 (July/August 1986): 39–41.

4. Luann R. Bell, "Nutrition Counseling—The Critically and Terminally Ill Patient," *Topics in Clinical Nutrition* 1, no. 1 (January 1986): 5.

5. Ibid., 1–6.

Chapter 14

Evaluation and Research

Self-evaluation and an evaluation of the ability of the patient and the patient's family to achieve desired goals should be a part of the dietitian's standard procedure during and after each counseling session. Only with evaluation can progress be noted and the nutritional care plan be modified as necessary. Evaluation of patient outcomes is the basis for honest self-evaluation and for research that will help dietitians become better providers of health care.

EVALUATION OF PATIENT OUTCOMES

Standards of care should be utilized by the dietitian when providing palliative nutritional care to terminally ill patients. A standard of care for the nutritional management of a terminally ill adult patient can be used in auditing patient care records (Table 14-1).

EVALUATION OF PALLIATIVE CARE PROGRAMS

Palliative care has been a vital force in health care since the 1970s in the United States. What have we learned about palliative care since its birth? Paul Torrens, a physician, professor, and noted researcher in evaluation and health care administration from Los Angeles has identified four major areas of learning from palliative care:[1]

1. We have learned much about death itself, particularly death from cancer.
2. We have learned a lot about how to care for the dying and their loved ones.
3. We have learned a lot about ourselves as health care professionals.
4. We have learned more about life.

Table 14-1 Standard of Care for Nutritional Management of a Terminally Ill Adult

TOPIC: Nutritional Management of the Terminally Ill Adult

OBJECTIVE: Provide individualized nutritional care (consistent with patient/caregiver goals and palliative care philosophy) that will enhance the patient's quality of life.

PATIENT SAMPLE: All adult patients, regardless of setting for delivery of care (home, hospital, day care center, long-term care facility, free-standing facility) who have been diagnosed as terminally ill and for whom the goals of palliative care (as opposed to curative care) have been established. It is recognized that at all times the patient or caregivers have the right to opt out of palliative care, choosing curative procedures if desired.

Elements	Standard	Exceptions	Special Instructions
I. Assessment of nutritional status that includes:			
A. Ability to chew, swallow, digest, absorb, and utilize nutrients	100%	1. Patient within 3 days of death 2. Patient/caregiver unable/unwilling to provide data	Nutritional assessment recorded in medical record on nutritional assessment form or in progress notes by R.D. Indicate exceptions.
B. Identification of the impediments to food consumption and mealtime enjoyment and their effects on quality of life (e.g., pain, depression, shortness of breath, sore mouth, nausea, vomiting, diarrhea, inability of caregiver to meet needs)	100%	1. Comatose patient 2. Patient within 3 days of death 3. Patient/caregiver unable/unwilling to provide data	Nutritional assessment recorded in medical record on nutritional assessment form or in progress notes by R.D. Indicate exceptions.
C. Identification of previous GI surgery, preventive treatment modalities, and chronic disease processes that may affect the patient's ability to eat and enjoy meals	100%	1. Comatose patient 2. Patient within 3 days of death 3. Patient/caregiver unable/unwilling to provide data	Nutritional assessment recorded in medical record on nutritional assessment form or in progress notes by R.D. Indicate exceptions.

continues

D. Identification of the patient/caregiver concerns regarding weight loss and food/fluid intake	100%	1. Patient within 3 days of death 2. Patient/caregiver unable/unwilling to provide data	Nutritional assessment recorded in medical record on nutritional assessment form or in progress notes by R.D. Indicate exceptions.
E. Identification of nutrient-drug interactions (e.g., pain medication causing constipation)	100%	1. Patient within 3 days of death	Nutritional assessment recorded in medical record on nutritional assessment form or in progress notes by R.D. Indicate exceptions.
F. Optional parameters including • height, weight, and other anthropometric measures; current and past weight history • nutrient intake: diet history, current and past nutrient intake compared to RDA or basic food group recommendations • biochemical values: serum albumin; total lymphocyte count; hemoglobin/hematocrit; transferrin or total iron-binding capacity; serum sodium, potassium, and calcium; fasting blood sugar; blood urea nitrogen and serum creatinine; serum osmolality • correlation of clinical signs and biochemical data with nutritional history and recent nutrient intake	Optional	1. Data unavailable 2. R.D. considers data not relevant to development of nutritional care plan or inappropriate to obtain from patient/caregiver or inappropriate in palliative care objectives and philosophy	R.D. decision regarding optional data to be recorded in medical record on nutritional assessment form or in progress notes.

Table 14-1 continued

Elements	Standard	Exceptions	Special Instructions
II. Provision and evaluation of individualized nutritional planning (plan of care) and treatment that includes			
A. Planning appropriate diet consistent with patient food tolerances, preferences, and palliative care objectives and philosophy (may include NPO order, limit po intake, nutritional supplements, tube feedings, parenteral nutrition, bolus feeding, constant infusion, cyclic infusion)	100%	1. Comatose or NPO patient 2. Patient within 3 days of death 3. Patient refuses to eat or drink 4. Patient's intake thwarted due to medical condition.	Progress notes by R.D. Indicate exceptions.
B. Providing an appropriate diet	100%	1. Comatose or NPO patient 2. Patient within 3 days of death 3. Patient refuses to eat or drink 4. Patient's intake thwarted due to medical condition.	Progress notes by R.D. Indicate exceptions.
C. Monitoring patient's intake	100%	1. Comatose or NPO patient 2. Patient within 3 days of death 3. Patient refuses to eat or drink 4. Patient's intake thwarted due to medical condition.	Progress notes by R.D. Indicate exceptions.
D. Evaluating the contribution of the plan of care to the patient's quality of life; revising as needed	100%	1. Comatose or NPO patient 2. Patient within 3 days of death 3. Patient refuses to eat or drink 4. Patient's intake thwarted due to medical condition.	Progress notes by R.D. Indicate exceptions.

E. Instructing the patient/caregiver on the plan of care as needed	100%	1. Comatose or NPO patient 2. Patient within 3 days of death 3. Patient refuses to eat or drink 4. Patient's intake thwarted due to medical condition.	Progress notes by R.D. Indicate exceptions.
III. Documentation of plan of care and provision of nutritional services that includes			
A. Documentation of plan of care	100%	None	Progress notes by R.D. Discharge notes by R.D. Notes should include reason(s) why provision of nutritional services could not be done.
B. Patient and caregiver acceptance of plan of care	100%	1. Comatose patient 2. Caregiver decision to discontinue program 3. Patient/caregiver unable to cope with instruction	Progress notes by R.D. Discharge notes by R.D. Notes should include reason(s) why provision of nutritional services could not be done.
C. Patient and caregiver understanding of plan of care and instruction	100%	1. Comatose patient 2. Caregiver decision to discontinue program 3. Patient/caregiver unable to cope with instruction	Progress notes by R.D. Discharge notes by R.D. Notes should include reason(s) why provision of nutritional services could not be done.
D. Documentation that patient and caregiver can demonstrate understanding of plan of care	100%	1. Comatose patient 2. Caregiver decision to discontinue program 3. Patient/caregiver unable to cope with instruction	Progress notes by R.D. Discharge notes by R.D. Notes should include reason(s) why provision of nutritional services could not be done.

continues

Table 14-1 continued

Elements	Standard	Exceptions	Special Instructions
IV. Development of plans for follow-up that includes			
A. Follow-up as needed	100%	1. Death of patient 2. Referral not needed 3. Referral not made 4. Patient/caregiver refuses referral	Discharge and progress notes by R.D.
B. Referral to other health care setting (e.g., home care, long-term care facility, or day care program)	100%	1. Death of patient 2. Referral not needed 3. Referral not made 4. Patient/caregiver refuses referral	Discharge and progress notes by R.D.
C. Provision of appropriate phone number to patient/caregiver	100%	1. Death of patient 2. Referral not needed 3. Referral not made 4. Patient/caregiver refuses referral	Discharge and progress notes by R.D.

By looking into the eyes of dying patients and their families for even a short period of time, we learn about death —what it is like to die and what it is like to have a loved one die. In caring for patients and families, we learn how to make the dying patient's final days more comfortable and more fulfilling. From our experiences, we have organized better programs of care and have enlisted a wide range of professional, nonprofessional, and lay workers, many of whom volunteer their services.

From our patients and our fellow workers, we learn a tremendous amount about ourselves. Patients and colleagues challenge us to look introspectively and to develop deeper personal insights. We examine our values, behaviors, and reasons for doing what we do. By becoming more comfortable with death, we learn more about life; through working with dying patients and families we develop a better sense of living.

From this knowledge has come several accomplishments.[2]

- A model of the better process of dying and a better program for the care of the dying has been developed.
- Palliative care programs have been replicated all over the world.
- The public and many professionals have been educated about death and dying.
- A quiet, gradual, and significant improvement in the programs of care for the dying in traditional health care institutions has been achieved.

Despite this learning and accomplishments, there are many things we have yet to learn and goals we have yet to accomplish. What have we not yet learned and not yet accomplished in palliative care work? Torrens identifies the following:[3]

- We have not documented in an exact, clear, and well-reported way whether programs for the care of the dying truly make a difference or are superior to the care of the dying in traditional settings. Several researchers, however, have suggested that palliative care programs are more effective than conventional medical programs in controlling the patient's pain and depression and in fostering open communication between patient, family and health care team.[4–11]
- We have not unequivocally documented the costs of what we are doing nor ascertained the cost effectiveness of our services. The recently published University of California at Los Angeles (UCLA) study[12] and the Kaiser-Permanente study[13] suggest that specialized palliative care programs can be, but are not necessarily, associated with reduction in health care costs.
- We have not learned as much about the dying process in other chronically ill patients as we have learned in cancer patients.

- We have not yet identified how to deal with the financial shortages that plague most palliative care programs.

What does the future hold for palliative care programs? Will they flourish? Will they become enmeshed in the traditional health care hierarchy and cease to be an entity of their own? The challenge is to evaluate what we are doing and to match what we can do to the needs of society. If we accept this challenge and serve as a catalyst for future developments palliative care programs can survive and prosper.

RESEARCH: OUR KEY TO THE FUTURE

Evaluation of palliative care is critical to its survival and to each discipline that is part of its program. Evaluation is accomplished through research. Only through evaluation of program and practice can a determination be made of (1) individual practices of various disciplines involved in palliative care, (2) past and projected expenses, and (3) expansion of facilities and programs.

Research in palliative care in general and in dietetics in particular is based on the assumption that practitioners seek to help patients and their families achieve the highest level of health care possible. Research problems focus on improving clinical knowledge and clinical judgment. Ultimately, better patient and family care occurs when clinical knowledge and judgment are improved.

The practice of palliative nutritional care therefore forms the basis of nutritional research in palliative care. The six steps in undertaking research have been well explained in a recent article by Elaine Monsen and Carrie Cheney[14] and simply stated by Joyce V. Zerwekh and Ann G. Blues as follows:[15]

1. identify the problem
2. state the problem
3. describe the significance of the problem to practice and theory
4. state the questions that must be answered in order to understand the problem
5. identify what data must be collected in order to answer the relevant questions
6. formulate the study and state the hypothesis

The choice of type of research design chosen is based on the kinds of questions posed. There are three types of research designs: (1) descriptive, (2) relationship and correlational, and (3) cause and effect. Examples of questions that are reasonable for research and would aid dietitians both in providing palliative care to patients and their families and in evaluating their contributions to palliative care programs are shown in Exhibit 14-1.

Overall, research is important to the dietitian because it keeps the dietitian accurate in what is said, provides guidance for clinical problem solving, and meets the societal need for information.

Exhibit 14-1 Examples of Nutrition-Related Research Questions Appropriate for Study in Palliative Care

Descriptive Questions
1. What are the major stresses identified by dietitians during their first year of full-time work with terminally ill patients?
2. What are the most common burdens and benefits of intravenous and enteral nutritional support from the patient's viewpoint? From the family's viewpoint? From the palliative care team's viewpoint?

Relationship and Correlational Questions
3. Do terminally ill patients with cachexia react differently to pain medications than do adequately nourished patients?
4. Are age, cultural/ethnic background, and socioeconomic status associated with the use of aggressive nutritional support in terminally ill patients?

Cause and Effect Research
5. Does administration of supplemental vitamin B complex improve depression in terminally ill patients?
6. Is an inhouse formula of bran and pectin as effective as more expensive commercial stool softeners in preventing constipation in patients receiving narcotics for pain?

Dietitians need to find better ways to increase patient's comfort. Studies are especially needed on the benefit versus the harm and the cost effectiveness of providing nutritional support to all patients, including those who are not imminently terminal, such as the elderly, the brain damaged, the comatose, the patient with acquired immune deficiency syndrome (AIDS) or motor neuron disease, and the mentally retarded.

As researchers, we must be clinically honest. We must not see only what we want to see, and we must not view what happens with patients in a way that confirms our theory. If we adhere to Arthur Lipman's admonition that:

good science in clinical care + *good tender loving care* = hospice success[16]

then our patients and our profession will be the ultimate beneficiaries of our efforts.

CHANGE: WHEN RESEARCH DEMANDS IT, HOW DO WE ACHIEVE IT?

Once evaluation or research indicates that a change in practice is needed, implementing change is often met with resistance from those who want to maintain the status quo. As has been said, "There is a thorny road that must be travelled by all health pioneers who would presume to bring change to the moss-grown tradition (author unknown)." Beaufort B. Longest[17] provides the following six suggestions for minimizing resistance to change caused by staff insecurity, misunderstanding, or turf protection:

1. Document the need for change.
2. Outline the problem, clarifying its symptoms and its basic cause.
3. Identify alternative methods for improvement.
4. Select the approach in consultation with those who will be affected by the change.
5. Implement change by
   a. making sure that everyone involved understands it and that enough time has passed for education
   b. disturbing as little as possible the existing customs and informal relationships
   c. providing information in advance and throughout the process about the relevance of the change and its progress and impact on the organization and people in it
   d. encouraging continual input from and ownership of the program with all involved
   e. providing for a means of releasing tension, doubts, and frustrations as the new program philosophy affects people, departments, or agencies
6. Evaluate the program and thus provide feedback that can lead to corrections and strengthen convictions.

While undergoing the process of change, we should remember the adage of Alfred North Whitehead that "the art of progress is to preserve order amid change and to preserve change amid order."[18]

It is upon the pillars of evaluation, research, and change that the future of palliative care and the dietitian's involvement in it rests. The dietitian and other health care professionals must seek new and better ways to accomplish the lofty goal of helping terminally ill patients live fully until they die. Our challenge is great, but the rewards are greater. Our patients and our future in palliative care depend on our acceptance and accomplishment of this challenge.

NOTES

1. Paul R. Torrens, "Achievement, Failure and the Future: Hospice Analysed," in *Hospice: The Living Idea*, ed. Dame Cicely Saunders, Dorothy H. Summers, and Neville Teller (London: Edward Arnold Ltd., 1981), 188-192.

2. Ibid., 188–192.

3. Ibid., 188–192.

4. John Hinton, "Comparison of Places and Policies for Terminal Care," *Lancet*, (6 January 1979): 29–32.

5. Colin Murray Parkes, "Terminal Care: Evaluation of Inpatient Service at St. Christopher's Hospice. Part I: Views of Surviving Spouse on Effects of the Service on the Patient," *Postgraduate Medicine* 55 (1979): 517–522.

6. Colin Murray Parkes, "Terminal Care: Evaluation of Inpatient Service at St. Christopher's Hospice. Part II: Self-Assessments of Effects of the Service on Surviving Spouses," *Postgraduate Medicine* 55 (1979): 523–527.

7. Colin Murray Parkes, "Terminal Care: Evaluation of an Advisory Domiciliary Service at St. Christopher's Hospice," *Postgraduate Medicine* 56 (1980): 685–689.

8. Susan Silver, "Evaluation of a Hospice Program: Effects on Terminally Ill Patients and Their Families," *Evaluation and the Health Professions* 4 (1981): 306–315.

9. Cicely M. Saunders, "Hospice Care," *American Journal of Medicine* 65 (1978): 726–728.

10. Glen W. Davidson, "Five Models for Hospice Care," *Quality Review Bulletin* 5, no. 5 (May 1979): 8–9.

11. Richard M. Dupee, "Hospice—Compassionate, Comprehensive Approach to Terminal Care," *Postgraduate Medicine* 72, no. 3 (September 1982): 239–241, 244–246.

12. Robert L. Kane, Jeffrey Wales, Leslie Bernstein, Arleen Leibowitz, and Stevan Kaplan, "A Randomized Controlled Trial of Hospice Care," *Lancet* 1, no. 8382 (21 April 1984): 890–894.

13. L.L. Kay, Mary A. Cummings, and M.B. Mundell, "Hospice: A Cost Analysis of Three Programs" (Kaiser-Permanente Medical Care Program, Southern California Region. Funded by National Cancer Institute, Contract No. 85375, July 1981), 18.

14. Elaine R. Monsen and Carrie L. Cheney, "Research Methods in Nutrition and Dietetics: Design, Data Analysis, and Presentation," *Journal of the American Dietetic Association* 88, no. 9 (September 1988): 1047–1065.

15. Joyce V. Zerwekh and Ann G. Blues, eds., *Hospice and Palliative Nursing Care* (Orlando, Fla.: Grune & Stratton, 1984), 318.

16. Arthur Lipman, "Pharmacological Needs of a Hospice Program" (Presentation at The First Annual American Conference on Hospice Care, Boston, 9 June 1985).

17. Beaufort B. Longest, *Management Practices for the Health Professional*, 2nd ed. (Reston, Va.: Reston Publishing Co., 1980), 233–237.

18. Alfred North Whitehead, *Essays in Science and Philosophy* (New York: Philosophical Library, 1948), 1.

Index

A

Acceptance, stage in grief, 265–266
Acute care hospital-based programs, 32
Adaptation to death/dying
  by family, 60–65
  by health care professionals, 83–86
Administrator, on palliative care team, 71
Admission criteria, 40
Adolescents, reactions to death, 22
Aggressive nutritional support, 124
  oral intake, 221–222
  tube feedings, 222–223
  See also Ethical issues.
Aging, 9–11
  physiological changes, 10–11
American Indians, health care practices, 136
Anemia, 144–145, 156
Anger, stage in grief, 264
Anorexia, 156–158, 218
  therapy for, 156–158
  treatment discussions, 219
Antidepressants, 208
Antiemetics, 152, 153, 154
Appetite enhancing drugs, 219
Asians, health care practices, 133–134

Assessment of patient. *See* Nutritional assessment
Autonomy, as ethical/legal issue, 231–233

B

Barber and Nejdl v. Superior Court, 252–253
Bargaining, stage in grief, 265
Belching, therapy for, 158–160
Bereavement, 15
  stages of, 17
  See also Grief and loss.
Blood transfusions, anemia, 145
Bouvia v. County of Riverside, California, 256
Breathing difficulty, 14
Brompton's cocktail, 207
Brophy v. New England Sinai Hospital, Massachusetts, 257–258
Bulk-formers, 146
Burnout
  causes of, 90–91
  prevention of, 91–93
  role overload and, 110
  signs of, 91

C

Cachexia, 160, 218
  causes of, 160
Calcitonin, 148
Care plan. *See* Nutritional care plan
Catastrophic Health Care Bill of 1988,
  47
Chemotherapy, pain management, 209
Children and death
  cognitive aspects, 20–22
  emotional reactions, 21, 22
  siblings, loss of, 23
  terminally ill children, 22–23
    counseling for, 268–270
Claire Conroy v. New Jersey Courts,
  253–254
Clergy, on palliative care team,
  72–73
Code of Ethics of the American Dietetic
  Association, dietitian's role defined,
  100–103
Committees
  planning committee, 35–37
  program committees, 42–44
Communication methods, dietitian,
  266–267
Community-based comprehensive home
  health agency programs, 33
Community-based independent
  programs, 33–34
Compazine, 152
Connecticut Hospice, 31–32
Constipation, 145–146
  narcotics and, 208
  therapy for, 160–163
Costs
  insurance coverage, 46
  Medicare, 47–49
  study of, 45–46
  variations in, 45–46
Cough, therapy for, 162–164
Counseling. *See* Dietitian as counselor
Cultural differences
  and palliative care, 138
  See also Health care practices.
Cupping, 133
Cyanosis, 14

D

Death, legal definition, 235
Death/dying
  adaptation process, health care
    professionals, 83–86
  causes of, 3
  changes in final days, 13–15
  cultural changes, 3–4
  denial of, 4–5
  final causes, 12
  malignancy, 11–12
  meaning of loss to patients/families,
    262–263
  questionnaire on, 80–81
  reactions, varieties of, 62
  starvation, 12
  symptoms, most common, 143
Decision-making
  ethical, 234
  palliative care team, 69
Dehydration
  ethical issues, 242–243
  narcotics and, 208
  sensations related to, 242
  therapy for, 165
Denial, stage in grief, 263–264
Dentists, on palliative care team, 73–74
Depression
  antidepressants, 208
  stage in grief, 265
Diarrhea, 146–147
  therapy for, 164–167
Dietitian
  ethical issues and, 240, 246, 247
  on palliative care team, 65–67,
    110–114
    group-supporting activities, 110–114
  position description, 107–108, 109
  role definition, 99–107
  role perception, 108, 110
Dietitian as counselor
  active listening, 266
  characteristics of good counselor,
    267–268
  communication methods, 266–267
  counseling after patient's death,
    270–271

and terminally ill child, 268–270
tips for, 271
Director of nursing, on palliative care
team, 71
Dry mouth. *See* Xerostomia
Durable power of attorney, 239
Dysgeusia, therapy for, 166–169
Dysphagia, therapy for, 168–171
Dyspnea, therapy for, 170–173

E

Eating, cessation, 13
Education, palliative care team,
88–89
Emotional reactions, to grief,
18–19
Ethical issues
bioethics in medicine, 230–235
autonomy, 231–233
ethical analysis, 234
Hippocratic Oath, 231
starting/stopping treatment, 233
current issues, 230
nutritional support
continuation of nutrition, 244
dehydration, 242–243
dietitian's role, 240, 246, 247
durable power of attorney, 239
force-feeding as benefit to patient,
241–242
force-feeding as burden to patient,
239, 240–241
issues for health care professionals,
245
ordinary and extraordinary care,
237–238
patient decision, 236–237
questions related to, 238–239
substituted judgment, 239
patient impairment, situations for,
232
patient suicide, 245–246
Evaluation
palliative care programs, 273, 279
palliative care team, 89
patient outcomes, 273

F

Family
adaptation, 60–62, 64–65
assessment of, 58, 60
as caregiver, 57–58
definition of, 56
home care
fears about, 59
needs of, 59–60
and palliative care team, 56–67
Fever, therapy for, 172–173
Fluid accumulation, therapy for, 172–175
Food, meanings of, 127–129
Food practices, Indochinese, 130–132
Force-feeding
as benefit to patient, 241–242
as burden to patient, 239, 240–241
Fungating tumors, therapy for, 174–175

G

Gate control theory, pain, 202–203
Golytely, 146
Grief and loss, 15–24
adolescents' reactions, 22
children's reactions, 20–24
emotional reactions, 18–19
grief work, 16
most susceptible individuals, 19–20
physiological reactions, 17–18
social reactions, 19–20
stages of, 263–266
acceptance, 265–266
anger, 264
bargaining, 265
denial, 263–264
depression, 264
typical situations, 16
Groupthink, 114

H

Halitosis, therapy for, 174–175
Harper, Bernice, 83
Health care practices
American Indians, 136
Asians, 133–134